Island Backroads

Hiking, Camping and Paddling on Vancouver Island

Richard K. Blier

Orca Book Publishers

Canadian Cataloguing in Publication Data
Blier, Richard K., 1952-
Island backroads

ISBN 1-55143-097-5
1. Vancouver Island (B.C.) – Guidebooks. 2. Outdoor recreation – British Columbia – Vancouver Island – Guidebooks. I. Title.
FC3844.2.B62 1998 917.11'2044 C97-911116-1 F1089.V3B62 1998

Library of Congress Catalog Card Number: 98-85281

Orca Book Publishers gratefully acknowledges the support of our publishing programs provided by the Department of Canadian Heritage.

Cover design by Christine Toller
Cover photographs and all interior photographs by the author
Printed and bound in Canada

Orca Book Publishers
PO Box 5626, Station B
Victoria, BC Canada
V8R 6S4

Orca Book Publishers
PO Box 468
Custer, WA USA
98240-0468

00 99 98 5 4 3 2 1

For M.L.

The author thanks the following persons whose timely and indispensable assistance helped create this book. For aid in compiling the mileages: R.T. Blier, Jon Chant, Chris Daniel, Tom Ebbs, Reg Geary, Ursulie Geary, Brenda Gerth, Bill Hadden, Graeme McFadyen, Janet McFadyen, Martin Nicholas, Alex Semple and M.L. Wightman. Thanks to the staff at BC government offices, logging companies and regional tourist information centres for their time and valuable information. Thanks to the Vancouver Island Highway Project for its maps and up-to-the minute progress reports on Island Highway improvements. Thanks to R.T. Mapping; Bill Hadden for photo submissions; M.L. Wightman for secretarial duties; and Reg Geary for maintaining my vehicle in logging-road readiness. Proofreading assistance: Jon Chant, Nancy Dewan, Bill Hadden and M.L. Wightman. Word-processing assistance: Brenda Gerth, Angelie VanderByl. Special thanks as always to Bob Tyrrell and the staff at Orca Book Publishers. And thanks again to all who contributed to my previous books.

CONTENTS

SECTION THREE: HIKING AND PADDLING DESTINATIONS

About this Book

Island Backroads describes dozens of backroading, hiking, canoeing, camping, fishing and outdoor destinations from the south end of Vancouver Island to the northern tip. These include wilderness lakes, scenic trails, BC Forest Service and logging company campsites, wilderness sites and serviced (and unserviced) provincial parks. Vehicular access is mainly via logging mainlines and rougher secondary roads. Some of the trips in this book describe areas that can only be reached on foot or by water. In a few cases I refer the reader to pertinent chapters of *More Island Adventures* (my second book), where more detailed descriptions of certain regions can be found.

Island Backroads' forty trip accounts fall under three headings:

Section One: The Paved Roads: Here you'll find lots of relatively easy-to-get-to destinations and lots of backroads close to the paved roads. This section covers Highway 28 (Gold River), Highways 1 & 19 (Victoria to Port Hardy), Highway 4 (Parksville to Long Beach), Highway 14 (The West Coast Road) and the Port Alice Highway.

Section Two: The Logging Roads: This section details well-travelled logging mainlines. Included are several day-trip loop drives and the backroads leading to Carmanah Walbran, Cape Scott and Raft Cove provincial parks and west-coast communities like Bamfield and Winter Harbour, among others. Most routes are seasonally suitable for passenger vehicles. There are plenty of challenging secondary roads for the more adventurous.

Section Three: Hiking and Paddling Destinations: Some of Vancouver Island's best wilderness hiking, camping and paddling adventures are featured here. Trips include several amphibious adventures. Four trailheads and/or launch points are reached by paved highways. Most road access is via gravel mainlines and secondary backroads. A number of trips require a canoe, kayak or boat for water access. Some destinations are best-suited for experienced travellers.

All trips are further divided into six sections:

1. In Brief: Each trip is introduced with a mention of key highlights, points of interest and what to expect.

2. Access: For quick reference, this section lists major access routes to each locale and gives road information (gravel, logging mainline, rough secondary spur etc.) with any entry restrictions.

3. Description: This section gives a detailed look at each trip, with distances in kilometres. (Slight variance in the mileage may be noted on slippery or frosty roads. No two vehicles are identical and everyone drives differently. Tire size may alter distance calculations slightly.) Also included are background information and suggested areas for further exploration.

4. **Contacts:** This listing will include sources for pre-trip planning: who to contact for regional access restrictions and road conditions, updates on hauling and active logging areas, and other key information. Listings may include district logging companies, the BC Forest Service and federal or provincial park offices. Always check with local Chambers of Commerce and Tourist Information Centres prior to a trip. Every effort has been made to include current phone numbers. Expect some discrepancies, as these listings frequently change.

5. **Maps/Guides:** Any relevant maps or guides will appear under this heading. Most logging companies publish recreational guides to their logging divisions. BC Forest Service pamphlets are also available. If you're the type of person who can spend hours studying maps and charts, you may want to purchase all the topographical sheets for your chosen backroads route. Not all maps are up-to-date. In many cases, using a topographical map alongside logging company road guides is practical. The maps included in *Island Backroads* are for reference purposes only. Not all roads are indicated. Always consult area topographical charts and detailed logging road guides.

6. **Nearest Services:** This listing tells where to find the closest gas, groceries and other services.

Off the Beaten Track

BACKROAD ADVENTURING

Everyone has a different perspective of Vancouver Island backroads. Those who rarely journey on gravel logging roads consider them rough and remote. Regular travellers have more tempered opinions. Logging mainlines and secondary roads lead to remote fishing and camping lakes, rivers and streams, hiking areas and great scenery. You might see old logging camps or decaying trestles. A short hike up an impassable spur road often leads to a spectacular vista or seascape. The less-travelled backroads are frequent haunts of black bears and other wildlife. It's relatively easy to discover your own favourite spot in Vancouver Island's forests.

Vancouver Island logging roads are the gateways to prime outdoor destinations. Most roads are open to the public (with some restrictions in active logging areas). Gravel mainlines are in seasonally good to fair shape. Secondary roads usually are rougher and could require a high-slung vehicle or 4 x 4. On some backroads you'll be sharing the road with industrial traffic. Logging company vehicles always have the right-of-way. Be alert and drive defensively. (Read the next section, Along the Logging Roads.) The frequency, location and hours of hauling operations vary throughout the year. Along some routes it's best to restrict your travels to after weekday working hours or on weekends and holidays. If you are new to backroads travel or if you would like further information, contact the nearest BC Forest Service office. Always travel with your headlights on.

Be prepared. Your vehicle should be in good condition. Carry engine oil, antifreeze or summer coolant, brake fluid, a set of tools and a repair manual. Good tires will reduce the chance of a flat. Check your spare tire prior to a trip. Secondary roads (and some mainlines) can be in bad shape, with sharp rocks that can easily pierce tires. Backroads can tax your vehicle's brakes, the suspension, cooling system and exhaust.

You could encounter confusing and unmarked side roads, steep, washboard hills, loose gravel, sharp rocks, switchbacks, potholes and deep puddles. Along secondary roads streams and heavy runoff can undercut roads and bridges to create weak spots and sinkholes. These are sometimes marked by ribbons or rocks. The routes may seem passable, but the weight of a car or truck could cave in the road. Should you frequent the older backroads, carry a shovel and a winch, or at least a come-along. In some areas, built-up gravel ridges may require a slow and careful straddling. Have someone guide you through to avoid scrapes to your vehicle's undercarriage. Low-slung vehicles could get hung up on protruding rocks. Avoid the temptation to continue downhill on really rough roads; sometimes it's not as easy getting back up again. In some places you may have to build up the roadway using logs and rocks.

Don't forget to fill up your gas tank before travelling into isolated regions. Bring extra food, water and warm clothing in case of a mechanical breakdown, even on day runs when you may not have overnight gear. (Most automobile association memberships do not cover logging road breakdowns.) Take your time on Vancouver Island backroads. A slower pace is easier on the nerves and you won't miss any scenery. Pull over and allow following traffic to pass. In dry weather, backroads are very dusty. Top off your vehicle's windshield washer fluid prior to a trip. Being sure you can see other travellers and they can see you is a good safety precaution.

Maps and guides are indispensable on the backroads. The BCFS publishes several pamphlets covering its Vancouver Island recreation sites. Most logging companies distribute recreation guides for their respective divisions. Pick up copies locally at regional offices. Some maps are available at local travel information centres. Use these maps in conjunction with topographical charts to lessen the chance of becoming lost. (Some National Topographical Series sheets are out-of-date. I update mine by hand, using any current maps for reference.) Not all roads are indicated on every map. If you're adventurous, you'll just have to scout out the unmarked routes by trial and error. Of course it's best to travel with someone who knows the area. Carry a notebook and jot down key junctions and cut-offs. (A steady hand is needed on the bumpy logging roads.) Regional marine charts and tidebooks complement any paddling or boating journey on the Island's inlets.

Public entry is not guaranteed in all regions nor should it be expected. Near population centres, public safety concerns, vandalism, security and litter problems – if you can call wrecked cars and other trash litter – sometimes prompt locked-gate policies. Access roads that run through private property or into fragile regions where 4 x 4 use is destroying vegetation are often closed. Co-operation among government, industry, private property owners and outdoor enthusiasts will ensure continued public access. Carry out your litter, follow seasonal fire, hunting and fishing regulations and don't cut trees. Take pride in our Observe, Record and Report and Wilderness Watch programs. Vancouver Islanders are gaining an envied reputation for monitoring their forestlands. If you spot a forest fire, contact the nearest BC Forest Service office or dial "O" and ask for Zenith 5555 (a toll-free number).

Island backroads are sometimes seasonally closed as a result of forest fire hazards or severe washouts and unsafe bridges. In many regions, road deactivation has rendered some roads impassable. Having an idea of expected road conditions is an important part of pre-trip planning. Check ahead with local BC Forest Service offices or logging companies. Remember that most Vancouver Island backroads are primarily industrial or forest service roads. Road conditions depend on the season. Most mainlines are regularly maintained. Some routes and secondary roads are not suitable for RVs or larger trailered boats.

ALONG THE LOGGING ROADS

Fifty years ago rail logging was prevalent in many Vancouver Island forests. With the advent of truck logging in the 1950s, the majority of the rail lines fell into disuse. Over the decades, networks of logging roads have penetrated Vancouver Island's old growth forests. In the 1960s, through the efforts of the Nanaimo and Victoria golf clubs, Alec Merriman and others, logging roads in tree farm licenses and private holdings were opened to the public. For the first time, wilderness adventurers could explore many of the backroads previously barred by locked gates.

There are several general classifications of Vancouver Island logging roads: restricted access, combined-use, inactive and deactivated roads. Some routes are signposted as Private Industrial Roads. Read and obey all posted notices on any backroad you venture down.

Restricted access roads (sometimes marked by a red, octagonal stop sign) run through active logging areas and can include mainlines where heavy hauling is ongoing. Public access is only permitted after working hours on weekdays or all day on weekends and holidays. Some active logging regions are closed to the public at all times for security and safety reasons. Private forest lands are usually gated.

Combined-use roads make up the bulk of Vancouver Island backroads. These arteries are open to the public twenty-four hours a day, but they are frequently used by logging vehicles. (A yellow, inverted triangle often identifies these roads.) Logging trucks and company vehicles have the right-of-way at all times on backroads. If you meet any, safely head to the nearest pullout (no matter what side of the road it's on) and signal your intentions to the other driver. Pull over and stop. Don't be in a hurry to get going again; there could be a second truck following the first. Always stop on the inside of any curves to avoid long sweeper logs (some over 20 m in length) that often extend out the back of the behemoth off-road haulers.

Industrial traffic may be frequent on some mainlines. Expect crummies (small buses which carry workers to and from work sites), heavy-duty company pickups, fuel carriers and both loaded and unloaded logging trucks. The loggers maintain radio contact with each other to pinpoint who pulls over and when. Signposted radio checkpoints are common on Vancouver Island backroads. If you don't fancy dodging loaded logging trucks or company buses, time your journey to after weekday working hours of the loggers. These hours vary. Logging trucks cool their brakes with water on downhill runs. In dry weather these telltale water marks are quite evident on the roads.

Inactive roads rarely have any logging traffic and are always open to the public. Lack of maintenance and washouts can render these roads rough or impassable, even with a 4 x 4. (These backroads are often signposted with a welcoming green circle.)

Deactivated roads are routes on which the logging companies have dug ditches and water-bars or removed bridges in compliance with Fisheries and Forestry guidelines. In many cases negotiating these roads requires a 4 x 4. Bridge closures or removal may render some routes impassable by vehicle.

Many districts are subject to periodic fire closures. Threats of poaching, vandalism and public safety concerns may also limit entry. For a time backroads may be impassable due to seasonal washouts, landslides, flooding or deep snows.

TIPS FOR OFF-SEASON TRAVEL

Over the summer, many BC Forest Service and logging company campsites and BC Parks campgrounds become tent and camper cities. If a less-crowded environment is your preference, consider an off-season trip. Sometimes in the early spring or late fall you'll be the only one around. Do your pre-trip planning well; some locations may be seasonally closed.

Expect foul weather and gear up sensibly. Most off-season travellers base in a camper, small trailer or van. Some stay in the back of a canopied pickup. Others stick with their tents. Whatever you do, be sure to have a suitable sleeping bag. Bring reliable, sturdy raingear that includes a rainproof coat, pants and water-resistant footwear. Gumboots are great in camp. Remember to layer your clothing in cold weather. (The dead air space insulates.) Wool will still keep you warm when you're wet. Avoid substantial heat loss from an uncovered head. Bring a hat or toque. Read up on hypothermia (rapid loss of body heat) and watch for the warning signs.

Off-season daylight hours are limited. Pack a good flashlight or two and extra batteries. Use candles in a secure holder. Another option is a lantern. In the off-season there are few bugs. The mosquitoes, deer flies and no-see-ums that plague summer outings disappear in cool weather. Always carry repellent (and some antihistamine lotion or similar bug-bite antidote) just in case you encounter a few stragglers.

Perishable food keeps better in the off-season. In colder weather you may not even need ice in your cooler. Secure your food before you leave camp for an extended period and when you turn in for the night. Rope all foodstuffs high in a tree or, if your vehicle is nearby, lock your goodies inside. Defend against hungry varmints, nighttime bandits and larger foragers by maintaining a clean camp.

Rope up a large tent fly or tarp between trees to provide a sheltered cooking area and somewhere to sit to escape any showers. Extra gear fits nicely under this makeshift roof. In the off-season, a campfire is essential, for heat and to boil water for coffee. Only damp wood may be available in the off-season, so bring firestarter.

Steady rain at lower elevations can turn into snow should you climb above the freezing line. Roads that were bare gravel during the day can frost over rapidly at sunset. If there's a chance you'll hit freezing temperatures, consider carrying chains and a small shovel. Sand or even kitty litter is good for traction. Watch the long-range weather forecasts prior to your trip. Showers and unsettled conditions are frequent in the off-season. Use common sense and shorten your trip if the weather deteriorates beyond reason. You can always come back another time.

HIKING AND CAMPING HINTS

Ask your friends where they like to camp, hike, fish, backroad or paddle. Personal accounts are helpful in pre-trip planning. Often you'll learn of clandestine Vancouver Island hideaways and hot fishing spots, but only after you've been sworn to secrecy. Always let someone reliable know your leaving and returning dates.

Make and keep checklists to use when you gather and organize your gear. Mine include canoeing, hiking, vehicle camping, tenting and 4 x 4 travel categories. A prepared list saves packing time and almost eliminates the chance of leaving anything behind. Still, I always find it takes longer to get everything ready than it does to go on a trip. Clean and sort your equipment as soon as possible on your return. Then start packing what you can for your next jaunt.

Just because the weather is fine when you leave, don't expect the same conditions toward the coast or up in the mountains. The weather is a fickle friend. Prepare for the worst and be adequately equipped. Carry full raingear, a hat and extra clothing that will keep you warm when it's wet. You can bring your suntanning paraphernalia, but sometimes it will stay in your pack. Use a reliable tent with a full-length fly. Tents with cap flies won't provide adequate protection in heavy rains. Beware of night dampness and fog that develops in low-lying areas. Seal susceptible gear in plastic bags.

Vary your food supplies according to personal preference and length and type of trip. A recipe for homemade beef jerky (economical to make and a treat on backpacking trips) is worth seeking out. Carry a supply of water in your vehicle and boil or treat all drinking water obtained from lakes, rivers and streams. Intestinal disorders can play havoc in the wilderness. One parasitic infection of the intestines, called giardia, is spread by animal and human waste.

Practise low-impact camping to help preserve the wilderness atmosphere. At user-maintained campsites remember to clean up your site before you leave. Some locations have limited garbage removal. Visitors can help maintain them by always carrying out their trash, whether there are garbage cans or not. This lessens unsightly overflow that could attract scavenging animals. Dispose of grey water well away from camp and at least 100 m from any stream, river or lake. Use existing toilet facilities whenever possible. The Outdoor Recreation Council of British Columbia publishes an excellent brochure, *Back Country Sanitation,* that covers disposal of human and camp waste.

On some hiking routes it's convenient to travel to your destination in two vehicles and leave one at each trailhead. Those concerned about vehicle security can have a friend drop them off and pick them up later, at a specific time. Leave no valuables in your car or truck and be sure to lock up.

Hiking times are directly related to the weather, trail conditions and an individual's own pace. Match the speed of your party's slowest member. Be patient and avoid frustration or anger under adverse trail conditions or when progress is slow and tedious. On longer trips, take advantage of extended weather breaks and dry out your wet gear.

Along many trails the water source is located some distance from the camping areas. Pack a small collapsible water container and gather your camp's drinking and cooking water in quantity. Don't forget a first-aid kit and include bug repellent and medication to treat bites and allergic reactions.

Vancouver Island's freshwater lakes support stocked and wild fish populations. Be selective about what you keep and always follow current regulations. Practise catch-and-release (particularly with larger fish) to help safeguard the fishery for future anglers. Hone your fish releasing techniques and use barbless hooks. Be gentle when handling fish and removing hooks. Use a haemostat to increase fish release success. This device's slender shape, curved tip and locking handle work great with deeply embedded hooks.

(Sometimes it's best to leave the hook in place and cut your fishing line. The hook will eventually rust out.) You can buy haemostats in medical supply outlets, outdoor stores and most fly-fishing shops. Don't keep the fish out of the water too long, and remember to revive your unhooked catch in the water.

WILDERNESS PADDLING

Exercise caution whenever you venture onto Vancouver Island's wilderness waters. The larger Vancouver Island lakes and inlets are usually the trickiest, yet even smaller paddling destinations should be treated with respect. Be wary on waters where contrary winds battle tides or river currents. Know your limitations and those of your kayak or canoe, travel with a compatible companion and be cognizant of weather shifts. Check long-range weather patterns prior to a trip, but bear in mind that high pressure sometimes brings strong winds with the clear skies. When in doubt, stay off the water. Always use a government-approved personal flotation device.

Winds generally spring up by late morning and can blow all day. In wider lakes and inlets, whitecapped rolling wave trains develop. Waves rebounding off steep shorelines induce confused sea conditions and dangerous chop. Get an early start to avoid the rougher water. Be prepared. The weather can turn ugly in minutes; you may become shorebound until the winds die down; at times they blow all night. Always carry extra food and supplies, just in case. From area topographical maps you can get an idea of possible landing and camping spots. These charts are good indicators of precipitous, inaccessible shorelines. Funnelled valley crosswinds can be problematic in these regions.

If the waves aren't too bad, keep just offshore and head upwind. Resist the urge to go with the wind and waves when you set out. Conditions could worsen later, leaving you with a tedious and often dangerous paddle back upwind. Many Vancouver Island lakes are dammed. Flooded areas may conceal stumps, snags and deadheads. Despite these dangers, stay close to shore in windy or wavy situations. Under favourable circumstances some paddlers rig up a sail and take advantage of the winds.

Go out on a local lake and practise. Work up to the larger lakes and more challenging water conditions. (My first big-lake canoeing was done on Nitinat and Cowichan lakes.) Contact local paddling clubs and take part in their outings. On wilderness trips it's best to journey with someone who knows the area well. Never travel alone. When developing your river-running and lake wave-paddling experience, leave all but your emergency gear and a daypack at a base camp and tackle the waters in a lighter, more manageable open canoe or unloaded kayak. On rivers, scout ahead for sweepers, impeding branches, deadheads, logjams and impassable rapids or waterfalls. Be familiar with rescue techniques and know how to swim.

When tidal camping on inlets, knowledge of the tides is essential. Information is available in the *Canadian Tide and Current Tables*, published by the Canadian Hydrographic Service. Tidal predictions are based on the assumption of calm seas; storms and winds may cause variances in tidal heights. Set up your tent above the high-tide line; build any fires below the high-tide line and erase any sign of your camp when you leave.

Canoeists should remember a bailer and sponge to remove any spray or rainwater that may accumulate in the bottom of the canoe. Tie in gear and lash a third paddle to a thwart in case of a capsize. Ensure painters (bow and stern ropes) are in good shape.

Reflected light off the water can increase sunburn danger significantly. Wear a hat and sunglasses and use sunscreen. Paddlers concerned about security can use a chain and lock to secure their craft to a tree. Conceal paddles somewhere away from your kayak or canoe. Watch and respect the weather, be aware of quick-changing water conditions and use common sense to ensure a safe journey.

CAMERAS AND CAMPING

Don't leave your camera behind on outings. Backpackers, in an effort to cut down on pack weight, will carry a minimum of filters and lenses. Paddlers and travellers who base near their vehicles have the luxury of including an extra lens or more. Some photographers bring along their tripods. Hikers may prefer a lighter, collapsible tripod.

Protection from dampness, dust and inevitable bumps and bangs will keep your camera operating. Cameras with electronic parts are particularly sensitive. If a padded camera case is too bulky, line your backpack with a heavy-duty plastic bag and place your photo gear inside an accessible top pocket, padded by towels or clothes.

Separate your camera, film, lens-cleaning supplies and lenses into Ziploc bags. Leave in some air for cushioning. Into each Ziploc bag put a small silica gel desiccant to absorb errant moisture. An empty film canister is an ideal container for backup batteries.

Cameras often malfunction in cold, damp or frosty weather. Lubricated parts may stick or seize up. You can often remedy these problems by warming your camera in your vehicle or camper.

SECTION ONE: THE PAVED ROADS

Trip 1: The West Coast Road

Victoria to Port Renfrew

IN BRIEF

The 93-km drive from Victoria's western outskirts to Port Renfrew has much to offer the outdoor enthusiast. The West Coast Road (Highway 14) is the gateway to Sooke, west-coast beaches and trails, the Juan de Fuca Marine Trail, French Beach Provincial Park, Port Renfrew and Botanical Beach.

ACCESS

Take the Trans-Canada Highway (Highway 1) west to the Colwood overpass and cut onto Highway 14 (Sooke exit). Continue about 2.5 km to Colwood Corners (the Goldstream Avenue intersection.)

DESCRIPTION

Whether you enjoy hiking, saltwater or freshwater fishing, backroading, camping or great west-coast scenery, a coastal jaunt along Vancouver Island's West Coast Road (Highway 14) has it all. Our starting point is Colwood Corners, in Victoria's Western Communities. Here, set your vehicle's trip meter to zero and head west to Sooke. The route is paved. Watch for narrow bridges, winding sections and some sharp corners.

The Galloping Goose Regional Trail crosses Highway 14 a number of times as it snakes from Victoria to Sooke and then up to Leechtown. The 59-km Capital Regional District trail is shared by hikers, cyclists and horse riders. *Hiking Trails I: Victoria and Vicinity*, published by the Vancouver Island Trails Information Society (VITIS), contains a description of the Galloping Goose Trail and many other southern Vancouver Island hiking destinations.

Saltwater anglers are familiar with Pedder Bay, Becher Bay and Sooke waters. Happy Valley, Metchosin and Kangaroo roads access marinas servicing the area. Just past the 17 Mile House, Gillespie Road (km 15.5) angles off to the left. Day hikers heading in to Roche Cove or East Sooke regional

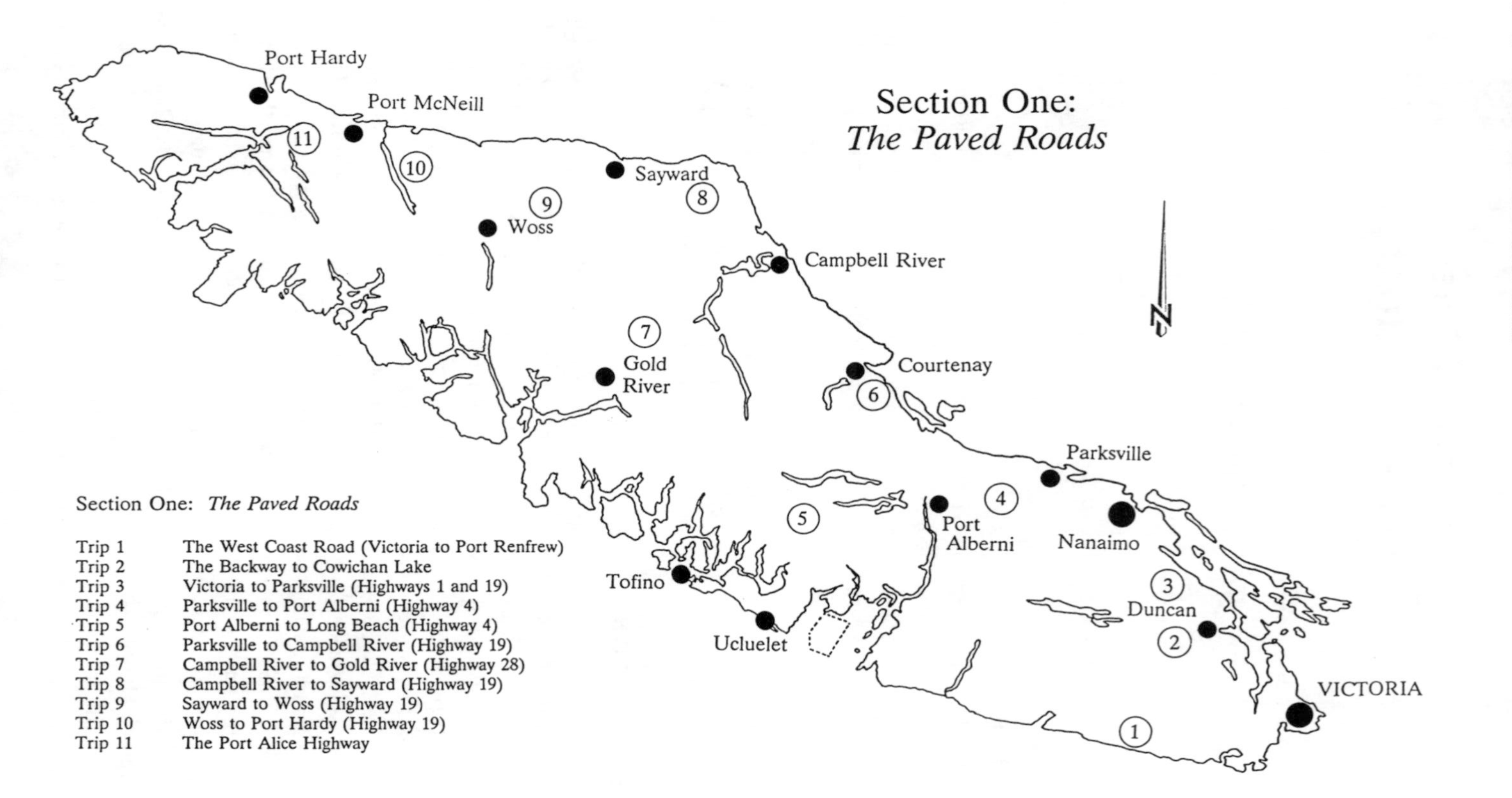
Section One:
The Paved Roads
N
Port Hardy
Port McNeill
11
10
Sayward
8
9
Woss
Campbell River
7
Gold River
Courtenay
6
Parksville
4
Port Alberni
Nanaimo
5
Tofino
Ucluelet
3
Duncan
2
VICTORIA
1
Section One: *The Paved Roads*
Trip 1 The West Coast Road (Victoria to Port Renfrew)
Trip 2 The Backway to Cowichan Lake
Trip 3 Victoria to Parksville (Highways 1 and 19)
Trip 4 Parksville to Port Alberni (Highway 4)
Trip 5 Port Alberni to Long Beach (Highway 4)
Trip 6 Parksville to Campbell River (Highway 19)
Trip 7 Campbell River to Gold River (Highway 28)
Trip 8 Campbell River to Sayward (Highway 19)
Trip 9 Sayward to Woss (Highway 19)
Trip 10 Woss to Port Hardy (Highway 19)
Trip 11 The Port Alice Highway

parks (two CRD parklands) will turn here. East Sooke Park features a variety of trails leading to mountain vistas and seaside cliffs. Old mine sites, petroglyphs and an outstanding view across Juan de Fuca Strait add to the park's unique charm. Some people hike to the coast and surfcast from the rocky shoreline near Beechey Head.

Just under the 19.5-km mark, look for Harbourview Road on the right. This leads to Sooke Mountain Provincial Park and three trout lakes, 10 km away and just outside the park boundaries. Sheilds, Grassie and Crabapple lakes hold feisty cutthroat and rainbows sought by fly casters. Options for climbers are Mount Manuel Quimper and Empress Mountain, north of Crabapple Lake. Driving in has been a problem on and off over the years; the gate at the bottom of Harbourview Road may be shut. Even when the road is open, a high-slung vehicle or 4 x 4 is needed on washed-out sections of the route. But you can always hike in or ride a mountain bike. For the past two years, a dedicated volunteer group calling themselves "The Rock Crawlers" have held an annual area cleanup that helps assure hiking access along Harbourview Road. Side roads in this region can be confusing, so be sure to carry maps. (See *More Island Adventures*, Trip 2.)

Sooke River Road (km 22) is just before the Sooke River bridge. Turn right here for Sooke Potholes Provincial Park, where you can swim, picnic and hike. Deep pools and river-carved potholes highlight the park. The Sooke Region Museum and tourist information office is located on Phillips Road (km 22.5), directly across the bridge. The staff have a wealth of local knowledge to share with visitors and you can inquire about points of interest in the Jordan River and Port Renfrew regions. Close to the museum are the fairgrounds for the summer All Sooke Day festivities. Challengers from New Zealand, Australia, the United States and Canada take part in the longest-running logging sports event in Canada. A community picnic features a salmon and beef barbecue using old-fashioned cooking methods.

At km 24 you'll reach the intersection with Otter Point Road in Sooke. This is the turn to take for Butler Main and the backroads in the Sooke Hills. *(*See Section Two: Trip 1.*)* Whiffen Spit Road (km 25.7) brings you down to a natural breakwater in Sooke Harbour. Constant wave action has breached the 1,200-m spit, although you can still walk out a fair distance at low tide. Birdwatchers and nature buffs will enjoy a walk along Whiffen Spit.

RVers and campers can base at the full-service campground at French Beach Provincial Park. Watch for the signposted entrance, just under the 45-km mark. There are sixty-nine spacious tent and RV sites, which can accommodate larger trailers and campers. The day-use area is wheelchair accessible and the park features woodland trails and a beautiful beach. Camping fees depend on the number of people and vehicles at each campsite.

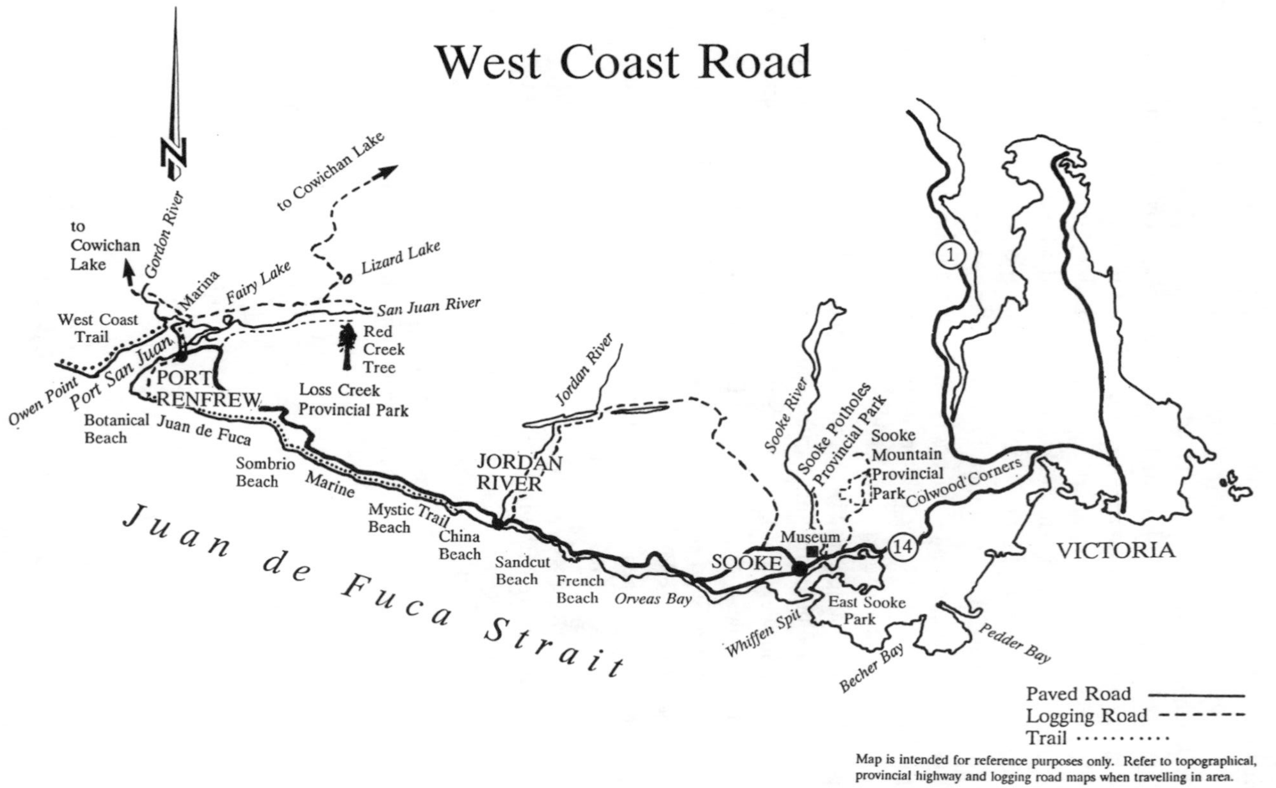
West Coast Road
to Cowichan Lake
Gordon River
to Cowichan Lake
Lizard Lake
Marina
Fairy Lake
San Juan River
West Coast Trail
Red Creek Tree
Owen Point
Port San Juan
PORT RENFREW
Loss Creek Provincial Park
Botanical Beach
Juan de Fuca
Sombrio Beach
Marine
Mystic Beach
Trail
China Beach
Jordan River
JORDAN RIVER
Sandcut Beach
French Beach
Orveas Bay
Juan de Fuca Strait
Sooke River
Sooke Potholes Provincial Park
Sooke Mountain Provincial Park
Colwood Corners
1
Museum
SOOKE
14
VICTORIA
Whiffen Spit
East Sooke Park
Becher Bay
Pedder Bay
Paved Road
Logging Road
Trail
Map is intended for reference purposes only. Refer to topographical, provincial highway and logging road maps when travelling in area.

Reservations are accepted by calling 1-800-689-9025.

Sandcut Beach (km 51.5) is reached by a short path that leads to a sand and cobble shore. Some hikers beachcomb all the way west to Jordan River. Point No Point, visible from Sandcut Beach, and the Olympic Mountains in Washington State are impressive on a clear day.

The highway drops down a steep grade at the logging community of Jordan River. The Western Forest Products office is at the bottom of the hill, on the left. On weekdays you can pop in for current access restrictions on its logging roads. WFP maintains a recreation site on the point of land right before the Jordan River bridge (km 55). This beachfront is filled with RVers over the summer and is a great base for day tripping. At certain times, large breakers roll in along the beach at Jordan River. This area is popular with surfers, who brave the chilling waters in wetsuits.

The entrance for China Beach Provincial Park is just under the 59-km mark. A trail from the parking lot winds sharply through the forest to the sea. No camping or open fires are allowed. The beach's wild nature is exposed when the wind is up and careening breakers pound the coastline. Weekend beachcombers frequent China Beach all year. BC Parks' Juan de Fuca Marine Trail starts here. This rugged coastal route extends 47 km from China Beach to Botanical Beach, near Port Renfrew. The trail, part of Juan de Fuca Provincial Park, is a welcome addition to the parks system. (See Section Three: Trip 1.)

The road drops down a hill and runs through Loss Creek Provincial Park (km 75). Rough trails extend along the creek. In 1996, and again in 1997, the road was covered by mudslides that slipped down the unstable bank on Loss Creek's north side. The Loss Creek bridge has since been relocated.

For Sombrio Beach, turn left onto a steep, bumpy spur road (just over the 78-km mark) and wind down through a logged area to the parking lot, about 2 km away. It's a short walk to the beach. Sombrio Beach, the second of four access points along the Juan de Fuca Marine Trail, has caves to explore and a picturesque waterfall. Surfers are often seen riding the west-coast swells. You can camp at the beach's east end. The Sombrio area was heavily logged in the mid-1980s. A stand of trees was left on the coastline, to bravely face the brunt of winter storms that at one time rolled over a sprawling forest of these aging veterans.

Down the road is Switchback Hill, a short, S-shaped corner. Before it was smoothed out, the hill was always rutted and bumpy and quite a jarring challenge for those travelling in smaller vehicles. Three of us once had to forcibly assist a friend's rebelling Volkswagen van up the final hump. No wonder it was considered by many backroad adventurers the worst part of the gravel stretch on the way to Port Renfrew.

The marked side road on the left at km 87.5 leads over 3.5 km to the

Commercial fishing fleets work out of many Vancouver Island locales.

Parkinson Creek access to the Juan de Fuca Marine Trail. As you descend another long grade near Port Renfrew, watch for the signposted cut-off (km 91) for the Red Creek Tree, one of Canada's largest-known Douglas firs. From the main road, travel around 12 km down an old railway bed to the parking area and trail to the ancient Douglas fir. The route in may be seasonally impassable. Red Creek Tree (73.8 m high; 12.3 m around) is estimated as being between 800 and 1,000 years old. A rival fir exists in the upper Coquitlam watershed. This tree measures 20 m taller than the Red Creek Tree, but is not as thick in circumference.

There is an important junction, just over the 93-km mark, where Deering Road meets the West Coast Road near the information centre. Straight ahead goes through the Port Renfrew townsite to terminate at the Port Renfrew Hotel and government dock. Cerantes Road, near the hotel, runs 3 km to the parking area at Botanical Beach Provincial Park, a major Port Renfrew attraction. The area is famous for its tidepools and easily viewed marine life. Remember to time your visit for a low tide. (See Section Three: Trip 2.) The Juan de Fuca Marine Trail begins its southeastern course nearby.

A right turn onto Deering Road leads to the white one-lane bridge over the San Juan River and passes a sandy beach on Port San Juan. There is a private wilderness campsite here operated by the local First Nations. Some paddlers head up the San Juan River to Fairy Lake. On the tidal, lower San Juan River, be knowledgeable of the tides and beware of tricky currents. Fallen trees and rogue deadheads may impede progress.

At km 94.5 the road splits. West Coast Trail hikers will cut left for another 2.5 km to the Parks Canada Gordon River trail registration and information centre. (See Section Three: Trip 5.) A right at km 94.5 leads to the Deering Bridge, spanning the north branch of the San Juan. On the north side of the river, turn left and continue for about a kilometre to the Port Renfrew Marina. Facilities include RV and tent campsites, well water and a sani-station. The boat launch and moorage floats accommodate larger boats.

Port Renfrew waters offer excellent bottom fishing – halibut are plentiful – and good crabbing. All species of salmon are present. Mooching for springs in the West Point (Owen Point) area is popular from early July to late August. Anglers with boats capable of tackling the sometimes rough seas near Carmanah Point will find good coho fishing in that vicinity. Zero tides are a problem at the shallow mouth of the Gordon River. Boaters usually can negotiate this spot at tides of 0.5 m or higher. Mornings are generally quiet on Port San Juan, though fog sometimes rolls in. By late afternoon, prevailing westerlies are up.

You can stay on the logging roads all the way to Cowichan Lake, or do as many people choose and head home the same way you came, along Vancouver Island's West Coast Road.

CONTACTS

- BC Parks (South Vancouver Island District): 250-391-2300
- Capital Regional District Parks (Victoria): 250-478-3344
- Pacific Forest Products (Cowichan Woodlands): 250-749-3796
- Port Renfrew Marina: 250-647-5430
- Sooke Region Museum: 250-642-6351
- Western Forest Products (Jordan River): 250-646-2031

MAPS/GUIDES

- BC Parks Juan de Fuca Marine Trail brochure
- Guide to Forest Lands of Southern Vancouver Island (Lake Cowichan Combined Fire Organization)
- Western Forest Products Visitors' Guide to Southern Vancouver Island
- National Topographical Series: 92C/8 Jordan River (1:50,000); 92C/9 Port Renfrew (1:50,000); 92B/5 Sooke (1:50,000);
- Provincial Maps: 92B/NW Victoria (1:125,000); 92C/NE Nitinat Lake (1:125,000)
- *Canadian Tide and Current Tables: Vols. 5 & 6* (Canadian Hydrographic Service)
- *Hiking Trails I: Victoria and Vicinity* (VITIS)

NEAREST SERVICES

Port Renfrew; Sooke; Western Communities.

Trip 2: The Back Way to Cowichan Lake

IN BRIEF

Instead of taking Highway 18 from Duncan to the village of Lake Cowichan, many visitors opt for an alternate drive along the backroads on the Cowichan River's north side. The route passes many river access points and the Stoltz Pool and Skutz Falls camping areas, part of Cowichan River Provincial Park.

ACCESS

From Highway 1 in Duncan turn west onto Trunk Road. (See Section One: Trip 3.) Trunk Road becomes Government Street. Turn left at Gibbons Road (the hospital turn) and continue to Menzies Road. Keep straight on Barnjum Road and then turn left onto Riverbottom Road. There are sharp corners and gravel stretches.

DESCRIPTION

Most people travel to Cowichan Lake via Highway 18, a road that meets Highway 19 just north of the city of Duncan. The 30-km route on Highway 18 runs through a demonstration forest and passes several forestry lookouts. Those who prefer a slower pace choose the backroads that meander along the Cowichan River's north side.

First you must find Riverbottom Road. In Duncan, turn west onto Trunk Road (at the first set of traffic lights north of the Cowichan River bridge) and reset your vehicle's trip meter to zero. *(See Section One: Trip 3.)* Trunk Road becomes Government Street and climbs a hill. At km 2 turn left onto Gibbons Road (near the hospital signpost) and continue to the intersection with Menzies Road (km 6.8). Go straight onto Barnjum Road. Near Wake Lake turn left onto Riverbottom Road (km 8.8).

At km 15 Riverbottom Road makes a sharp left; straight ahead is a dead end. The route passes Sahtlam Lodge and hits the gravel at km 16.4. At km 16.7 you'll reach the Stoltz Pool campground, part of Cowichan River Provincial Park. Opened in July 1997, the park stretches along the Cowichan River and includes the Stoltz Pool and Skutz Falls camping areas. At the Stoltz Pool locale you'll find forty-three sites, including four walk-in, five double and two pull-in spots to fit larger RVs. Firewood is provided. There are riverside trails, a picnic area and a boat launch on a riverbank susceptible to river scouring. A daily fee is charged and the gates are closed at night. Check with the BC Parks South Vancouver Island District for current information. The park is already proving itself popular. In its first summer of operation the Stoltz Pool campsite was often filled to capacity.

Stoltz Road (km 18.3) swings in on the right. At km 20.8 watch for the entrance to Cowichan River Provincial Park's Marie Canyon day-use area (once a BC Forest Service site) overlooking the precipitous canyon. Take care when viewing the gorge from the cliffside paths – the forest floor can be slippery. Many park visitors camp in the Skutz Falls area (km 23). The day-use parking lot (km 23.5) is closer to the falls, just beyond Mayo Road.

There are many riverside trails to follow, including the Cowichan River Footpath that crosses to the Cowichan's north side via a Forest Service bridge near Skutz Falls. This bridge, built to provide small logging contractors with a road connection to the woodlands on the Cowichan River's south side, replaced a suspension footbridge. Existing foundations were incorporated so as not to disturb the riverbed.

The Cowichan River Footpath, originally an angler's trail, runs 30 km along the Cowichan River, from Glenora (near Duncan) almost to the village of Lake Cowichan. If you plan on hiking all or part of the Cowichan River Footpath, it's an idea to park your vehicle at one end and have a friend drop you off at your starting point. Volunteers from the Outdoor Club of Victoria, the Duncan Sierra Club and the Cowichan Valley Naturalists clear overgrown sections and re-flag parts of the route. Upstream sections of the footpath from Skutz Falls may be difficult to locate. See *Hiking Trails II: Southeastern Vancouver Island* (VITIS) for further details.

From its start in the village of Lake Cowichan, the Cowichan River flows 58 km and drops 168 m before finally emerging in the tidal flatlands of Cowichan Bay. Along the winding route are a series of steep falls and over a hundred sets of rapids. The river is inaccessible in some places due to sheer rock walls, such as those in the Marie Canyon area.

The Cowichan River was once called the gateway to Cowichan Lake. Log drives were common on its waters in the late 1800s. The loggers had to use the river. There was no functional road on which to move the huge timbers and the projected E & N rail link was still years away.

The Cowichan River's first drive took place in the winter of 1890-1891. There were problems from the start. The untried river displayed its force by scattering a high percentage of the logs into the trees. Farther downstream, the river was deflected by a jam and changed its course, flooding some lowland areas. The Duncan road bridge was swept away and the railway span was in danger of suffering the same fate.

Once hauled along primitive skid roads to the Cowichan River, the logs (with branches and bark removed) were marked with their respective owner's stamp and then boomed and stored. Initially, oxen were used to shift the fallen trees, giving way over the next decade to horses, then steam-driven donkey engines. The donkey engines were mobile and could be quickly set up and dismantled at various camps along the river where grounded logs were retrieved. Despite many objections, the "new-fangled contraptions" became prevalent in the Cowichan Valley.

A river has many moods, always changeable and as fickle as the weather. For a successful drive, the water level had to be just right: neither too high nor low. It followed that spring and fall were driving times. When favourable conditions existed, logs were floated down the Cowichan River to a mill located at Genoa Bay.

Early BC loggers took a page from the books of log drives on the Ottawa River in Ontario and the St. Maurice River, near Trois Rivieres, Quebec. A big difference was log size; west coast logs were almost eight times as large as their counterparts back east. The length of BC logs ran around sixty feet, though the occasional one-hundred-footer was sent down. These larger logs contributed to many log jams. One pileup was caused by the accidental release of a series of four booming logs.

When a jam occurred, men would attempt to pry obstructing logs loose with peaveys, winches and pulleys. Armed with these cumbersome implements and wearing caulked boots, the men would scurry out onto the heaving snarl to try and free key logs. The blockage could suddenly surge free, becoming a thundering mass of water and logs. Dynamite was a last resort. Loggers, dangling at the end of ropes, were lowered into the tangled mess of timbers to place the charges. Slippery logs, ice and the river's powerful hydraulics were all pitted against a man's determination, skill and daring.

In 1906, Joe Vipond headed one of the largest runs ever on the Cowichan River. His camp (located near Nixon Creek, on Cowichan Lake's south side) utilized Vancouver Island's biggest donkey engine. Under the direction of Vipond, his chief engineer Joe Jordan and able-bodied men like Bazil Kier, they brought out a record twelve million board feet of timber. The success of this endeavour was not without tragedy; one man was lost near Sahtlam. His body was found in a log jam, downstream from where he had been sucked into the current while rolling logs.

The Cowichan River's last log drive occurred in the winter of 1909. Harry McGargle had been warned that the river's level was far too high, yet he disregarded the wary advice of others and proceeded with the drive. Although his summer logging brought in $10,000, a tidy sum in those days, McGargle saw all his profits end up in the woods, ensuring his bankruptcy. That same year, construction began on the E & N rail link from Duncan to Cowichan Lake, and logging in the region slowed. A few years later the rail line opened, providing a safer means of transporting logs to the mill and ending the practicality of the Cowichan River log drives.

Today the river is seasonally used by several canoe and kayak clubs. There are countless swimming holes and picnic sites on both the north and south shores. Access is easier from the north side, where roads lead to the river. Winter steelheaders are familiar with the Cowichan River. During the steelhead season drift boats float the river. Many anglers hire one of the knowledgeable Cowichan River fishing guides.

The road veers away from Skutz Falls area and goes 3 km north to Highway 18. Just before the Highway 18 intersection, swing left onto Old Lake Cowichan Road and continue another 7 km to the village of Lake Cowichan. The upper end of the Cowichan River Footpath emerges onto this road about 3 km from the townsite.

CONTACTS

- BC Forest Service (South Island Forest District): 250-724-9205
- BC Parks (South Vancouver Island District): 250-391-2300

MAPS/GUIDES

- BC Forest Service Duncan Forest District Recreation Map
- Cowichan Lake brochure (Cowichan Lake District Chamber of Commerce)
- Cowichan River Footpath Map and Fishing Guide (Cowichan Fish and Game Association)
- Community maps of North Cowichan and South Cowichan (LRH Ventures)
- National Topographical Series: 92C/16 Cowichan Lake (1:50,000); 92B/3 Duncan (1:50,000)
- Provincial Maps: 92B/NW Victoria (1:125,000); 92C/NE Nitinat Lake (1:125,000)
- *Hiking Trails II: Southeastern Vancouver Island* (VITIS)

NEAREST SERVICES

Duncan; Lake Cowichan.

Trip 3: Victoria to Parksville

(Highways 1 & 19)

IN BRIEF

Travel from Victoria to Parksville is now easier (and quicker) than ever since highway improvements were made to the Trans-Canada (Highway 1) on Victoria's western approaches and farther up-Island on sections of Highway 19. The 18.5-km Nanaimo Parkway, on Nanaimo's west side, is a treat to drive. Many well-known provincial parks are just minutes from the paved roads. The route is close to several logging road networks.

ACCESS

Take Highway 1 west from Victoria to the traffic lights at Spencer Road, just west of the Millstream Road interchange. Reset your vehicle's trip meter to zero at the Spencer Road lights and head north.

DESCRIPTION

This trip follows the Island Highway (Highways 1 and 19) from Victoria to Parksville. Many provincial parks, wilderness campsites, hiking destinations and logging-road networks are fairly close to the paved roads. We'll begin at the Spencer Road/Trans-Canada Highway intersection, just north of Millstream Road in Victoria's western outskirts. Reset your vehicle's trip meter to zero at the Spencer Road lights and continue north. At km 2.7 turn left onto Sooke Lake Road and follow the signposts to Goldstream Provincial Park. You can confirm a spot at one of the park's 159 serviced campsites by calling the BC Parks Discover Camping Campground Reservation Service at 1-800-689-9025 (in Vancouver, dial the last seven digits only). Campsites are also available on a first-come, first-served basis.

From Sooke Lake Road the highway drops down a hill to pass Goldstream Park's day-use section and picnic area (km 5), along the Goldstream River. It's a great spot to view spawning fall salmon. Hundreds of bald eagles flock to the river estuary between December and February. Call 250-478-9414 for information on the park's annual Eagle Extravaganza. The Visitor Centre schedules seasonal interpretative programs and nature displays. A path on the west side of the highway winds to Vancouver Island's own Niagara Falls, where Niagara Creek catapults over a mossy cliff to a canyon

Nanaimo Parkway

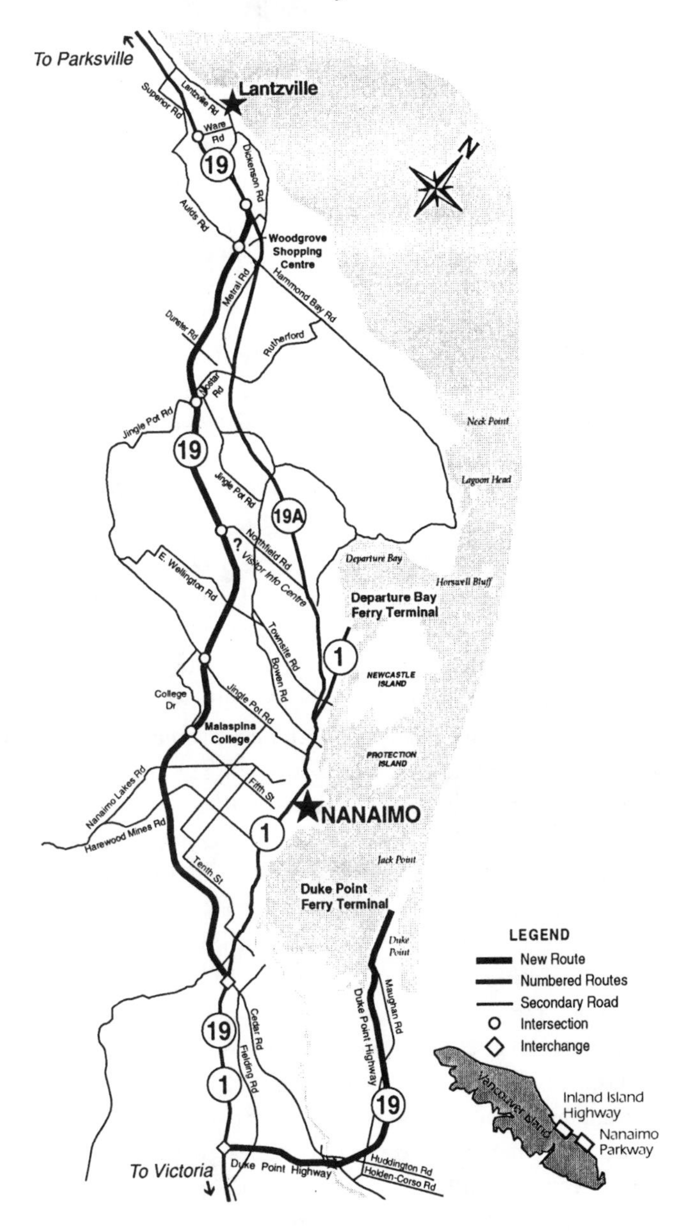

Map courtesy of the Vancouver Island Highway Project.

pool. Best time to visit is following heavy rains. Be prepared for spray.

Near the top of the Malahat, just north of the South Shawnigan Lake cut-off, watch for the signposted turn (on the left at km 15.4) for Spectacle Lake Provincial Park. Spectacle Lake, named for its shape, has a fine swimming beach at its east end. The lake is stocked with Eastern brook trout and many anglers use the hiking trail that circles the lake. At the Malahat Summit (352 m above sea level) a viewpoint overlooks Finlayson Arm. Two more lookouts follow, with views of Brentwood Bay, Haro Strait and (on clear days) the often snowy heights of Mount Baker in Washington State.

Bamberton Provincial Park (km 22.5), another favourite destination for family campers, has fifty campsites, a large picnic area and supplied wood and water. A fabulous 225-m sandy beach fronts Saanich Inlet. The park participates in BC Parks Discover Camping Reservation System.

At km 27.5 you'll reach the Shawnigan Lake turn in Mill Bay. Gravel roads extend beyond Shawnigan Lake's northwest end to access the Kinsol trestle, Koksilah River Provincial Park and the backroads to Weeks Lake. Four-wheelers might opt for the rugged seasonal route from Weeks Lake to Butler Main, closer to Sooke. (See Section Two: Trip 1.)

You can cut off Highway 1 just over the 34-km mark and journey in to Cowichan Bay, a scenic alternate drive through rolling farmlands near Duncan. There is a saltwater boat ramp at Cowichan Bay. Turn left onto Koksilah Road (km 38) and follow the signs to Bright Angel Provincial Park. The suspension footbridge over the Koksilah River is a big feature. The park has riverside trails and a fine picnic site with tables and a covered barbecue pit.

Highway 1 drops down a hill to cross the Koksilah River just south of Duncan. A left at the light at the Allenby Road intersection (km 43.5) is the turn for the Cowichan River Footpath's Glenora trailhead. This is also the turn for the backroads in MacMillan Bloedel's Cowichan Division. Take Allenby Road, then Indian Road and Glenora Road to the Deerholme gate. (You can also take the Bright Angel Park turn on Highway 1 and follow Koksilah Road and Miller Road to Glenora Road.) Mainlines are in good to fair shape, with some steep hills; secondary roads could require a 4 x 4. The area is subject to fire closures. Public access is permitted only on weekends and holidays, and visitors must check in at the watchman's gatehouse and pay a small entry fee. The gate is locked at night. Call ahead for current information. Remember to camp only in designated campsites.

Several Shawnigan Division lakes provide good spring and fall fishing. Keating, Lois and Wild Deer lakes are excellent May fly-casting destinations. Wild Deer Lake has a wilderness campsite. Note that some of the region's smaller lakes are catch-and-release only. Check the current regulations carefully. (See *More Island Adventures*, Trip 5.)

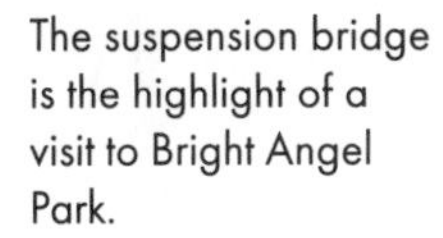
The suspension bridge is the highlight of a visit to Bright Angel Park.

Ladysmith, on the 49th parallel, has some of the steepest streets of any community on Vancouver Island. North of Ladysmith turn right onto the south end of Cedar Road (km 78) for Quennell Lake, with its many arms, and Holden Lake. In Cassidy, the Nanaimo Lakes Road meets Highway 1 at km 83. This paved road runs about 22 km west to the gravel backroads in TimberWest's Nanaimo Lakes region, a favourite with campers, anglers and backroad adventurers. Public access is restricted to weekends and holidays and visitors must sign in. (See Section Two: Trip 4.)

At the Duke Point ferry terminal interchange (km 87), Highway 19 meets Highway 1 and swings north with the Trans-Canada to the start of the Nanaimo Parkway, at the next interchange near the north end of Cedar Road (km 88.5). Stay on Highway 1 for Petroglyph Provincial Park, just south of Nanaimo. From the parking area short trails lead to rock carvings dating back thousands of years. In downtown Nanaimo, watch for the signs indicating the turn for the Newcastle Island ferry. This boat takes foot passengers over to Newcastle Island, a marine park accessible only by water. There is a campsite there and many trails to explore. The island was once a producer of coal, and two quarries operated there years ago. The ferry dock is behind the hockey arena. Highway 1 runs north to the Departure Bay BC Ferries terminal. Stay on what is now called Highway 19A to reconnect with Highway 19, near the Woodgrove Shopping Centre.

From its start at Cedar Road's north end, the Nanaimo Parkway skirts Nanaimo's west side to its northern terminus (km 107) just north of the Aulds Road/Hammond Bay Road intersection. A bike path runs along part of the parkway. At km 108.5 you'll reach the Lantzville turn at Ware Road. MacMillan Bloedel's Northwest Bay Main meets Highway 19 at the km-122 traffic lights. This gravel mainline accesses a number of trout lakes in the hills northwest of Nanaimo. Some spurs are unmaintained and may require high-slung vehicles or 4 x 4s. Boomerang, Blackjack and Kidney lakes contain cutthroat or rainbow trout; some have both species. Check with MacBlo for current access restrictions.

The Inland Island Highway section of Highway 19 begins at the Craig's Crossing interchange (around the km-123 mark). (Section One: Trip 6 follows Highway 19 north from Parksville to Campbell River.) Stay on Highway 19 and head northwest for 5.5 km to the Highway 4A interchange and exit for Parksville. Many visitors cut onto Highway 19A at Craig's Crossing for Rathtrevor Beach Provincial Park (headquarters for BC Parks Strathcona District) and downtown Parksville.

Rathtrevor Beach Provincial Park has 174 serviced campsites surrounded by Douglas fir, a group camping area, picnic tables, a children's playground, a sani-station for recreational vehicles and hot showers. The park's warm, shallow beach is ideal for swimming or seeking sand dollars on the sandy flats. Over the summer an open-air amphitheatre is used for interpretative park programs. Arrive early to ensure a campsite or reserve a space through the BC Parks Discover Camping Campground Reservation Service.

In downtown Parksville, at the Alberni Highway and Highway 19A junction, turn left for Port Alberni and Long Beach. The drive along Highway 4 from Parksville to Port Alberni and west to Pacific Rim National Park is described in Section One: Trips 4 & 5. Stay on Highway 19A to follow the oceanside route north from Parksville to Qualicum Beach, Qualicum Bay, Deep Bay and Bowser, Vancouver Island's lighthouse country. (See Section One: Trip 6.)

CONTACTS

- BC Forest Service (South Island Forest District): 250-724-9205
- BC Parks (South Vancouver Island District): 250-391-2300
- BC Parks (Strathcona District): 250-954-4600
- Local Chambers of Commerce and Tourist Information Centres
- MacMillan Bloedel (Cowichan Division): 250-245-6300/ 250-746-1078 (watchman's gate)
- MacMillan Bloedel (Northwest Bay Division): 250-468-7621
- TimberWest (Nanaimo Lakes security gate): 250-754-3032

MAPS/GUIDES

- Community maps of North and South Cowichan (LRH Ventures)
- Guide to Forest Lands of Southern Vancouver Island (Lake Cowichan Combined Fire Organization)
- MacMillan Bloedel Recreation and Logging Road Guide to the Cowichan Division
- TimberWest Nanaimo Lakes Logging Road Guide
- National Topographical Series: 92B/13 Duncan (1:50,000); 92G/4 Nanaimo (1:50,000); 92F/1 Nanaimo Lakes (1:50,000); 92F/8 Parksville (1:50,000); 92B/12 Shawnigan Lake (1:50,000)
- Provincial Maps: 92F/SE Port Alberni (1:125,000); 92B/NW Victoria (1:125,000)
- *Backroading Vancouver Island* (Neering/Whitecap)
- *Hiking Trails I* and *Hiking Trails II* (VITIS)
- *Parks of British Columbia & The Yukon* (Paquet/Maia)

NEAREST SERVICES

Various communities along the route.

Trip 4: Parksville to Port Alberni

(Highway 4)

IN BRIEF

Depending on which exit you take from Highway 19 (Inland Island Highway) to reach Highway 4 (Alberni Highway), you can visit two popular riverside provincial parks (Englishman River and Little Qualicum Falls). Highway 4 passes Cameron Lake, runs through Cathedral Grove and accesses the backroads to Mount Arrowsmith Regional Park and Labour Day Lake.

ACCESS

Take Highway 19 from Craig's Crossing (just south of Parksville, where Highway 19A hooks into the Island Highway) to the Highway 4A interchange, about 5.5 km away. (See Section One: Trip 3.) Exit and head about 10 km west on Highway 4A to the junction with Highway 4. You can also continue north for 8.5 km on Highway 19 to the Highway 4 interchange to access our starting point, just west of Coombs. Gravel mainlines extending off Highway 4 are seasonally in good to fair shape. Active logging may restrict public access on some backroads.

DESCRIPTION

We'll begin our run at the junction of highways 4 and 4A, west of Parksville. There are two approaches from the Island Highway. Take the Coombs/Parksville exit (5.5 km from Craig's Crossing) and continue west on Highway 4A for about 3 km to Errington Road, the access to Englishman River Falls Provincial Park. There are 105 tent and RV sites here. The waterfall and river ravine intrigue countless visitors at this serviced family campsite. Reservations can be made through the BC Parks Discover Camping Campground Reservation Service at 1-800-689-9025. Highway 4A runs through Coombs to the junction with Highway 4, about 10 km from the Inland Island Highway.

If you choose Highway 19's Qualicum Beach/Port Alberni exit, about 14 km from Craig's Crossing, follow Highway 4 toward Port Alberni for 2.5 km to the Highway 4A junction, west of Coombs. Reset your vehicle's trip meter to zero here.

Keep right at km 6.7 for Little Qualicum Falls Provincial Park. The park features swimming holes and a gravel beach. Avoid the area below the waterfalls; treacherous currents make swimming here dangerous. There are over ninety camping spots at this location. A daily fee is in place from April to October. Trails extend beyond the park boundaries, with one route leading up Wesley Ridge.

Cameron Lake, a popular sailboarding destination, is bordered by steep mountains and has two picnic sites on its south side. The first is at the lake's east end (km 10.8). A steep trail up Mount Arrowsmith starts close by. The second picnic site is just over 2.5 km farther west. Cameron Lake (477 ha) contains rainbow, cutthroat and brown trout as well as kokanee.

The look of Cathedral Grove (km 16.4), part of MacMillan Park and one of the more popular stops of interest, was forever changed in January 1997 when a severe windstorm whipped through the narrow Cameron Valley and caused scattered blowdowns, some between 30 and 45 m wide. The 15-ha Cathedral Grove section of the park, famous for its huge 500- to 800-year-old Douglas fir, received damage to ten percent of its trees. The storm's havoc spread around Cameron Lake and as far east as Little Qualicum Falls Park. Surprisingly, the Horne Lake area, one valley to the north, escaped relatively unscathed. A BC Parks self-guided interpretative trail through the windfall helps inform visitors about forest regeneration. Future improvements may include a new, safer parking area (away from the highway) and an information centre. The BC Forest Service publishes *Parksville to Pacific Rim*, an informative pamphlet that describes Highway 4 and its logging history.

Highway 4 climbs to the Alberni summit (375 m). Should you choose to explore the backroads near Mount Arrowsmith, watch for the Mount Arrowsmith Regional Park turn (km 26) and cut left. Area gravel mainlines are usually in good to fair shape. Washouts and snows may render some roads seasonally impassable. Follow the River Road mainline to the Cameron River bridge and the nearby Pass Main junction, about 10.5 km from Highway 4. Pass Main, with steep, long grades and several switchbacks, snakes a farther 10 km to the entrance to Mount Arrowsmith Regional Park and area hiking trails. You can stay on Pass Main to a viewpoint of the Strait of Georgia and Hornby, Denman and Texada islands. Anglers can continue on to St. Mary's Lake for rainbow and cutthroat trout fishing. You usually can't get to the lake until June, after the ice and snow melt.

From the Pass Main junction, anglers and hikers often travel east on Lake Road (for just over 13 km up the Cameron River Valley) to the Labour Day Lake trail, near Mount Moriarty. You'll encounter confusing forks and unmarked intersections on the way and the road is seasonally rough. (See *More Island Adventures*, Trip 14 for more detailed directions.) Labour Day

A sailboarder tests the winds on Cameron Lake.

Lake is a higher-elevation rainbow trout fishing destination at the 899-m level. A trail circles the lake and there are a couple of user-maintained wilderness campsites. Experienced hikers can seek out the route east from Labour Day Lake that leads to Indian Lake and then drops into TimberWest's Nanaimo Lakes territory.

Once over the hump (as locals refer to the summit), Highway 4 twists down to Port Alberni, situated at the head of Alberni Inlet. On Port Alberni's eastern outskirts (km 31.5) keep left for Bamfield. This turn is close to the Port Alberni Tourist Info Centre. Highway 4 swings right to the foot of Johnston Street and the Somass River (km 36). (See Section One: Trip 5 for a look at what awaits you along Highway 4 from Port Alberni to Long Beach.)

Call the Alberni Forest Information Centre at 250-724-7890 for updated summer hours and schedules for annual public logging tours available by reservation to school groups and through advance booking. Stop in and pick up a copy of MacMillan Bloedel's *Recreation and Logging Road Guide to*

TFL 44, a detailed map that covers backroads in the Alberni Valley, Nitinat and Long Beach regions.

CONTACTS

- Alberni Forest Information Centre (Port Alberni): 250-724-7890
- BC Forest Service (South Island Forest District): 250-724-9205
- BC Parks (Strathcona District): 250-954-4600
- MacMillan Bloedel (Franklin Operations): 250-720-4200

MAPS/GUIDES

- BC Forest Service *Parksville to Pacific Rim* brochure
- BC Forest Service Port Alberni Forest District Recreation Map
- Guide to Forest Lands of Southern Vancouver Island (Lake Cowichan Combined Fire Organization)
- MacMillan Bloedel Recreation and Logging Road Guide to TFL 44
- National Topographical Series: 92F/2 Alberni Inlet (1:50,000); 92F/7 Horne Lake (1:50,000); 92F/1 Nanaimo Lakes (1:50,000); 92F/8 Parksville (1:50,000)
- Provincial Map: Regional Map #2 Parksville/Tofino (1:125,000)
- *Hiking Trails II* (VITIS)
- *Southern Vancouver Island Hiking Trails* (Rogers/Heritage House)

NEAREST SERVICES

Coombs; Parksville; Port Alberni.

Trip 5: Port Alberni to Long Beach

(Highway 4)

IN BRIEF

The 88-km jaunt along Highway 4 from Port Alberni to the Long Beach area is one of the most spectacular drives on Vancouver Island. The mountain and river scenery is breathtaking and the route accesses freshwater lakes and area backroads.

ACCESS

Drive through Port Alberni on Highway 4 to the foot of Johnston Street. (See Section One: Trip 4.) Swing right at the T-junction near the Somass River onto River Road and follow the Tofino/Ucluelet signposts. Gravel logging mainlines accessed along Highway 4 are in good to fair shape. Secondary roads are best suited for a high-slung vehicle or 4 x 4.

DESCRIPTION

The Port Alberni-to-Long Beach run starts in Port Alberni at the foot of Johnston Street. (See Section One: Trip 4.) At the T-junction close to the Somass River, turn right onto River Road and reset your vehicle's trip meter to zero.

To reach Stamp Falls Provincial Park, swing right onto Beaver Creek Road (km 0.3) and continue 12 km to the entrance. This park, open from April to October, is a great place to view the fall salmon runs. One riverside trail starts near the campsites and leads to a spectacular view of the river canyon. Some trails are used by shorecasters. A farther 6.2 km north on Beaver Creek Road runs to the junction of Somers and Woolsey roads. A secondary gravel road starts nearby. This route snakes through woodlands on Lanternman Creek's east side to connect with the logging road network to Courtenay. (See Section Two: Trip 10.)

Highway 4 meets Mission Road around the 3-km mark. Cross the Somass River bridge and cut left onto Mission Road for the backroads to Nahmint or Sproat lakes. (See Section Two: Trips 7 & 8.) The highway crosses the Sproat River bridge (km 8) and then curves to Great Central Road (km 10). A right here runs 7.5 km to the foot of Great Central Lake. The Robertson Creek hatchery is a kilometre before the lake. Tours can be arranged at this facility, which rears young chinook and coho salmon. The backroad network from the Port Alberni area to Courtenay begins at Great Central Lake. The nearby Ark Resort is one starting point for adventurers heading to Della Falls, Canada's highest waterfall. (See Section Three: Trip 6.)

Sproat Lake Provincial Park (km 10.3) is one of Vancouver Island's most popular family camping destinations. There are showers, firewood and a sani-station. The fifty-nine sites at this serviced locale are split between two camping areas. RVs and large trailers are best suited for the sites near the lake. Those with small camper units and tents will find the forested spots on the north side of Highway 4 more to their liking. The latter are accessed from Great Central Road.

Sproat Lake Park has a large picnic area, an extensive beachfront, a boat launch and moorage. There are several hiking trails. One path leads to petroglyphs on a lakeside cliff face. Many people opt to base camp at the park and day-trip to local attractions. Lakeshore Road, near the park entrance, runs west to Bomber Base Road and Sproat Lake's water bomber base, home to the Martin Mars water bombers. Over the summer, the Martin Mars (used to combat Island forest fires) moor offshore in Sproat Lake and are easily viewed from Sproat Lake Park.

Highway 4 follows along the north side of Sproat Lake, with many excellent vistas. Taylor Arm Provincial Park (km 19.3) is undeveloped and intended for group outings. Reservations for a gate key may be made through the BC Parks Strathcona District office in Parksville. The park is open from April to October and there is no fee. Trails connect the camping area with the park's day-use area on Sproat Lake, on the south side of Highway 4.

At km 30.4 an unmarked industrial road meets Highway 4. Turn left for a wilderness campsite and natural boat ramp near the mouth of the Taylor River. This river is Sproat Lake's largest tributary, with a watershed of forty square kilometres. It was named after Charles Taylor, Port Alberni's first settler (1864). Near the rest area and picnic site (km 37.8) the Taylor River has formed a deep pool. An information signpost adjacent to the parking area describes area fish and provides historical background.

Highway 4 crosses the Taylor River bridge to an industrial road (km 38.5). Turn left for the backroad that winds along Sproat Lake's south side. (See Section Two: Trip 8.) The highway climbs through Sutton Pass (km 43), 175 m above sea level. The deep canyons of the Kennedy River highlight this part of the route. One riverside pulloff is on the right at km 51.8. Here you can watch the river as it drops through a chute. Following heavy rains, the Kennedy River explodes into roiling whitewater.

Watch for the sign that indicates a salmon enhancement trail at km 59.5. A kilometre away is a riverside highway rest stop. About 64.5 km west of

The Stamp River is popular with steelheaders.

Port Alberni, Highway 4 passes a rough boat access on an eastern arm of Kennedy Lake. Then it's up via the switchbacks to a panoramic view west. First-time visitors often mistake the wide expanse of Kennedy Lake, the largest in area (6,475 ha) on Vancouver Island, for the Pacific Ocean. The road hugs the cliffs, twists down to lakeside and levels out to run alongside Kennedy Lake.

Look for a logging road on the left that begins to parallel the highway. This key junction (km 76), where the signposted Maggie Lake Forest Service Road (Toquart Road) meets Highway 4, is the starting point for the 16-km backroads run to the BC Forest Service wilderness campsite on Toquart Bay. Just before this turn, watch for a bright yellow highway sign indicating the logging road. (Section Two: Trip 9 covers the backroads to Toquart Bay's beautiful west-coast beach.)

Highway 4 heads 4 km west to a natural boat launch on Kennedy Lake (km 79.7). One January, I spotted a group of five or six otters cavorting on a wooden raft just offshore. By the time I had parked and zipped back for some photos, the sleek animals had returned to the chilly lake waters and were gliding west. Just over 6 km from the Toquart Bay turn, watch for the access road (on the right just past the 82-km mark) for Kennedy Lake Beach, a popular swimming destination. The sandy beach in a pocket cove on Kennedy Lake is part of Pacific Rim National Park Reserve and intended for day use only; no camping is permitted.

MacMillan Bloedel's West Main (km 86.3) meets the highway 10.5 km west of the Toquart Bay cut-off. Close by is the Walk in the Forest interpretative trail constructed by the Share the Clayoquot Society. You can turn right here and drive to some great paddling, backroading and fishing areas in the southern forests of Clayoquot Sound. (See Section Two: Trip 9.)

From the West Main intersection, it's only 1.5 km to the T-junction where Ucluelet travellers cut south; those going to Pacific Rim National Park Reserve and Tofino bear north. It's 18 km to the turn for the Grice Bay public boat launch, 21.4 km to the road to the Radar Hill viewpoint. Radar Hill, a Pacific Rim National Park Reserve landmark, almost had a name change in 1996. Bemused local residents were not even contacted by the federal government about the idea. Later, it was decided to honour the Canadian war effort at Kap'yong Hill, Korea, with a monumental plaque on Radar Hill.

Radar Hill offers a spectacular panorama of the inlets, islands, mountains and coastal temperate rainforests that make up Clayoquot Sound. In late 1996, 133 countries supported the United Nations Educational Scientific and Cultural Organization (UNESCO) designation of Clayoquot Sound as an international biosphere reserve.

CONTACTS

- Alberni Forest Information Centre (Port Alberni): 250-724-7890
- BC Forest Service (South Island Forest District): 250-724-9205
- BC Parks (Strathcona District): 250-954-4600
- MacMillan Bloedel (Sproat Operations): 250-720-4100
- Pacific Rim National Park Reserve (Ucluelet): 250-726-7721
- Rainforest Interpretative Centre (Tofino): 250) 725-2560

MAPS/GUIDES:

- BC Forest Service *Parksville to Pacific Rim* brochure
- BC Forest Service Port Alberni Forest District Recreation Map
- MacMillan Bloedel Recreation and Logging Road Guide to TFL 44
- National Topographical Series: 92F/3 Effingham River (1:50,000); 92F/6 Great Central Lake (1:50,000); 92F/7 Horne Lake (1:50,000); 92F/4 Tofino (1:50,000)
- Provincial Map: Regional Map #2 Parksville/Tofino (1:125,000)
- *Pacific Rim Explorer* (Obee/Whitecap)
- *Hiking Trails III* (VITIS)

NEAREST SERVICES

Port Alberni; Tofino; Ucluelet.

Trip 6: Parksville to Campbell River

(Highway 19)

IN BRIEF

The Inland Island Highway section of Highway 19 extends 43.5 km from Craig's Crossing, south of Parksville, to Mud Bay, near Rosewall Creek Provincial Park. From Mud Bay to Campbell River, Highway 19 winds north along Vancouver Island's east coast. At the time of this writing (1998), the northern section of the Inland Island Highway (from Mud Bay to the southern outskirts of Campbell River) was not completed. When this highway opens in stages through the year 2001, the entire oceanside route from Craig's Crossing to Campbell River will be designated Highway 19A.

ACCESS

Take Highway 19 to the Craig's Crossing interchange, just south of Parksville. (See Section One: Trip 3.) Head north on Highway 19.

DESCRIPTION

For this trip take the Inland Island Highway north from Parksville to Mud Bay. Distances between the highway interchanges were tabulated at points where the roads crossed. Drivers will notice variances at on-ramps and exits. Other highway junctions and access roads are signalled intersections. Until the last section of the new highway is finished, Highway 19 will follow the coastal route from Mud Bay to Campbell River.

From Craig's Crossing (km 0), near Parksville, Highway 19 heads west for about 5.5 km to the Highway 4A interchange. Exit here and swing north for Parksville; travel west on Highway 4A for Englishman River Falls Provincial Park, Errington, Coombs and the junction with Highway 4. (See Section One: Trip 4.)

From the Highway 4A interchange, stay on the Inland Island Highway to the Highway 4 interchange (km 14). Take Highway 4 (Alberni Highway) 2.5 km to the Highway 4A junction, west of Coombs. (See Section One: Trip 4.) Cut north on Memorial Avenue for Highway 19A and Qualicum Beach. Summer sunsets along the waterfront are a delight.

At km 28 you'll reach the Horne Lake Road intersection. This is the turn for Bowser and Qualicum Bay. Many visitors fish or swim at Horne

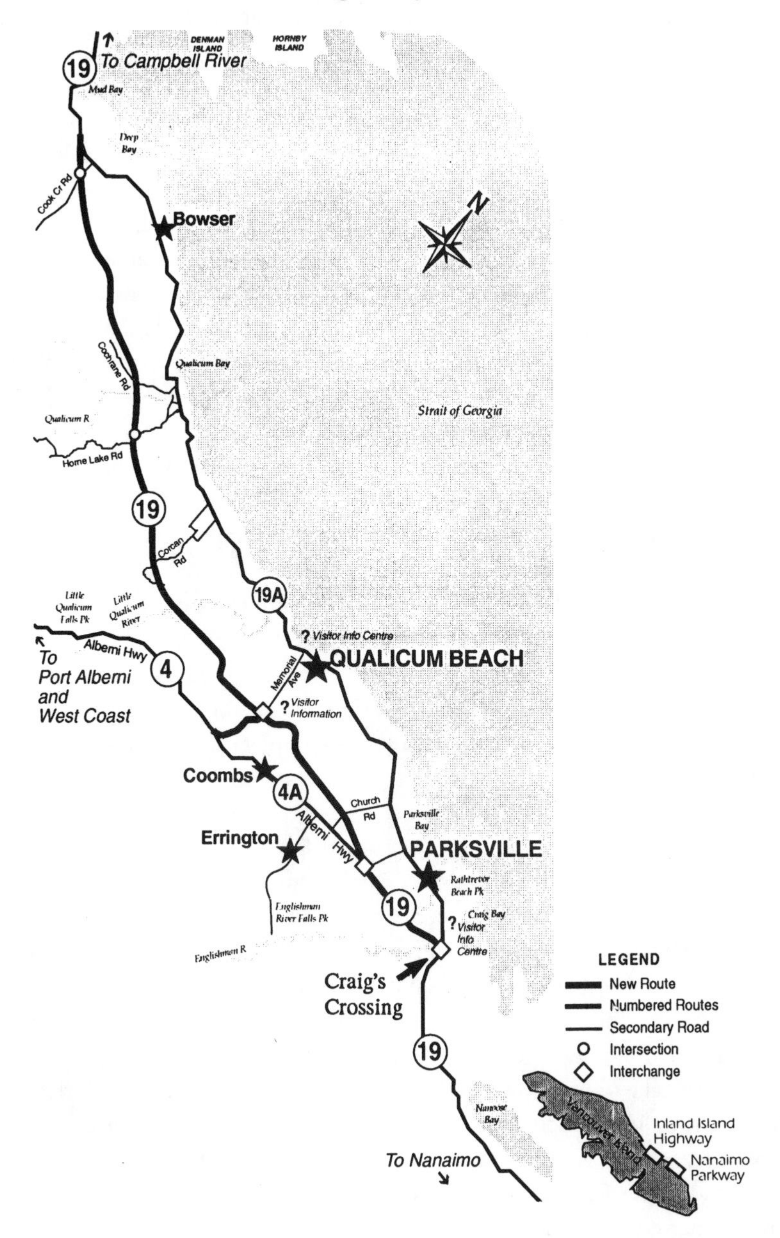

Map courtesy of the Vancouver Island Highway Project.

Lake, or picnic at nearby Spider Lake Provincial Park. At the west end of Horne Lake, spelunkers explore cave networks at Horne Lake Caves Provincial Park, near the Big Qualicum River.

Turn left at the Horne Lake Road intersection and follow the signs for 6 km to Spider Lake Provincial Park. The park is accessed via Turnbull and Lakeview roads. A small parking area is located on Spider Lake's southeast fringe. The main parking lot is just down the road. Spider Lake Provincial Park, created in 1981, is intended for day use only. The gate remains locked between 11 p.m. and 7 a.m. Lakeside trails, a gently sloping, grassy shoreline and a sandy beach for summer swimming make Spider Lake a perfect spot for a family picnic. Canoes, kayaks and rowboats are ideal on the lake. A boat launch is available for small cartoppers. No power boats are allowed. Rainbow and cutthroat trout, kokanee and steelhead inhabit Spider Lake (57 ha), which also provides good smallmouth bass fishing. Check current freshwater regulations carefully.

For Horne Lake, turn west from Highway 19 and follow the Horne Lake Caves signs. Near the one-lane bridge over the Big Qualicum River anglers will find water access. Small trailered boats can be launched with care from the rough shoreline. Near the launch point a dam blocks the natural flow into the Big Qualicum River. A sluice gate controls water volume from Horne Lake and water temperature is regulated from three water intake levels, effectively protecting the Big Qualicum River from flood and drought. This greatly increases the survival rates of fish fry. All species of salmon return to the river, as do steelhead and sea-run cutthroat trout. A trip to the Horne Lake area is not complete without a stop at the Big Qualicum Hatchery. The signposted access road is just off Highway 19A, north of the Spider Lake/Horne Lake cut-off. In the fall, visitors can view spawning salmon through a window below the river's surface.

Horne Lake (848 ha) contains cutthroat and rainbow trout, steelhead and kokanee. You can fish year round, but peak times are in the late spring and fall. Powerful winds deflect off the cliffs of Mount Mark. Horne Lake waters can turn ugly in minutes; small boaters and paddlers beware. Many visitors base at the private campsite at Horne Lake's west end and day-trip. The campground has a good boat launch that accommodates larger boats.

Horne Lake Caves Provincial Park, created in 1971, is about 12 km from the Highway 19 junction. From the parking area near the Big Qualicum River footbridge, a trail winds along the river to the cave mouths. The Horne Lake Main and Lower Caves are open for self-guided tours. Reservations and details on summer guided tours of the Riverbend Cave (gated to prevent vandalism) can be obtained through the Horne Lake Caves Info Line at 250-757-8687. Call 250-248-7829 for information on more advanced guided tours.

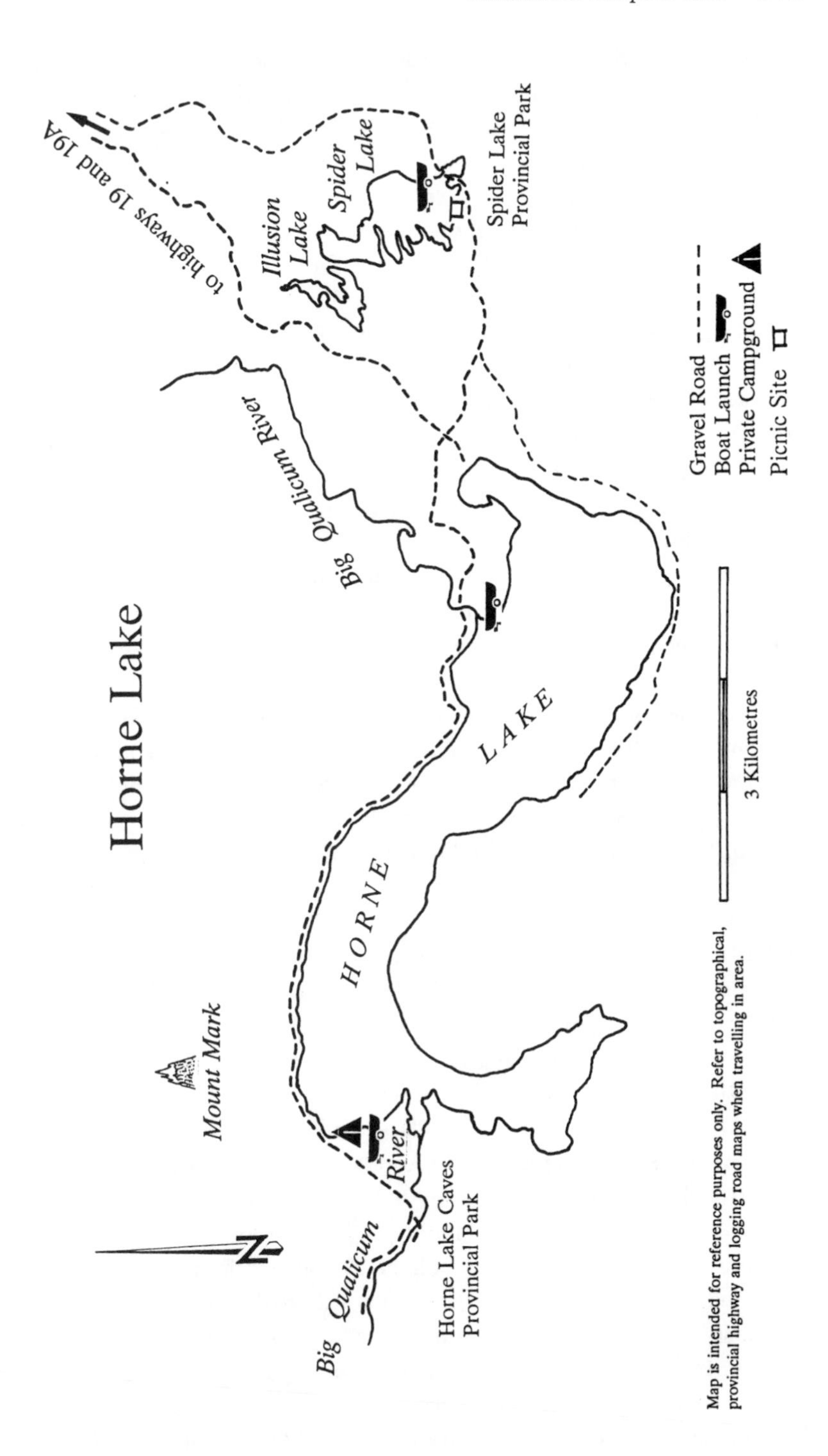
Horne Lake
to highways 19 and 19A
Illusion Lake
Spider Lake
Spider Lake Provincial Park
Big Qualicum River
HORNE LAKE
Mount Mark
Big Qualicum
River
Horne Lake Caves Provincial Park
Gravel Road
Boat Launch
Private Campground
Picnic Site
3 Kilometres
Map is intended for reference purposes only. Refer to topographical, provincial highway and logging road maps when travelling in area.

Continue north of the Horne Lake Road intersection to Cook Creek Road, just under the 40-km mark. Turn here to connect with Highway 19A near Mud Bay. This is also the cut-off for Deep Bay and Rosewall Creek Provincial Park, a wintering area for waterfowl. The Inland Island Highway meets the north end of Highway 19A, the scenic oceanside route, at km 43.5. (This access point will be closed when the new section of the Inland Highway opens.) From here Highway 19 hugs the coast to Courtenay.

Around the 52.5-km mark is the Denman Island ferry terminal at Buckley Bay. A second ferry departs Denman Island for the smaller Hornby Island. Denman Island's Fillongley Provincial Park is a popular destination, even with its limited number of camping sites. Hornby's two provincial parks (Tribune Bay and Helliwell) are for day use only. Tribune Bay's warm, shallow beach attracts sunbathers and swimmers; Helliwell Park features a bluff trail that overlooks the Strait of Georgia. Both islands have hiking trails.

At the Royston lights at km 68 swing left for Cumberland, once a coal-mining centre. The Cumberland Museum is full of historical relics from the mining days. Drive through Cumberland and follow the signs to the Comox Lake's southeast shore and a convenient boat launch. You can camp or picnic nearby.

Courtenay is next, with an economy based on farming, logging, fishing and tourism. Saltwater anglers often base in the Courtenay/Comox district for fishing vacations. You can take Lake Trail Road from Courtenay west to the logging roads near Comox Lake and the Willemar Lake region. One backroad connects with the mainlines in the Port Alberni area. (See Section Two: Trip 10.)

In Courtenay, at km 73, Highway 19 swings right to cross the 17th Street bridge. Follow the Campbell River signs to the Ryan Road intersection. Cut right on Ryan Road for Little River and the Powell River ferry. Keep straight ahead for Campbell River. At the km-75 traffic light, swing right on Highway 19 for Campbell River. Straight through, on Headquarters Road, leads to the Mount Washington and the Forbidden Plateau ski areas. Over the summer Forbidden Plateau hiking trails are a popular destination. (See Section Three: Trip 8.) Another access to the ski areas is north of Courtenay, at Howard Road (km 90). From this point it's 13 km along a zigzag course to the bottom of Mount Washington Road.

Miracle Beach Provincial Park, a large 193-site serviced facility, is at km 97. Turn right from Highway 19 and continue east to the park entrance. There is a great beach here. Over the summer, visitor programs are featured in the open-air amphitheatre. Arrive early in the morning so you can secure a spot at this fine family campground. A fee is charged from mid-May to September. Miracle Beach Provincial Park participates in the BC Parks Discover Camping

Campground Reservation Service. Call 1-800-689-9025 for information.

At km 103 you'll reach Oyster Bay Shoreline Park, a bird sanctuary. Cut left at km 110.5 onto the Jubilee Parkway, a 4.5-km link to the Inland Island Highway's Campbell River bypass. At km 122 you'll reach the Willis Road intersection. Less than 3 km ahead is the junction with Highway 19A and Highway 28.

Some visitors prefer to drive north from the Jubilee Parkway turn and take the oceanside route to Campbell River (Highway 19A). You'll pass Big Rock, a huge glacier-deposited erratic left from the last Ice Age. Across Discovery Passage you'll identify Quadra Island and the Cape Mudge lighthouse. This stretch has many resorts and charter-boat businesses that cater to area salmon fishermen. Campbell River's Discovery Pier is a great spot for beginners and seasoned shorecasters to try their luck. Some good-sized fish have been caught from the pier, which extends 183 m out from the shore.

The Quadra Island ferry terminal is located on Highway 19A, near Campbell River's downtown core. Some people day-trip to Quadra Island and visit First Nations petroglyphs near the Cape Mudge lighthouse. Beautiful Rebecca Spit Provincial Park (a marine park) has safe moorage for boaters. You can also drive to this day-use park and walk the length of its long, sandy beach. Quadra Island's Main Lake Canoe Route and Village Bay Lake Provincial Park are excellent paddling destinations.

About 13 km from the Jubilee Parkway turn, Highway 19A reaches the junction with Highway 19 and Highway 28, near the Campbell River bridge. Take Highway 28 west for Gold River. (See Section One: Trip 7.) For North Island points, stay on Highway 19 and cross the Campbell River bridge. (See Section One: Trip 8 for an account of the run along Highway 19 from Campbell River to Sayward.)

Let's backtrack now to Craig's Crossing for a brief look at the 39.5-km oceanside route along Highway 19A from Parksville to Cook Creek Road. At Craig's Crossing cut onto Highway 19A to pass the Parksville area Tourist Information Centre and Rathtrevor Beach Provincial Park. (See Section One: Trip 3.) In downtown Parksville, the Alberni Highway meets Highway 19A, 5 km from Craig's Crossing. About 24 km from the Alberni Highway junction, turn left onto Horne Lake Road for Spider Lake and Horne Lake Caves provincial parks.

Highway 19A parallels Vancouver Island's east coast to spectacular seascapes; on clear days mainland mountain ranges form a striking backdrop for Lasqueti and Texada islands, in the Strait of Georgia. The tiny communities along the highway (from the Horne Lake area north to Qualicum Bay, Bowser and Deep Bay) are collectively known as Vancouver Island's lighthouse country. The area is extremely popular with salmon anglers.

Fishing resorts line the highway, offering boat rentals, accommodation and knowledgeable fishing guides. Highway 19A meets Cook Creek Road around 42 km from Craig's Crossing. Turn left for Highway 19 or continue north for 2.5 km to Rosewall Creek Provincial Park.

CONTACTS

- BC Forest Service (South Island Forest District): 250-724-9205
- BC Parks (Strathcona District): 250-954-4600
- Big Qualicum Hatchery: 250-757-8412
- Horne Lake Caves Info Line: 250-757-8687
- Local Chambers of Commerce and Tourist Information Centres

MAPS/GUIDES

- BC Forest Service Port Alberni Forest District Recreation Map
- BC Parks Horne Lake Caves brochure
- National Topographical Series: 92F/10 Comox (1:50,000); 92F/11 Forbidden Plateau (1:50,000); 92F/7 Horne Lake (1:50,000); 92F/14 Oyster River (1:50,000); 92F/8 Parksville (1:50,000); 92K/3 Quadra Island (1:50,000)
- Provincial Maps: 92F/NW Buttle Lake (1:125,000); 92F/SE Port Alberni (1:125,000); 92F/NE Powell River (1:125,000)
- *Hiking Trails III* (VITIS)
- *Parks of British Columbia & The Yukon* (Paquet/Maia)

NEAREST SERVICES

Various communities along the route.

Trip 7: Campbell River to Gold River

(Highway 28)

IN BRIEF

Highway 28 snakes 87 km from Campbell River to Gold River to access several provincial parks, fishing and paddling lakes, challenging hiking trails and spectacular Strathcona Park mountain scenery. And there are plenty of backroads along the way.

ACCESS

Highway 28 starts on the outskirts of Campbell River, at the junction of Highway l9 and Highway 19A. (See Section One: Trip 6.) North Island travellers will stay north on Highway 19 to cross the Campbell River bridge. For Gold River cut west onto Highway 28. The road is narrow, with sharp curves. Industrial traffic is frequent. Logging mainlines accessed along Highway 28 are in good shape; secondary roads are good to fair. Some older roads may require a high-slung vehicle or 4 x 4. Fire closures and active logging may restrict public access.

DESCRIPTION

Highway 28 winds from Campbell River to Gold River and provides access to provincial parks, fishing lakes, wilderness campsites, nature walks and hiking trails. At the junction of Highway 19 and Highway 19A, near the Campbell River bridge, head onto Highway 28 and reset your vehicle's trip meter to zero.

At km 1.5 watch for the signposted entrance to Elk Falls Provincial Park. This large campground is fully serviced with 121 tent and vehicle sites. A fee is charged from mid-May to September. Located on the banks of the Quinsam River, it's a good spot to base camp while visiting the Campbell River region. A forested trail runs from the campsite to the DFO Quinsam River salmon hatchery.

The highway skirts the Campbell River and climbs a long hill to the day-use section of the park (km 4.4). Tall Douglas fir and a series of river waterfalls (Moose, Deer and Elk) will enchant visitors. If you continue over the John Hart Dam, the road hooks into the backroads on (Lower) Campbell Lake's north side. This is the quickest and best route to Loveland Bay Provincial Park, especially if you are driving a large RV or pulling trailered boats.

Next is the signposted entrance for McIvor Lake, part of Campbell Lake. Popular with swimmers, boaters and anglers, McIvor Lake has great beaches and a boat launch. The lake holds cutthroat and rainbow trout, as well as Dolly Varden (char). The highway winds by Echo Lake (24 ha), where there is cartop boat access at a tiny recreation site. Electric motors only may be used on the lake. Anglers shorecast for two trout species and Dolly Varden. Sunset fishing can be productive when risers dimple lake waters. At the west end of Echo Lake, near a TimberWest logging yard, Elk River Main, an active hauling road, intersects Highway 28 (km 16). This is one of several logging-road routes into the Sayward Forest *(See Section Two: Trip 12)*.

Argonaut Main meets Highway 28 at km 17.7. This industrial artery accesses Wokas Lake and Upper Quinsam Lake. Gooseneck Lake and Middle Quinsam Lake are reached via bumpy secondary roads. Area lakes (many with tiny user-maintained wilderness campsites and rough boat launches) contain cutthroat and rainbow trout and Dolly Varden. Small dams and spillways regulate water flow in district lakes and rivers. These diversions are part of the elaborate drainage system that maintains water levels for BC Hydro power stations nearer Campbell River.

Be ready to get lost – there are confusing, unmarked spurs. Side roads have many dips and dives on which you could scrape your vehicle's undercarriage. Off-season waterholes may impede progress. Heavy industrial traffic may be encountered on Argonaut Main. The first stretch of the route, though wide, can be extremely muddy in wet weather; large ore trucks from the Quinsam Coal Mine haul down Argonaut Main and frequently churn things up. (See *More Island Adventures,* Trip 18 for a more detailed look at these backroads.)

Turn right off Highway 28 at km 28.7 for Strathcona Dam. Cross the dam and take the Greenstone Forestry Road to the Sayward Forest. The Greenstone road is not suitable for large trailered boats or RVs. The highway follows the east side of Upper Campbell Lake to Strathcona Park Lodge (km 40.7), the well-known outdoor education centre and resort. The boundary of Strathcona Park is marked by the east portal, near a picnic site. At km 47.4, Highway 28 turns right to cross the bridge at Buttle Narrows, a short section of the Campbell River that connects Upper Campbell Lake with Buttle Lake. Seasonal headquarters (summer) for Strathcona Park are close by.

Before we continue on to Gold River, let's take a side trip down Westmin Road, into the heart of Strathcona Park's towering mountains. At Buttle Narrows keep straight ahead to parallel Buttle Lake's east side. Just ahead is a lakeside picnic site and boat launch, within easy range of Rainbow Island's four-site marine campsite. The Titus, Wolf River, Marblerock and Phillips Creek marine campsites, on Buttle Lake's west side, can only be reached by boat, kayak or canoe. A trail starts at the Phillips Creek site and switchbacks up to Marble Meadows, near Marble Peak.

From the Highway 28 junction to Buttle Lake's south end, the route passes a number of picnic sites and relatively easy nature trails at Lupin Falls, Auger Point and Karst Creek. The latter has a boat launch. Being dammed, Buttle Lake harbours sunken stumps and deadheads. Both Buttle Lake (4,204 ha) and Upper Campbell Lake (2,400 ha) are prone to strong winds. Use caution out on the water. The lakes contain rainbow and cutthroat trout and Dolly Varden.

The Ralph River Campsite, 26 km from Highway 28, has 76 user-maintained campsites, firewood and comfort stations. The Wild Ginger nature trail is just north of the campsite; the Shepherd Creek trailhead and the start of a challenging hike into the Comox Glacier Nature Conservancy Area is to the south. Just below Henshaw Creek watch for the trail to Flower Ridge.

At Buttle Lake's south end (34.5 km from Highway 28) the road crosses the Thelwood Creek bridge, close to the Price Creek Trail parking area. This trail goes 7 km up Price Creek Valley to deteriorate into a strenuous route to Cream Lake. Half a kilometre west of Thelwood Creek, take Jim Mitchell Lake Road for about 7 km to the Bedwell Lake Trail. Beyond Bedwell Lake a hiking route climbs to Cream Lake. Another rugged route heads down the Bedwell (Oinmitis) River Valley to terminate at the head of Bedwell Sound, in Clayoquot Sound. This trail, although regularly maintained by Friends of Strathcona, is not up to park standards.

A few years ago, a friend and I day-hiked along the Bedwell Lake Trail. We climbed as far as Bedwell Lake before foul weather set in. We put away our cameras, ate a hasty lunch on a bluff and began the 600-m descent to trailhead just as the fine drizzle turned to heavy showers. About halfway down, my friend inexplicably backed into me and kept slowly retreating. The reason for his strange behaviour lay just ahead. A very close, very large black bear sat blocking the trail. Our increasingly loud talking did little, except move the animal into the bushes just off the path, where he or she sat down again, seemingly content to scrutinize us some more. Finally, after we sang a few choruses of "Drunken Sailor," the bear had endured enough caterwauling and sauntered away deeper into the forest. Our hiking pace increased as we surged out to the trailhead.

Continue beyond Jim Mitchell Road for about a kilometre to the Myra Falls Trail. Watch for loose rock on the steep hill down to the series of waterfalls on Myra Creek. From here it's just under 4 km (through the Westmin Resources mine site) to the visitor parking area for the Phillips Ridge, Tennent Lake and Upper Myra Falls trails. Be sure to consult the BC Parks *Strathcona Provincial Park* brochure prior to any hikes. It includes trail maps and hiking hints and cautions. All Strathcona Park trails are closed to horses and mountain bikes. *Hiking Trails III: Central and Northern Vancouver Island and Quadra Island*, published by the Vancouver Island Trails Information Society, contains detailed maps and descriptions of the park's trails and routes.

Back now to the km-47.4 mark of Highway 28, at Buttle Narrows. Cross the bridge for the Buttle Lake Campsite, on Buttle Lake's west side, and Gold River. This site has eighty-five campsites, water, firewood, a nearby boat launch, a sandy beach and an adventure playground for the kids. Highway 28 skirts the west arm of Upper Campbell Lake. From the Lady Falls parking lot (on the left at km 64) visitors can hike up a short but steep trail to a picturesque cascade on Cervus Creek.

Around the 71-km mark, watch for the Elk River Trail signpost and follow the signs to the trailhead. The Elk River Trail climbs 555 m up the Elk River Valley to Landslide Lake. Years ago, the trailhead was relocated to avoid a crumbling cliff face and canyon. Newer bridges have replaced some tricky log crossings. Beyond Volcano Creek, at the top of a long hill, the path levels off and skirts the base of a waterfall. To protect water quality, camping is no longer permitted at Volcano Creek or Landslide Lake. Instead, use the gravel flats en route.

Highway 28 passes the Drum Lakes, part of the Campbell River hydro development. Lake water levels fluctuate periodically. Nearby, the 5-km Crest Mountain Trail goes up to a ridge offering commanding views of the Elk and Heber river valleys. At km 87 you'll reach Gold River. In the mid-1960s, the community was relocated from the mouth of the Gold River to its present location. Pacific Forest Products then constructed a pulp mill near the old townsite on Muchalat Inlet.

If you have a 4 x 4 you can attempt the backroads up to Donner Lake, inside Strathcona Park's western boundary. The lake, approximately 12 km east of Gold River, is close to Mount Donner; to the southwest tower the heights of Golden Hinde (2,200 m), Vancouver Island's highest mountain. Access is via Ucona Road and a series of branch roads. The route passes Kunlin Lake, a destination for summer cutthroat anglers. The last 5 km to 564 m-high Donner Lake can be rough. A short hike leads to lakeside. Cutthroat fishing at Donner Lake peaks in July and August. No power boats are permitted.

You can drive from Gold River to the end of Highway 28 at Muchalat Inlet. Rocky cliffs and towering mountains make the ride a scenic delight. Peppercorn Park, just outside the town limits, runs along the banks of the Gold River. Riverside trails go to a number of swimming beaches. About 2.7 km from Gold River, at the Big Bend picnic site, visitors often shorecast the

Gold River's deep pools. Many anglers base at the Lion's Club campsite during steelheading season. Stop in at the Pacific Forest Products office (just off the highway) and pick up a recreation and logging road guide to area backroads. PFP is a leader in genetic research that leads to taller trees of better quality. Its seed orchard and research centre are located in Saanich.

Finding a parking spot at the end of Highway 28 is difficult during the salmon season. Boaters with smaller craft should be alert for prevailing west winds, which funnel up Muchalat Inlet. Heavy chop is prevalent when the winds are contrary to an ebbing tide. At the Avenor pulp mill you might see trucks hauling timber off-load into the inlet, where scurrying dozer boats boom the logs. Steam and smoke billow from the mill as the rumble of heavy machinery drones in the background. Finished products from the mill are loaded directly onto sea-going ships. The M.V. *Uchuck III* docks nearby. On its scheduled run, freight and passengers are carried to isolated west-coast communities such as Tahsis, Zeballos and Kyuquot. The vessel (once an American minesweeper) was built in Portland, Oregon, in the 1940s.

From Gold River the Head Bay Forest Road passes the Upana Caves on its way to Tahsis. Another logging road, Gold River Main, heads north to Woss. (For a close look at the backroads from Gold River to Woss, see Section Two: Trip 13.)

CONTACTS

- BC Forest Service (Campbell River): 250-286-9300
- BC Parks (Strathcona District): 250-954-4600
- TimberWest (Oyster River Division): 250-287-7979
- Pacific Forest Products (Gold River): 250) 283-2221

MAPS/GUIDES

- BC Forest Service Campbell River Forest District Recreation Map
- BC Parks Strathcona Provincial Park brochure
- Campbell River Search and Rescue Society Logging and Highway Road Map
- Pacific Forest Products Recreation and Logging Road Guide to the Forest Lands of West Vancouver Island
- National Topographical Series: 92K/3 Quadra Island (1:50,000); 92F/l4 Oyster River (1:50,000); 92F/l3 Upper Campbell Lake (1:50,000); 92F/l2 Buttle Lake (1:50,000); 92E/l6 Gold River (1:50,000); 92E/9 Muchalat Inlet (1:50,000)
- Provincial Map: 92F/NW Buttle Lake (1:125,000)
- *Adventuring Around Vancouver Island* (Lebrecht/Noppe/Greystone)

- *Adventuring in British Columbia* (Nanton/Simpson/Douglas & McIntyre)
- *Hiking Trails III* (VITIS)
- *Parks of British Columbia & The Yukon* (Paquet/Maia)

NEAREST SERVICES

Campbell River; Gold River.

Trip 8: Campbell River to Sayward

(Highway 19)

IN BRIEF

Highway 19 stretches 64 km north from Campbell River to Sayward. Travellers will find countless trout lakes to visit and a variety of wilderness campsites, hiking trails and backroads to explore.

ACCESS

In Campbell River, at the junction of Highway 19, Highway 19A and Highway 28, take Highway 19 and head north to Sayward. (See Section One: Trip 6.) Gravel mainlines along Highway 19 are in good to fair shape. Expect some hauling in certain areas. Active logging could restrict public access. Secondary roads are rough and may require a truck or 4 x 4.

DESCRIPTION

Drive through Campbell River to the junction of Highway 19, Highway 19A and Highway 28. Take Highway 19 north for Sayward and reset your vehicle's trip meter to zero at the Campbell River bridge. The Seymour Narrows viewpoint (km 11) looks out on Discovery Passage and Race Point. On April 5, 1958, in the world's largest non-nuclear explosion, high explosives were used to blow up Ripple Rock, a submerged rock outcropping below the surface of the narrows. Over the years, more than 120 vessels had sustained damage when they struck or ran aground on Ripple Rock. You can take a closer look at the historical site along the Ripple Rock Trail, a 4-km trail to a bluff that overlooks Seymour Narrows. Surging tides in this waterway create whirlpools and standing waves that still demand respect from boaters negotiating the channel. Watch for the trailhead signpost, about 6 km north of the lookout.

MacMillan Bloedel's Menzies (Salmon River) Main (km 14.5) is the primary access to the Sayward Forest, northwest of Campbell River. Several backroad routes off Highway 28 (Gold River Highway) wind in from the south. This provincial forest (Crown land) consists mainly of second growth. Extensive rail logging decades ago removed many of the older stands of trees. Swaths of forest were destroyed in the Campbell River fire of 1938. The Sayward Forest has almost more BC Forest Service campsites than

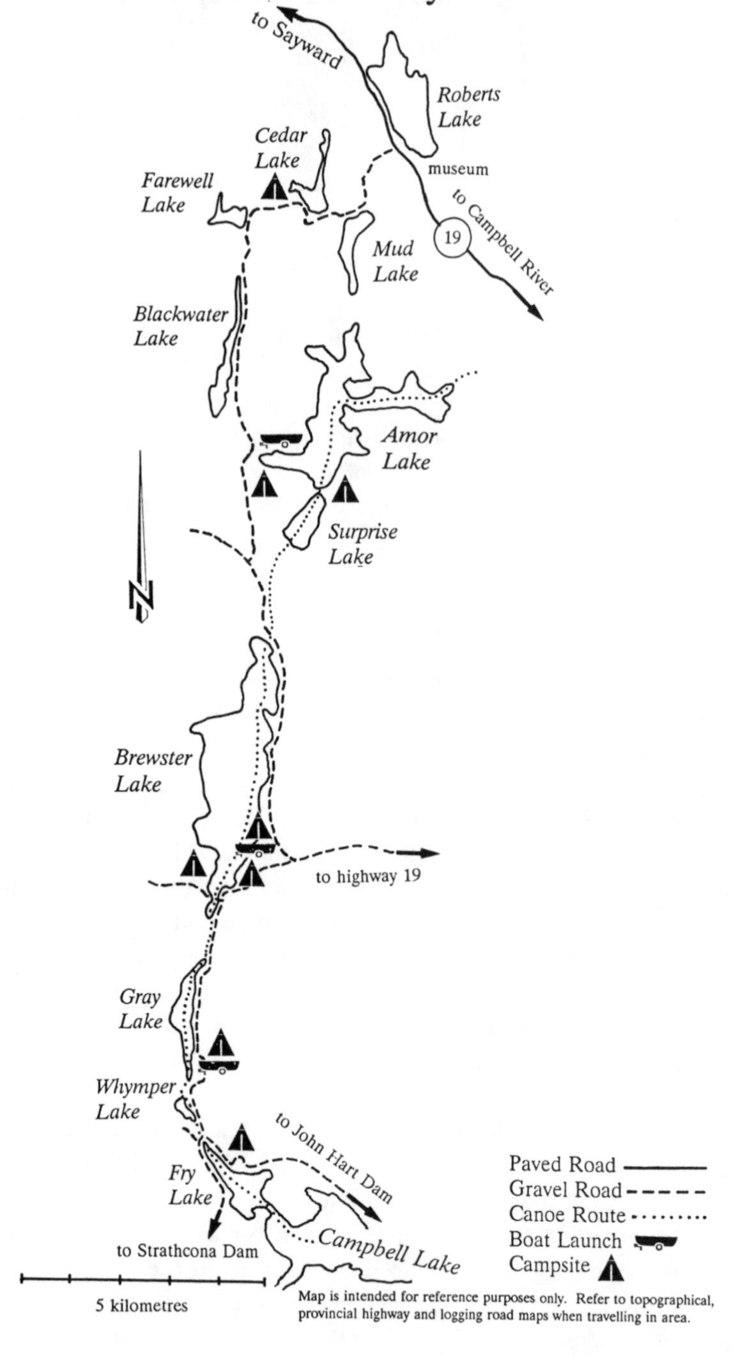
Amor Lake to Gray Lake
to Sayward
Roberts Lake
Cedar Lake
Farewell Lake
museum
to Campbell River
19
Mud Lake
Blackwater Lake
Amor Lake
Surprise Lake
Brewster Lake
to highway 19
Gray Lake
Whymper Lake
to John Hart Dam
Fry Lake
to Strathcona Dam
Campbell Lake
Paved Road
Gravel Road
Canoe Route
Boat Launch
Campsite
5 kilometres
Map is intended for reference purposes only. Refer to topographical, provincial highway and logging road maps when travelling in area.

fishing lakes. (See Section Two: Trip 12.)

Two more approaches to the Sayward Forest lie along Highway 19; both are secondary roads with seasonal rough spots. These routes are not recommended for trailers, RVs or low-slung vehicles. At km 24.7 Mohun Lake West Road swings by 28-ha Twin Lake (a popular cutthroat trout destination) to parallel Mohun Lake's west shore to Menzies Main. Both lakes have a two-site BCFS campsite and boat launch. Mohun Lake (191 ha) contains rainbow and cutthroat trout and Dolly Varden (char). These lakes are part of the Sayward Forest Canoe Route, a challenging 47.2-km paddling circuit that intersects the heart of the Sayward Forest. (See Section Three: Trip 9.)

Just over 30 km from the Campbell River bridge (near Roberts Lake), watch for a signposted BCFS road (Mud Lake Road) on the left. You can work your way about 18.5 km to Menzies Main, near Brewster Lake. Cedar Lake (33 ha) has a tiny wilderness campsite. Anglers with cartoppers seek the lake's cutthroat trout. At the 4.5-km mark turn left at a T-junction onto Blackwater Lake Road and head south to pass several lakes (Amor, Brewster, Gray and Whymper) along the Sayward Forest Canoe Route.

The BCFS Amor Lake campsite (km 9.7) is a good access point for paddlers, though parking is limited. This user-maintained site has a natural boat launch. A small cartop boat or canoe helps anglers test the waters of Amor Lake's many arms. Early morning and sundown are good times to be out on the water; sometimes the bite is sporadic. In addition to cutthroat trout, Amor Lake (362 ha) contains Dolly Varden (char) and kokanee salmon. Average size of the cutthroat is a little over 30 cm, but sometimes you'll hook into a slightly larger fish. Many area anglers practise voluntary catch-and-release.

From Amor Lake the road runs south to MacBlo's Long Lake Main (km 12.2). Turn left onto Long Lake Main, a bumpy road that skirts Brewster Lake's eastern fringe. An overgrown spur, just under a kilometre away, is a portage route up to Surprise Lake, part of the Sayward Forest Canoe Route. The BCFS maintains area portage trails seasonally. From a viewpoint at Brewster Lake (km 14) you can see Victoria Peak, one of Vancouver Island's highest mountains. (See Section One: Trip 9. More detailed information on a logging-road loop near Victoria Peak is found in *More Island Adventures*, Trip 21.)

At the Menzies Main junction (km 18.4) turn left and take Menzies Main east to Highway 19, just south of the Ripple Rock trailhead. If you swing west on Menzies Main you can connect with the backroad on (Lower) Campbell Lake's north side. Just under 2 km from Long Lake Road, turn left onto Gray Lake Road (just before the bridge at Brewster Lake's south end) for Campbell Lake Road. (See Section Two: Trip 12.)

Back on Highway 19, head north from the BCFS road to the Roberts Lake Resort and the Link and Pin Museum (km 30.5). The museum highlights the Sayward Forest logging history and features an extensive collection of kerosene lamps. The log building was moved to the Roberts Lake site from its original location near Sayward to save the structure from floods. A stop at the museum (open seasonally from June to September) is worth consideration.

Just north of Roberts Lake, backroad adventurers can explore four BC Forest Service roads to BCFS wilderness campsites at Stella, Pye and McCreight lakes. Stella South (km 32), Pye East (km 34) and Pye West (km 37) forestry roads are rough, seasonal routes. Their condition depends on the amount of maintenance received and the time of year. Call the Campbell River Forest Service for updated road information. Just north of the Pye East cut-off, Highway 19 passes the start of the McNair Lake Trail (km 34.3). This 1.8-km path follows an old railway grade to McNair Lake.

Rock Bay Road (km 40) is the principal route to area lakes. McCreight Lake has three wilderness campsites under 4 km from Highway 19. These include Sitka Spruce Beach (a small walk-in site at the lake's south end), Aldergrove and McCreight Lake. The latter has a steep boat launch. Friends and I sometimes overnight at McCreight Lake en route to North Island points. Rough secondary roads east of McCreight Lake lead to three Pye Lake perimeter campsites; stay on Rock Bay Road for the campsite on Stella Lake's west side. Area boat launches are rough and intended for cartop boats.

McCreight Lake (272 ha) and Stella Lake (423 ha) contain rainbow and cutthroat trout and Dolly Varden; McCreight also holds kokanee salmon. Pye Lake (370 ha) has char and cutthroat trout. Spring and fall are the best times to fish these lakes. Rock Bay Road accesses the forestry road to Little Bear Bay and a six-site user-maintained campsite, about 16 km from Highway 19. A trail leads to a nearby waterfall. Saltwater anglers bring small cartoppers to launch into the saltchuck at the rough boat ramp fronting the Thurlow islands.

Highway 19 passes the Big Tree Creek rest area (km 45.9) to the Dalrymple Trail (km 49.7). From the parking area a 500-m interpretative forest path winds through private MacBlo land near Dalrymple Creek to a picnic site near Gail's Falls. More challenging is the Salmon Lookout (km 54.8), a steep trail that climbs 3 km to an old forestry lookout. Hikers are rewarded with a panoramic view of the Salmon River Valley.

At the Sayward junction (km 63.7), turn right for Sayward and Kelsey Bay, about 10 km away. Old ships form a breakwater close to the dock on expansive Johnstone Strait. (Stay north on Highway 19 for Woss, a trip described in Section One: Trip 9.)

CONTACTS

- BC Forest Service (Campbell River): 250-286-9300
- MacMillan Bloedel (Menzies Operations): 250-287-5000

MAPS/GUIDES

- BC Forest Service Campbell River Forest District Recreation Map
- BC Forest Service Sayward Forest Canoe Route pamphlet
- Campbell River Search and Rescue Society Logging and Highway Road Map
- MacMillan Bloedel Campbell River/Sayward Recreation and Logging Road Guide
- MacMillan Bloedel Dalrymple Creek Nature Trail Guide
- National Topographical Series: 92K/4 Brewster Lake (1:50,000); 92K/3 Quadra Island (1:50,000); 92K/5 Sayward (1:50,000)
- Provincial Map: 92L Alert Bay (1:250,000)

NEAREST SERVICES

Campbell River; Sayward.

Trip 9: Sayward To Woss

(Highway 19)

IN BRIEF

The 65 km stretch of Highway 19 north from Sayward to Woss accesses two routes to Schoen Lake Provincial Park, two gravel mainlines to Gold River and some great paddling, fishing, hiking and camping spots.

ACCESS

This trip starts along Highway 19, at the Sayward Junction. (See Section One: Trip 8.) Gravel mainlines along Highway 19 are in good to fair condition. Fire closures and active logging may restrict public access in some areas.

DESCRIPTION

At the Sayward Junction, reset your vehicle's trip meter to zero and take Highway 19 north to the Keta Lake rest area, about 9 km from the Sayward Junction. At km 9.7, Upper Adam Road crosses the paved road. Left turns are prohibited from the highway. Take the logging road on the right and backtrack across Highway 19 on the Upper Adam Road bridge. This is the start of a backroads loop within MacMillan Bloedel's Kelsey Bay Operations.

The 61-km Adam River/White River loop offers spectacular mountain scenery among some of Vancouver Island's highest peaks, including Victoria Peak (2163 m). Heavy industrial traffic may be encountered on some area backroads. MacBlo recommends you travel after 5:30 p.m. on weekdays.

The Upper Adam Road logging mainline climbs 21.4 km to the Schoen Lake Provincial Park trail that leads through Nisnak Meadows to Nisnak Lake and on to Schoen Lake's unroaded east end. (See Section Three: Trip 10.) Upper Adam Road connects with the backroads to Tlowils and Stewart lakes, popular angling destinations. Tlowils Lake (26 ha) holds cutthroat and rainbow trout. Stewart Lake (46 ha) has cutthroat trout, Dolly Varden (char) and kokanee. Both lakes have small wilderness campsites and rough boat launches. Only electric motors may be used at these lakes. Check the current freshwater fishing regulations for Stewart Lake; additional restrictions apply. The White River Valley features rocky canyons, deep pools and a picturesque waterfall in its lower reaches. (For more in-depth information

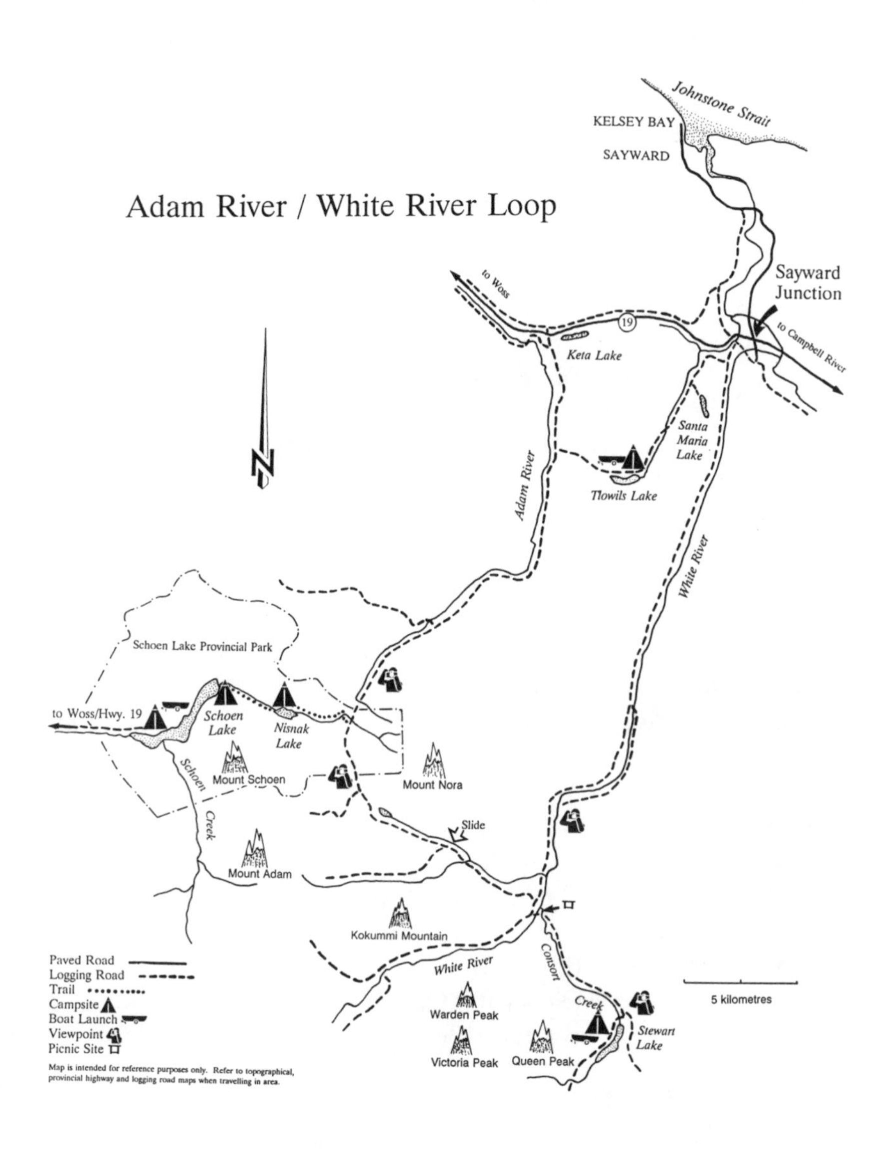

Adam River / White River Loop
Johnstone Strait
KELSEY BAY
SAYWARD
Sayward Junction
to Woss
19
to Campbell River
Keta Lake
Santa Maria Lake
Tlowils Lake
Adam River
White River
Schoen Lake Provincial Park
to Woss/Hwy. 19
Schoen Lake
Nisnak Lake
Mount Schoen
Schoen Creek
Mount Nora
Slide
Mount Adam
Kokummi Mountain
White River
Consort Creek
Warden Peak
Victoria Peak
Queen Peak
Stewart Lake
5 kilometres
Paved Road
Logging Road
Trail
Campsite
Boat Launch
Viewpoint
Picnic Site
Map is intended for reference purposes only. Refer to topographical, provincial highway and logging road maps when travelling in area.

on the Adam River/White River backroads see *More Island Adventures*, Trip 21.)

Rooney Lake (16 ha), on the right at the 20.5-km mark, contains cutthroat trout and Dolly Varden (char). Shorecasters will find easy access close to Highway 19. Turn right onto Rooney Lake Road (km 22.5) to reach a tiny MacBlo wilderness campsite (with a boat launch) on the lake's north shore. The main access to MacBlo's Eve River Operations meets Highway 19 just over the 26-km mark. You can take Main Line or East Main down the Eve River Valley to private user-maintained wilderness campsites, picnic sites, river fishing holes and a boat launch on Johnstone Strait. Check with MacBlo for current access restrictions and hauling information.

Approximately two-thirds of the way to Woss, Highway 19 swings south in the upper Tsitika River Valley and leaves MacBlo woodlands to enter Canadian Forest Products territory. Watch for the signpost at km 54.5 that indicates the cut-off for Schoen Lake Provincial Park (and the lake's west-end campsite) and Mount Cain. (See Section Three: Trip 10.) This is also the turn for the logging road to the Klaklakama Lakes and a backroads route to Vernon Lake and Gold River. (See Section Two: Trip 13.)

At the Hoomak Lake rest stop (km 58.5) there are picnic tables, a cartop boat launch and Canfor's 3-km interpretative forest trail. Hoomak Lake (94 ha) has cutthroat trout and Dolly Varden (char). Like most area lakes, the best fishing occurs in the spring or fall.

The Woss turnoff is at km 65. Woss is Canfor headquarters. Stop in at their office for a copy of the Englewood Logging Division (TFL 37) recreation map. From Woss you can follow logging roads south to Gold River. (A trip from Gold River to Woss is described in Section Two: Trip 13.)

CONTACTS

- BC Forest Service (Port McNeill): 250-956-5000
- BC Parks (Strathcona District): 250-954-4600
- Canadian Forest Products (Woss): 250-281-2300
- MacMillan Bloedel (Eve River Operations): 250-287-7473
- MacMillan Bloedel (Kelsey Bay Operations): 250-282-3100
- North Island Forestry Centre (Beaver Cove): 250-956-3844

MAPS/GUIDES

- BC Forest Service Port McNeill Forest District Recreation Map
- Canadian Forest Products Englewood Logging Division (TFL 37) Recreation Map
- MacMillan Bloedel Campbell River/Sayward Recreation and Logging Road Guide

- Pacific Forest Products Recreation and Logging Road Guide to the Forest Lands of West Vancouver Island
- National Topographical Series: 92L/8 Adam River (1:50,000); 92K/5 Sayward (1:50,000); 92L/1 Schoen Lake (1:50,000); 92L/2 Woss Lake (1:50,000)
- Provincial Map: 92L Alert Bay (1:250,000)
- *Hiking Trails III* (VITIS)

NEAREST SERVICES

Sayward; Woss.

Trip 10: Woss to Port Hardy

(Highway 19)

IN BRIEF

From Woss to Port Hardy (about 100 km), Highway 19 runs through the heart of northern Vancouver Island. Paved roads lead to Port Alice, Port Hardy and Port McNeill. Logging roads branch off the highway to regional and provincial parks, wilderness campsites, fishing and paddling lakes and remote coastal communities.

ACCESS

This trip begins at the Woss turn on Highway 19. (See Section One: Trip 9.) Mainlines along Highway 19 are in seasonally good to fair shape; expect industrial traffic on some routes. Seasonal fire closures and active logging can restrict public access. A 4 x 4 may be required on secondary roads. Deactivated roads may be impassable.

DESCRIPTION

We'll start this run at the Woss turn on Highway 19. (See Section One: Trip 9.) Near the Zeballos turnoff (about 21 km north of the Woss cut-off) many backroad adventurers take the 44.5-km logging-road route that skirts Bonanza and Ida lakes to Beaver Cove and Telegraph Cove. Wilderness campsites (co-managed by the BC Forest Service and TimberWest) are en route, as are several trout-fishing destinations. From Highway 19, on the south side of the Steele Creek bridge, cut right onto the logging road, reset your trip meter to zero and swing east. Area roads are not suitable for RVs or large trailered boats.

The Bonanza Lake South wilderness campsite (km 15.5) has fourteen user-maintained camping spots and a nearby boat launch. Bonanza Lake (901 ha) is habitat for rainbow and cutthroat trout, Dolly Varden (char) and kokanee salmon. Summer steelhead trout and coho salmon pass through the lake. Late spring and early fall are prime fishing times. Watch the winds and weather when boating or paddling. Anglers should be aware of the mandatory release of wild rainbow over 50 cm caught in Bonanza Lake and Ida Lake to the north. Check the current regulations carefully.

At a junction near Bonanza Lake's top end (just under the 25-km mark)

Bonanza Lake

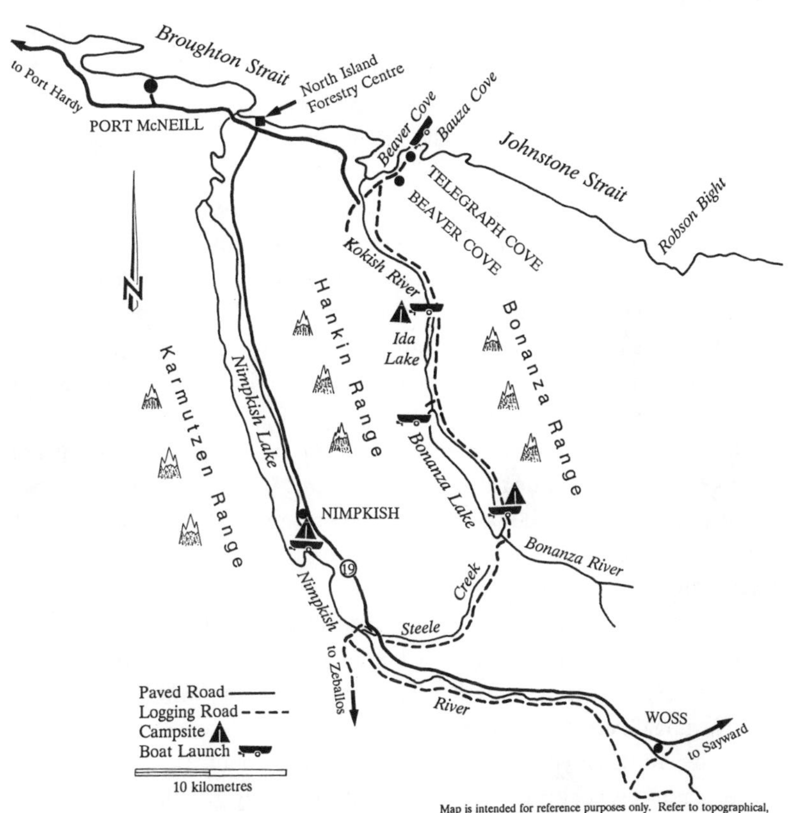

turn left from Main Road South and cross the Bonanza River bridge to the Bonanza Lake North recreation site, with a picnic area and three tiny campsites. This area, known for spring birdwatching, is an ideal launch point for canoes, kayaks and small cartoppers. Pilings from a disused booming ground stand out in the lake. The Ida Lake (108 ha) wilderness campsite and boat launch is a few kilometres north on the mainline, near a demonstration forest.

Main Road South parallels the Kokish River. Rock canyons limit winter steelhead migration to the river's lower reaches. When water levels are right, a tiny run of summer steelhead works upriver and through Ida and Bonanza lakes. (For a closer look at the Bonanza Lake backroads run, see *More Island Adventures*, Trip 23.) Just over the 42-km mark you'll reach a junction. Turn left for the paved road and the North Island Forestry Centre, close to Highway 19. Keep straight ahead for Beaver Cove, TimberWest's Beaver Cove logging office and the picturesque village of Telegraph Cove, about 2.5 km away.

Before the Island Highway was completed in the late 1970s, Beaver Cove was the northern end of a BC Ferries route from Kelsey Bay. Beaver Cove remains a bustling place. Canfor's Beaver Cove dryland sort is the northern end of one of the last operating logging railways in the world. The line stretches south from Beaver Cove to Vernon and crosses Highway 19 a number of times. TimberWest logs are trucked to Beaver Cove, sorted and then towed to mainland mills.

Telegraph Cove, nestled on a tiny bay fronting Johnstone Strait, sits on pilings connected by a boardwalk. The historic (now idle) sawmill started by the pioneering Wastell family is a stop of interest. Sport fishing, whale watching (Telegraph Cove is near Robson Bight) and diving opportunities draw many summer visitors.

Back on Highway 19, take the Zeballos turn (on the north side of the Steele Creek bridge) for more trout lakes (Atluck and Anutz lakes provide anglers with good spring and fall fishing), wilderness campsites, Little Huson Cave Regional Park and more intriguing backroads. Reset your vehicle's trip meter to zero when you cut onto Zeballos Road, about 21 km from Woss. The Nimpkish River bridge is 2 km from the highway. At km 2.7 bear left to follow the south side of the Nimpkish River back to Woss. This 24-km route is subject to periodic bridge and road closures. Anglers can reach river pools (with a little bushwhacking) from numerous points along this backroad. Experienced kayakers put in at the confluence of the Nimpkish River and Kaipit Creek for a challenging ride down the river to Nimpkish Lake.

Keep right at the km-2.7 junction for Zeballos. At km 3, turn right for the Canfor campsite at Anutz Lake. Many visitors stop at this wilderness campsite (once a logging camp) and base here for area angling and backroad explorations. A rough boat ramp accommodates small, trailered boats. Anutz Lake (98 ha) contains rainbow trout. Paddlers can explore a connecting stream from Anutz Lake to the south end of Nimpkish Lake.

Continue beyond Anutz Lake to Little Huson Cave Regional Park, about 6 km from Highway 19. (On most maps and signposts the park is incorrectly spelled as Little Hustan Cave Park.) Located on Atluck Creek, park highlights include rock arches, caves and a natural rock bridge in the Atluck Canyon. Limestone formations like these are common on northern Vancouver Island; the features at Little Huson Cave Regional Park are some of the most accessible. Nearby Huson Lake has both rainbow and cutthroat trout and a boat launch at its south end.

Back on Zeballos Road, cut right at km 9 onto Atluck Road and watch for the signs for Atluck Lake. This route is close to Mukwilla Lake (42 ha), a good rainbow trout fishing destination in the late spring or early fall. This lake also holds kokanee. Wolfe Lake (20 ha), to the south, is habitat for rainbow and cutthroat trout and Dolly Varden. Both lakes have cartop boat access.

Atluck Lake (308 ha) has a five-site BCFS/Canfor campsite and boat launch on its eastern fringe. Watch for the entrance just under the 13-km mark. Pinder Peak's lofty heights make a stunning backdrop for spring and fall anglers seeking the lake's rainbow and cutthroat trout. Dolly Varden is also present. Atluck Lake is narrow and surrounded by steep mountains. Sudden winds can create heavy chop and dangerous whitecaps in minutes. Use caution in smaller craft. The mainline parallels the cliffs on Atluck Lake's north shore to a boat launch and picnic site near lakehead. (For a look at the backroads from Atluck Lake's west end to Tahsish Inlet, an area reference map and an account of a paddling adventure in Tahsish/Kwois Provincial Park, see Section Three: Trip 11.)

A left at the km-9 junction onto Pinder and Zeballos mainlines leads another 32 km to Zeballos. These roads are travelled by industrial traffic and not recommended for RVs. Zeballos, once a booming iron and gold-mining centre, is a port-of-call for the M.V. *Uchuck III*, out of Gold River. A serpentine logging mainline runs farther west to Fair Harbour, the former site of a logging camp. It was dismantled in 1969 and relocated at Zeballos. Today, Fair Harbour is the saltwater launch point for Kyuquot, the tiny west-coast community on outer Kyuquot Sound. Many ocean paddlers begin explorations of Kyuquot Sound waters at Fair Harbour. Some travellers base at the BCFS user-maintained campsite, near the federal dock. There are twenty-five camping spots here and a boat launch. This recreation site is managed by the BCFS Campbell River District office.

Highway 19 heads north from the Zeballos cut-off to the community of

The North Island has plenty of fishing lakes.

Nimpkish (km 29.3). Turn left and follow the signs down the hill for the BCFS/Canfor Nimpkish Lake campsite. Located on Nimpkish Lake, close to the mouth of the Nimpkish River, this twenty-site user-maintained locale can be ideal for windsurfers. Strong daily thermals create excellent sailboarding conditions. Blustery winds usually come up by mid-morning and persist till late afternoon. Lake waters can get rough. When on Nimpkish Lake, stay close to the shore and keep an eye on the weather, especially if you're paddling an open canoe. Nimpkish Lake, 25 km in length, contains cutthroat trout and Dolly Varden. Gang trolls are effective at the creekmouths.

The mountain scenery across the lake from the recreation site is part of Nimpkish Lake Provincial Park, established to protect an old-growth western hemlock forest in the Tlakwa Creek watershed. A little north of the community of Nimpkish, turn left off Highway 19 for the BCFS/Canfor Kinman Creek Recreation Site, located in a tall second-growth forest. A trail goes to Nimpkish Lake. Next, Highway 19 runs above Nimpkish Lake's east side to provide spectacular views of the jagged mountains of the Karmutzen Range, on the west shore. At the Beaver Cove Road junction (km 55), swing right and continue for about 13 km to Beaver Cove, 15.5 km to Telegraph Cove. The North Island Forestry Information Centre is located at this turn. Stop in and inquire about logging-road maps, forestry information and schedules for a variety of seasonal logging tours. The office is open from June through August.

Highway 19 crosses the Nimpkish River bridge just past the 56-km mark. Lower Nimpkish has Provincial Park protects most of the steep Nimpkish River Valley, downstream from the foot of Nimpkish Lake to the river flats south of the highway bridge. This prime habitat for black bear and salmon is visited by experienced kayakers and canoeists who challenge the lower Nimpkish River's tricky tidal and river currents. Beware of large mid-stream boulders.

At km 62, turn right for Port McNeill, a logging and fishing town. A ferry runs to Cormorant Island and the village of Alert Bay, noted for its tall totem poles. The ferry also services Sointula, a fishing community on Malcolm Island. Just under 4 km north of the Port McNeill turn are MacMillan Bloedel's Port McNeill Division headquarters. The world's largest burl marks the entrance to the office complex. Nearby, West Main intersects Highway 19 (km 66). Turn left onto West Main to access more wilderness hiking, paddling and fishing destinations. (See Section Two: Trip 14.) The Port Alice Highway meets Highway 19 just under the 86-km mark, about halfway between Port McNeill and Port Hardy. (See Section One: Trip 11 for a description of the 30-km drive to Port Alice, on Neroutsos Inlet.)

Highway 19 terminates in Port Hardy, situated on Hardy Bay, a small coastal indentation of Queen Charlotte Strait. Adjacent Bear Cove is the southern terminus of the BC Ferries Prince Rupert and Bella Coola runs. Many of Port Hardy's residents are engaged in logging or fishing. Area waters provide excellent saltwater angling.

At nearby Fort Rupert, the Tex Lyon Trail snakes north along Beaver Harbour to Dillon Point, with spectacular seascapes en route. The 7-km (one-way) hike to Dillon Point starts near Beaver Harbour Park's boat launch, at the end of the long, sandy beach. Precise knowledge of the tides is essential when rounding the rock bluff, about twenty minutes from the trailhead. Always time your travels for an ebb tide. Consult the *Canadian Tide and Current Tables: Vol. 6* published by the Canadian Hydrographic Service. From the bluff to Dillon Point, allow four hours' hiking time. Some sections of the coastal trail are rough. Dillon Point, with easy boat access, has a picnic and barbecue area.

Logging roads extend west from Port Hardy to Holberg, Winter Harbour and Raft Cove and Cape Scott provincial parks. (See Section Two: Trip 16.)

CONTACTS

- BC Forest Service (Campbell River): 250-286-9300
- BC Forest Service (Port McNeill): 250-956-5000
- BC Parks (Strathcona District): 250-954-4600
- Canadian Forest Products (Woss): 250-281-2300
- Local Chambers of Commerce and Tourist Information Centres
- MacMillan Bloedel (Port McNeill Division): 250-956-5200
- North Island Forestry Centre (Beaver Cove): 250-956-3844
- TimberWest (Beaver Cove Division): 250-928-3023

- Western Forest Products (Port McNeill) 250-956-3391
- Regional District of Mount Waddington (Port McNeill): 250-956-3301

MAPS/GUIDES

- BC Forest Service Port McNeill Forest District Recreation Map
- BC Forest Service Campbell River Forest District Recreation Map
- Canadian Forest Products Englewood Logging Division (TFL 37) Recreation Map
- MacMillan Bloedel Port McNeill/Port Hardy Recreation and Logging Road Guide
- Pacific Forest Products Recreation and Logging Road Guide to the Forest Lands of West Vancouver Island
- TimberWest Beaver Cove Logging Road Guide
- Western Forest Products Visitors' Guide to Northern Vancouver Island
- National Topographical Series: 92L/10 Alert Bay (1:50,000); 92L/7 Nimpkish Lake (1:50,000); 92L/11 Port McNeill (1:50,000); 92L/2 Woss Lake (1:50,000)
- Provincial Map: 92L Alert Bay (1:250,000)
- *Canadian Tide and Current Tables: Vol. 6* (Canadian Hydrographic Service)
- *Whitewater Trips for Kayakers, Canoeists and Rafters on Vancouver Island* (Pratt-Johnson/Soules)

NEAREST SERVICES

Nimpkish; Port McNeill; Telegraph Cove; Woss.

Trip 11: The Port Alice Highway

IN BRIEF

From Highway 19, about halfway between Port McNeill and Port Hardy, the Port Alice Highway snakes 31 km through rolling hills to Port Alice, on Neroutsos Inlet. You'll pass Marble River Provincial Park and the Marble River campsite, a base for many visitors. Area backroads lead to fishing lakes, day-use recreation sites and wilderness campsites.

ACCESS

On Highway 19, drive just less than 24 km northwest of the Port McNeill cut-off to the Port Alice Road. (See Section One: Trip 10.) The route is a paved highway with blind hills and winding sections. Gravel mainlines accessed along the highway are in good to fair shape. Secondary roads are rough. Deactivated roads may be impassable. Active logging and fire closures may limit public access.

DESCRIPTION

The Port Alice Highway meets Highway 19 midway between Port McNeill and Port Hardy. (See Section One: Trip 10.) It's a pleasant 30-minute drive to Port Alice, which, like Gold River, was one of BC's instant towns, dependent on the forest industry. Reset your vehicle's trip meter to zero at the highway junction. The Beaver Lake recreation site, maintained by Western Forest Products and the BC Forest Service, is on the right at km 0.5. This day-use area has a swimming float, a beach and picnic tables. Beaver Lake (7 ha) contains cutthroat and rainbow trout and Dolly Varden (char). No angling from power boats is permitted. Across the highway, a short (just under a kilometre) WFP interpretative trail winds through a demonstration forest.

Port Hardy Main intersects the highway at km 10.3. Turn left for West Main, just over a kilometre from the highway. Swing east on West Main for WFP's O'Connor Lake day-use recreation site with a boat launch and picnic tables. O'Connor Lake (42 ha) holds both rainbow and cutthroat trout. Head south on Port Hardy Main for 8 km to the branch road that accesses the Alice Lake wilderness campsite. There are ten user-maintained sites here and a natural boat launch. Alice Lake Main runs south to a three-vehicle campsite at Pinch Creek. These locations are co-managed by the BCFS and MacMillan Bloedel. Alice Lake Main meets WFP's South East Main, near the Benson River bridge. (For a look at how to reach this point along MacBlo's West Main and Benson Main, see Section Two: Trip 14.)

The Port Alice Highway passes Sarah Lake and then crosses the Marble River bridge. At km 14.5 you'll reach the entrance to the BCFS/WFP Marble River user-maintained campsite. Many people set up a base camp and day-trip on area backroads. There are thirty-three campsites, comfort stations and a picnic area. Riverside hiking trails lead down to the Marble River rapids, a scenic highlight.

Marble River Provincial Park, created in 1995, protects the Marble River canyon and the estuary near Varney Bay. Paddlers and boaters can access Alice Lake (1,218 ha) at the boat ramp. The nearby Marble River salmon hatchery is worth a visit. Alice Lake, known for its cutthroat trout, is also habitat for rainbow trout and Dolly Varden (char). No wild rainbow trout over 50 cm in length may be kept. Steelheading is productive at certain times of the year in the Marble River. On the river below Alice Lake, a bait ban applies all year.

Just over the 25-km mark, cut left onto South East Main and follow the signs to the Regional District of Mount Waddington's Link River Regional Park. Located on Alice Lake's south end, this popular park has forty-two campsites, excellent sandy beaches, a boat launch, sheltered cooking areas and fire pits. Link River (the section of the Marble River that connects Victoria and Alice lakes) is a catch-and-release stream, limited to fly-fishing only.

Just over the 29-km mark, swing right onto Quarry Main for WFP's Port Alice office at Jeune Landing. Stop in for updates on hauling and road conditions and to pick up a copy of its logging-road guide. Quarry Main continues to the WFP dryland sort on Neroutsos Inlet. This long arm of Quatsino Sound was named after C.D. Neroutsos, a former manager of BC Steamships. The inlet provides water access to the Port Alice mill for sea-going freighters. Decades ago a coastal steamer service out of Victoria ran along the coast to Port Alice. The *Princess Norah* and *Princess Maquinna* were two vessels employed on the route.

Port Alice was named after Alice Whalen, whose five sons founded the Whalen Pulp and Paper Company. It is one of the oldest operating kraft pulp mills on the BC coast. Many owners have come and gone since operations began in 1918. In 1936, BC Pulp and Paper was the proprietor. Its Spry Camp on Neroutsos Inlet consisted of camp buildings and homes strung out on a massive log float. Today the mill is run by Western Pulp. In the mid-1960s, the original townsite near the mill was razed and the community moved to its new location. A full-service marina, boat launch, public wharf and RV campground are close by. The Port Alice region offers fishing and diving in the inlet and hunting and hiking in the nearby mountains.

Beyond the mill you can take WFP's West Main to Victoria Lake (1,556 ha), one of Vancouver Island's largest. The lake contains rainbow and cutthroat trout and Dolly Varden (char). WFP's Victoria Lake day-use recreation site, halfway down the lake's west side, has a boat launch and picnic tables. A more remote four-site campsite, at Spruce Bay, lies about two-thirds down Victoria Lake's east side. Active hauling may limit public access, so it's best to check with WFP beforehand. The mainline around Victoria Lake's south end may be impassable due to a condemned bridge. Logging roads extend beyond the Port Alice mill to the Mahatta River area and the west coast. (See Section Two: Trip 15 for details.)

CONTACTS

- BC Forest Service (Port McNeill): 250-956-5000
- BC Parks (Strathcona District): 250-954-4600
- MacMillan Bloedel (Port McNeill Division): 250-956-5200
- Regional District of Mount Waddington (Port McNeill): 250-956-3301
- Western Forest Products (Port Alice): 250-284-3395
- Western Forest Products (Port McNeill): 250-956-3391

MAPS/GUIDES

- BC Forest Service Port McNeill Forest District Recreation Map
- MacMillan Bloedel Port McNeill/Port Hardy Recreation and Logging Road Guide
- Western Forest Products Visitors' Guide to Northern Vancouver Island
- National Topographical Series: 92L/6 Alice Lake (1:50,000); 92L/11 Port McNeill (1:50,000)
- Provincial Map: 92L Alert Bay (1:250,000)

NEAREST SERVICES

Port Alice.

Section Two:
The Logging Roads
Port Hardy
Port McNeill
Sayward
Woss
Campbell River
Gold
River
Courtenay
Parksville
Port
Alberni
Nanaimo
Tofino
Ucluelet
Duncan
VICTORIA
1
2
3
4
5
6
7
8
9
10
11
12
13
14
15
16
N
Section Two: The Logging Roads
Trip 1 Sooke To Shawnigan
Trip 2 Port Renfrew to Cowichan Lake
Trip 3 The Cowichan Lake Loop
Trip 4 The Nanaimo Lakes Region
Trip 5 Cowichan Lake to Port Alberni
Trip 6 Backroads to Bamfield
Trip 7 The Nahmint Lake Loop
Trip 8 The Sproat Lake Loop
Trip 9 Clayoquot Sound Backroads
Trip 10 Port Alberni to Courtenay
Trip 11 Courtenay to Campbell River
Trip 12 The Sayward Forest Loop
Trip 13 Gold River to Woss
Trip 14 Port McNeill Backroads
Trip 15 The Mahatta River Region
Trip 16 Port Hardy to Cape Scott

Section Two: The Logging Roads

Trip 1: Sooke To Shawnigan Lake

IN BRIEF

Some of the best-known southern Vancouver Island backroads snake through the mountains north of Sooke. You can take logging mainlines from either Shawnigan Lake or Sooke to access a popular hydro reservoir (known for its rainbow trout) and several higher-elevation fishing lakes. A few destinations you can't even get to with a 4 x 4, yet impassable road conditions don't stop determined anglers who hike in.

ACCESS

From Sooke: Drive to Sooke and take Otter Point Road to Young Lake Road. (See Section One: Trip 1.) Take Young Lake Road to Camp Barnard. Swing right onto Butler Main logging road. From Shawnigan Lake: Travel west from the Trans-Canada (Highway 1) to Shawnigan Lake's northwest tip and the junction of Renfrew Road and West Shawnigan Lake Road. (See Section One: Trip 3.) Gravel mainlines are in good to fair shape. There are some narrow sections and steep hills. Secondary roads may be overgrown or seasonally rough and may require a 4 x 4. Deactivated roads could be impassable. The area is subject to fire closures. Active logging may restrict public access. Times and locations of mainline hauling vary. Call ahead for current access restrictions and road information.

DESCRIPTION

Bounded on the east by the Greater Victoria Water Supply Area (with restricted public access), the Sooke backroads are regularly travelled by anglers, hunters, backroaders and mountain bikers. Loggers are here, too. When Western Forest Products or Pacific Forest Products hauls down area mainlines, public entry is restricted to after weekday working hours.

Sooke's gateway is the Butler Main logging road. From Victoria, follow

Sooke to Shawnigan Lake

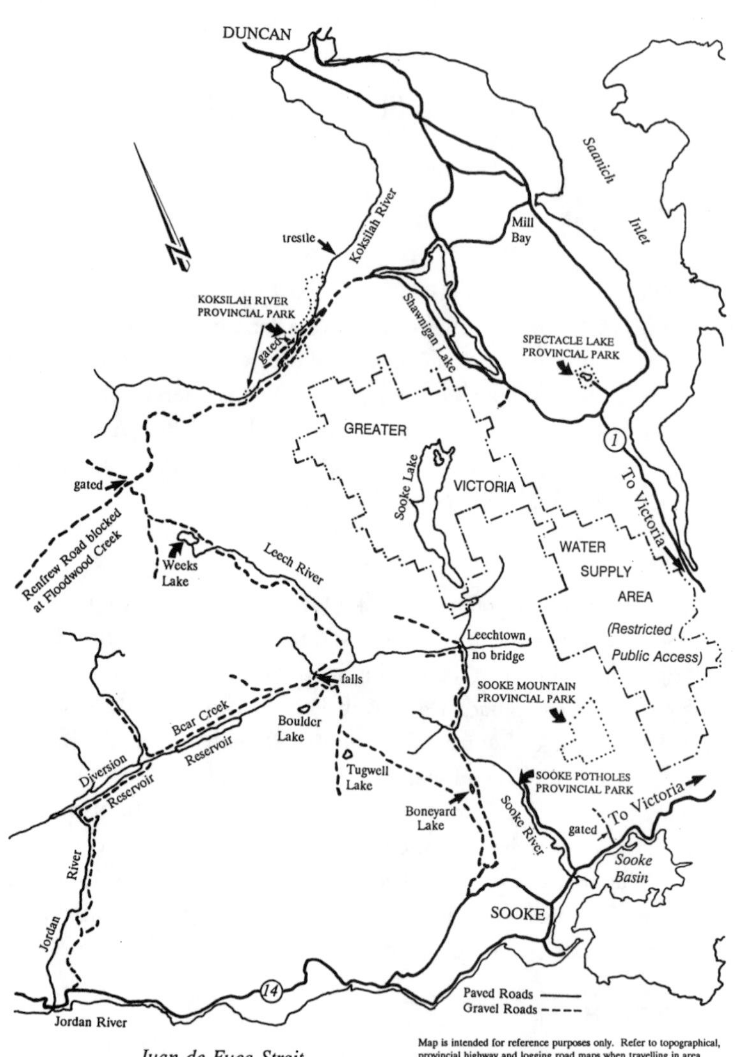

Highway 14 to Sooke. (See Section One: Trip 1.) Take Otter Point Road through the golf course to Young Lake Road. Follow Young Lake Road to the entrance of Camp Barnard, swing right onto Butler Main and reset your vehicle's trip meter to zero. At km 1, Boneyard Main cuts through a gravel pit to run 12 km up the west side of the Sooke River Valley to Leechtown. When PFP is using Boneyard Main, access is restricted. Boneyard Lake is 5 km from the pit.

The Capital Regional District's Galloping Goose Regional Trail winds along the Sooke River's east side. This 59-km recreation corridor stretches from Victoria to Leechtown and is shared by hikers, cyclists and horse riders. Parts of the route run through private property; in these sensitive areas users are reminded to stay on the trail.

At Leechtown the road curves left and deteriorates farther up the Leech River Valley. Cragg Main crosses the Leech River bridge to an active PFP logging area. Gold was discovered in the Leech River back in 1864. For a time, Leechtown and nearby Boulder City became gold boom towns. Little remains of these settlements today. Legends of clandestine Spanish treasure in the hills abound; one story tells of a hidden gold cache reached by descending a series of carved stone steps on a mountainside.

Butler Main heads north from the Boneyard Main cut-off and begins a long climb. Around the 10.5-km mark watch for a jumble of rocks and boulders on the left. You can scramble almost a kilometre up this barely discernible washed-out spur road to Tugwell Lake and shorecast along game trails. Watch out for snags; lakeside trees and bushes have strong appetites for spoons and spinners. Tugwell Main meets Butler Main around the 11.5-km mark. A left here leads to the rugged spur climbing 4 km to Ranger Lake. Perched above the 700-m level, Ranger Lake is often iced over late into the spring.

Butler Main passes a roadside pond and turns sharply to the west. A viewpoint looks out over the Leech River Valley. On a clear day you can gaze eastward across the stark slopes of Survey Mountain and ribbons of logging roads to the snowy heights of Mount Baker in Washington State. Washouts near the bottom of the secondary road for Boulder Lake (on the left at km 14) may even preclude 4 x 4s. Many anglers park and hike about 2 km uphill to the lakeside. It's easy to see how Boulder Lake was named – large rocks lie scattered about its waters and around the centre island. A trail leads along the lake to rainbow trout fishing spots. Area fly casters prefer a Royal Coachman or shrimp imitation; some anglers use small spinners.

The Weeks Lake turn, marked by a painted rockface, is at km 15. We'll look at a seasonal route from Shawnigan Lake to this cut-off later. If you take the Weeks Lake turn and continue about a kilometre to a bridge, you can explore the West Leech Falls area. The cascade is impressive after heavy rains. Just over the 19-km mark, watch for rough side roads going down to user-maintained campsites on Bear Creek Reservoir's north side. Negotiating a few of these spurs may require a 4 x 4 or high-slung vehicle. Trailered boats are not recommended. The 18-m-high earth dam at the reservoir's west end, completed in 1912, created one of three water storage areas for BC Hydro's Jordan River generating station. Diversion Reservoir is to the west; the Elliot Reservoir lies farther down the Jordan River Valley.

Best fishing times at Bear Creek Reservoir (stocked annually with rainbow trout) occur in the late spring and fall. A cartop boat or canoe will nicely complement your visit. BC Hydro signs warn against the use of outboard motors. The waters of both Bear Creek and Diversion reservoirs harbour sunken stumps and branches. At times these hazards are just below the surface due to fluctuating water levels. Funnelled winds frequently create lumpy water conditions, so it's easy to get hung up. Be cautious out on the water.

Make a sharp left a little over the 23-km mark for Diversion Reservoir; straight ahead on Jordan Main leads to the headwaters of the Jordan River. The road crosses the Bear Creek bridge and skirts a short section of the Jordan River. These are great paddling waters when the river is free from drifting reservoir deadheads. There are several rough water accesses on Diversion Reservoir's south side. Diversion Dam (km 28) was finished in 1913. Occasional water release from this impressive structure sends a cascading white arc of water through a large valve to the riverbed below. The Jordan River development is one of ten BC Hydro sites undergoing provincial evaluation to discover how hydro dam diversions affect downstream salmon habitat. From Diversion Dam the road turns south to follow East Main down the Jordan River Valley to the community of Jordan River, 12 km away.

You can get to Weeks Lake and the Sooke backroad network from the Shawnigan Lake area. A profusion of logging roads and unmarked intersections often confuses first-time visitors. If you can't arrange to travel with someone who knows the roads, be sure to consult an updated Guide to Forest Lands of Southern Vancouver Island, published by the Lake Cowichan Combined Fire Organization.

Take either the South Shawnigan Lake cut-off (close to Spectacle Lake Provincial Park and its eastern brook trout fishing) or the Mill Bay turn on Highway 1. (See Section One: Trip 3.) Travel to Shawnigan Lake's northwest end and take Renfrew Road to the junction with West Shawnigan Lake Road. Here, reset your vehicle's trip meter to zero. Up until late 1987 you could drive the Renfrew Road all the way from Shawnigan Lake to Port Renfrew. A highlight of the drive was the Bedspring suspension bridge over

The Kinsol trestle spans a deep gorge of the Koksilah River.

the 45-m-deep Williams Creek ravine. The bridge, when deemed unsafe, was barricaded and later dismantled, severing a popular backroads route. The Floodwood Creek bridge, farther east, was blocked only a few years ago.

At km 1.3, the road curves where it meets an abandoned CNR right-of-way. A 2-km hike north along the right-of-way goes to the Kinsol trestle: the highest (44.2 m) and longest (187.2 m) wooden railway bridge in Canada. The bridge spans a deep gorge of the Koksilah River and access is limited. Respect the privacy of area residents.

The trestle's name, short for King Solomon, comes from the Kinsol copper mine that operated in the area in the early 1900s. Canadian Northern Pacific initiated work on a rail line in 1911 and bridge work was completed by the CNR in 1920. The line, instrumental to the success of the Cowichan Valley's early forest industry, was used to bring in equipment and supplies and to carry out Cowichan Lake timber to Victoria mills. In 1979, the last train crossed the Kinsol trestle with a four-car load of cedar poles. The line was abandoned a year later. The bridge is in disrepair and both ends are blocked. Recurring plans to restore the bridge and make the area an historic viewing site or part of a linear park remain thwarted by the high cost of restorations and maintenance and the liabilities for public safety. The opportunity to preserve the Kinsol trestle in its beautiful setting still exists, though some estimates show that without expedient attention, the structure could collapse within two decades. For more information on the Kinsol trestle, contact the Ecomuseum in Duncan, at 250-746-1611.

Just over the 5-km mark, you'll reach what is known as Burnt Bridge, at Koksilah River Provincial Park. The bridge is blocked by a huge gate to prevent further vandalism on the river's north side and on private forest land outside park boundaries. This undeveloped wilderness park (comprising 210 ha in three sections) was established in 1959. Old roads lead to hiking, fishing, picnicking and swimming spots. The park is particularly scenic when the Koksilah River is running high. BC Parks recently cleared out old stumps, improved the roads and replanted trees as part of a cleanup and restoration effort, and has established a number of designated tent pads.

At Burnt Bridge keep left, up the hill, for Weeks Lake. The smallest section of Koksilah River Provincial Park is ahead, identified by a wide pull-off on the right. At km 11, a usually gated private road cuts off on the left. Continue up a long grade. At the top is a fine view over to Mount Lazar. Keep straight ahead at a crossroads at km 15.8. At a major junction just over the 19-km mark, swing left for Weeks Lake. Watch for two small bridges just before this turn. At km 21.6, go left again. The next part of the route is subject to flooding. A little beyond a gravel pit is a bumpy secondary road down to Weeks Lake (km 23.6).

Weeks Lake (24 ha), an excellent paddling lake and favourite angling destination, sits at an elevation of 518 m, near Jordan Meadows. Cartop boats can be launched at a natural boat ramp. Sometimes, you can roam around Weeks for hours without a strike or any sign of fish, although you might be able to hook one by dragging a worm along the bottom. Fly casters look for those special days when the lake's surface is speckled with rings. Weeks Lake is regularly stocked with rainbow trout. On its south shore, tall trees camouflage an hourglass-shaped pond. You can easily portage a canoe over a primitive trail that leads in, although you'll encounter deadfall en route.

From Weeks Lake, Leech Main links with Butler Main via the Leech River Valley, just west of Survey Mountain. Washouts and snows may block this 13.7-km route in the off-season. A long grade winds up to a viewpoint overlooking the lower Leech River Valley. The road then drops down a hill to the West Leech River bridge, near West Leech Falls. At km 37.3 you'll reach Butler Main, about 4 km east of Bear Creek Reservoir.

Holidays and weekends are ideal times to explore the Sooke logging roads. Following heavy winter snowfall, spring can arrive late in many areas. As you'll discover, on the Sooke backroads what you see is what you get.

CONTACTS

- BC Forest Service (South Island Forest District): 250-724-9205
- BC Parks (South Vancouver Island District): 250-391-2300
- Pacific Forest Products (Cowichan Division): 250-749-3796
- Western Forest Products (Jordan River): 250-646-2031

MAPS/GUIDES

- Guide to Forest Lands of Southern Vancouver Island (Lake Cowichan Combined Fire Organization)
- Community map of South Cowichan (LRH Ventures)
- Western Forest Products Visitors' Guide to Southern Vancouver Island
- National Topographical Series: 92B/12 Shawnigan Lake (1:50,000); 92B/5 Sooke (1:50,000)
- Provincial Map: 92B/NW Victoria (1:125,000)
- *Hiking Trails II* (VITIS)

NEAREST SERVICES

Sooke; Shawnigan Lake.

Trip 2:
Port Renfrew to Cowichan Lake

IN BRIEF

There are two logging mainlines from Port Renfrew to Cowichan Lake. One route follows the Gordon River Valley to a pocket stand of old growth and a rugged trail up Mount Sutton. The second backroad runs through the Harris Creek and Robertson River valleys and accesses several river swimming holes, trout lakes and user-maintained campsites. The mainlines hook into Cowichan Lake's South Shore Road. Four-wheelers tackle the secondary spurs to several vistas.

ACCESS

Follow the West Coast Road (Highway 14) to Port Renfrew. At Deering Road, turn right and cross the white bridge over the San Juan River, near Harris Cove. At a second river crossing (the Deering Bridge, on the San Juan River's north branch), you'll reach a signposted T-junction. (See Section One: Trip 1.) Gravel mainlines are in good to fair shape; secondary spurs may require a high-slung vehicle or 4 x 4. Deactivated roads may be impassable. Winter snows periodically block some routes. Active hauling may restrict public travel to after weekday working hours.

DESCRIPTION

If you feel like taking the backroads from Port Renfrew to Cowichan Lake, you have a choice of routes, and they both start at the same place, just outside Port Renfrew. Take Highway 14 (West Coast Road) to Port Renfrew, cut right onto Deering Road and follow the marina/West Coast Trail signposts. (See Section One: Trip 1.) At Harris Cove, cross the white San Juan River bridge to a second span (the Deering Bridge) over the river's north branch. Reset your vehicle's trip meter to zero at the signposted T-junction. Heavy industrial traffic is frequent on some routes; area logging companies suggest visitors time their travels to after weekday working hours or weekends and holidays.

For the Gordon River Valley route, swing left at the T-junction and travel about one kilometre to the Port Renfrew marina, established in 1988. From the marina entrance, the mainline crosses Browns Creek to the Gordon River bridge, just over the 5-km mark. Cut left and cross the bridge. Straight ahead are Grierson and Pandora mainlines. When passable, these mainlines lead to great views of Port San Juan and area mountains. Most area spur roads require a high-slung truck or 4 x 4. Deactivated roads are often impassable.

On the west side of the Gordon River bridge, stay right on Gordon Main for Cowichan Lake. At km 12.7, Bugaboo Main swings off to the left at Bugaboo Creek. Near Loup Creek, Branch 4000 leads to a trail through a small stand of old-growth Douglas fir and western red cedar known as Grant's Grove. Watch for an overgrown Gordon River trestle around the 27.5-km mark. Just over the 31-km mark you'll reach TimberWest's Gordon River camp.

Continue through the camp on Gordon River Main to a junction where the road splits (km 35.5). Go left onto the Caycuse/Gordon River Hookup (Caycuse Crossover) for 11 km to Cowichan Lake's South Shore Road, just east of Caycuse. You can keep right at the 35.5-km mark and journey about 13 km down the Sutton Creek Valley to meet the South Shore Road at Honeymoon Bay.

Just south of the Caycuse/Gordon River Hookup is the start of the Mount Sutton Trail. Park where the mainline widens, next to a stand of alders. A cable car crosses the Gordon River near a box canyon. Adventurous hikers will continue up a flagged route (steep in spots) to Mount Sutton's summit. It's best to hike with someone who knows the area; it's easy to become lost. *Hiking Trails II: Southeastern Vancouver Island*, published by the Vancouver Island Trails Information Society, describes the Mount Sutton Trail.

Back now to the Deering bridge, near Port Renfrew, and a second route to Cowichan Lake. Turn right at the signpost for Cowichan Lake. There are stretches of intermittent pavement. Logging has always been a primary industry of the San Juan River Valley. The British Canadian Lumber Company (1912–1914) ran a rail line from Fairy Lake to the mouth of the Gordon River. A second line extended along the southern banks of the San Juan River, from Harris Creek to the Gordon River. A number of hiking trails follow the old railway grades and lead to San Juan River fishing and swimming holes. Consult the BC Forest Service *Duncan Forest District Recreation Map* for more information on a wide variety of Port Renfrew area trails.

The San Juan area was once the homestead of Vander Waver, a Dutch settler. Rhubarb thrived in his garden and he entered some samples at the Chicago World's Fair in 1933. His entry won first prize. In the late 1920s, The Rainbow Farm (a religious commune comprised of Stratford Bible students) was set up, to farm and raise cattle. With the onset of the Great Depression, monetary problems forced the commune to close.

The Fairy Lake campsite (km 3) has almost two dozen forested camp-

The Fairy Lake campsite is a favourite destination for paddlers and anglers.

sites, two developed beach areas, fire rings, picnic tables and an anchored float that doubles as a swimming and sunning platform. Firewood is provided during the summer months. In the off-season, low-lying campsites and those at lakeside are prone to flooding. Camp with caution.

Fairy Lake (33 ha) is a popular destination for spring and fall anglers, who launch small cartoppers and cast for resident and sea-run cutthroat trout and Dolly Varden (char). Between October 15th and April 30th, only artificial flies may be used and a trout and char catch-and-release applies. Between May 1st and October 14th, the daily possession limit is two trout or char. In addition, there is an outboard engine limit of 7.5 hp. Always check current regulations carefully.

Fairy Lake is fed by two creeks. Fairy Creek enters the lake near the campsite and can be reached by a shoreline trail. Renfrew (Granite) Creek pours in on Fairy Lake's east side. A short outlet stream connects the lake with the San Juan River. Paddlers and boaters do head out into the river. Be wary. The San Juan River's lower stretches are tidal. Watch for tricky, changeable currents and know the tides.

The road skirts Fairy Lake's northern fringe and heads east to the junction with Harris Creek Main (km 12.5). Lens Creek Main, the road to the right that parallels the San Juan River, used to connect with the Shawnigan Lake area. The link was severed in 1987 when the Williams Creek suspension bridge was blocked off. (It has since been removed.) There are still plenty of things to see on the backroad east of Harris Creek Main. About 2.5 km away, Lens Main provides access to the short spur to Pixie Lake, with a rough camping area and water access for cartop boats. Tiny Pixie Lake (2 ha) contains rainbow trout.

Just over 4.5 km from Harris Creek Main you'll reach the San Juan Bridge wilderness campsite where the road used to cross the San Juan River on a black suspension bridge. This suspension bridge, like the one over Williams Creek, was deemed unsafe for vehicles, barricaded and replaced. There are six user-maintained sites here, fire rings, a gravel beach and a picnic area.

For Cowichan Lake, keep left at the Harris Creek Main junction (km 12.5) and head up the Harris Creek Valley. At km 14 you'll reach the Lizard Lake Recreation Site with twenty user-maintained campsites at the west end, picnic tables, fire rings, a day-use area and a natural boat launch. Four more campsites are on the lake's east side. These sites are open seasonally from the May long weekend through Labour Day. Lizard Lake (9 ha) is habitat for rainbow trout, though the fish can be hard to catch as there is plenty of food already available to them. The lake's east side can be a hotspot. Lizard Lake derives its name from a thriving newt population. Surfacing newts can easily be mistaken for fish sign. The Lizard Lake, Fairy Lake and San Juan Bridge campsites are co-managed by the BC Forest Service and TimberWest.

At the 18.5-km mark (near the confluence of Harris and Hemmingsen creeks) a bridge crosses a deep canyon on Harris Creek. Just over the 21-km mark, watch for an overgrown spur at the site of a former Harris Creek logging camp. Years ago area logging companies relocated a large spruce stump to the old camp as a point of interest. The large butt log was cut down in 1958 along the San Juan River flats, an area renowned for supplying spruce for wartime airplane production. At km 23 a trail winds in to a giant spruce that still stands near Harris Creek. An information signpost describes area spring wildflowers.

The road follows Harris Creek to more great swimming holes in deep pools where the river bends. On days when the weather is scorching and the driving dusty, a quick dip in one of these natural bathtubs is a refreshing break. Keep right onto Hillcrest Main (around the 30-km mark) for Cowichan Lake. At this point, the road leaves TimberWest woodlands and enters Pacific Forest Products territory. These roads are active hauling routes. If you prefer not to share the backroads with logging trucks, travel after weekday working hours or on weekends and holidays.

Hillcrest Main climbs a steep grade to an area where the mountaintops are denuded of trees. The bare rocky summits reflect stark evidence of the consequences of early logging practices, a devastating forest fire in the 1950s and the ravages of time, wind and rain. At km 41 Lens Main comes in on the right. Hillcrest Main levels out substantially in the Robertson River Valley. Drive by a Pacific Forest Products logging yard to reach the South Shore Road in Mesachie Lake, at the flashing amber light (km 49).

CONTACTS

- BC Forest Service (South Island Forest District): 250-724-9205
- Pacific Forest Products (Cowichan Division): 250-749-3796
- TimberWest (Honeymoon Bay Operations): 250-749-6805

MAPS/GUIDES

- BC Forest Service Duncan Forest District Recreation Map
- Guide to Forest Lands of Southern Vancouver Island (Lake Cowichan Combined Fire Organization)
- National Topographical Series: 92C/16 Lake Cowichan (1:50,000); 92C/9 Port Renfrew (1:50,000)
- Provincial Maps: 92C/NE Nitinat Lake (1:125,000); 92B/NW Victoria (1:125,000)
- *Hiking Trails II* (VITIS)

NEAREST SERVICES

Honeymoon Bay; Lake Cowichan; Mesachie Lake; Port Renfrew.

Trip 3:
The Cowichan Lake Loop

IN BRIEF

Starting at the community of Lake Cowichan, the 75-km loop drive around Cowichan Lake (half on paved roads, the remainder on logging mainlines) leads to a variety of camping, hiking, fishing and paddling destinations. TimberWest maintains a couple of lakeside campsites: one (Caycuse) on the south shore; the second (Heather) at the head of the lake. BC Forest Service wilderness campgrounds (Nixon Creek, Maple Grove and Pine Point) draw tenters and those with smaller trailers and camper units. Most of these sites have natural boat launches, ideal for cartop boats. Gordon Bay Provincial Park can accommodate larger RVs, trailers and boats.

ACCESS

From Highway 1, north of Duncan, turn west onto Highway 18 (Cowichan Valley Highway) for 30 km to the village of Lake Cowichan. (See Section One: Trip 3.) The lake perimeter roads are used by logging trucks; yield the right-of-way to any industrial traffic.

DESCRIPTION

A loop tour around Cowichan Lake begins in the village of Lake Cowichan, at the Cowichan River bridge. Stop in at the Travel Infocentre near the Kaatza Museum for information and a copy of the *Guide to Forest Lands of Southern Vancouver Island*. Its Cowichan Lake brochure features area maps. Lakeview Park is a semi-wilderness campground operated by the Lake Cowichan Parks Committee. A daily fee is charged with firewood included. Watch for the signposted entrance 2 km from the bridge.

The village of Mesachie Lake, 6 km west of Lake Cowichan, is home to the Cowichan Lake Forestry Research Station, situated at the end of Forestry Road. You can arrange a group tour by calling 250-749-6811. Visitors can view the province's main centre for genetic tree research, seed orchards and tree improvement projects. The world's largest Douglas fir breeding plantations are nearby. The station was established in 1929, on Cowichan Lake's South Arm, with a second plot of land on the lake's north side added later. A bunkhouse and cookhouse from the 1940s are heritage buildings.

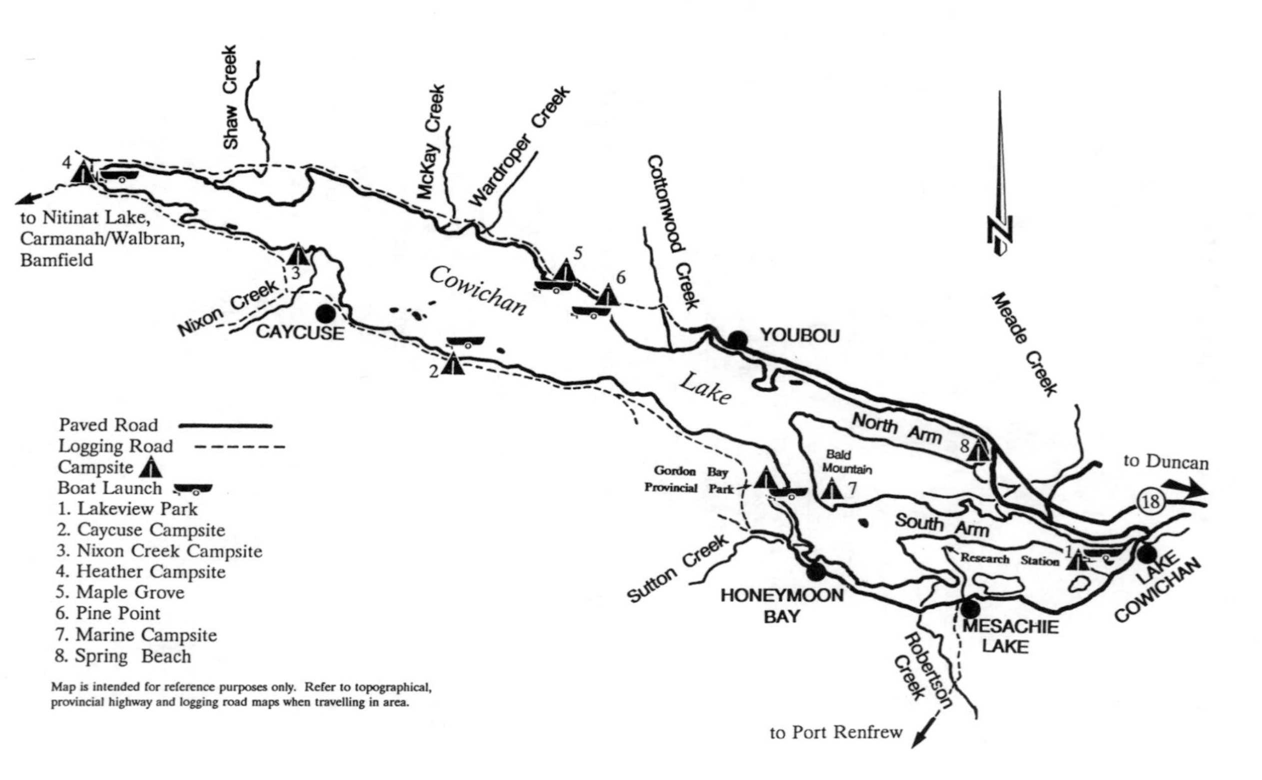
Cowichan Lake
Shaw Creek
McKay Creek
Wardroper Creek
Cottonwood Creek
Meade Creek
to Nitinat Lake, Carmanah/Walbran, Bamfield
Nixon Creek
CAYCUSE
Cowichan
Lake
YOUBOU
North Arm
South Arm
Bald Mountain
Gordon Bay Provincial Park
Sutton Creek
HONEYMOON BAY
Research Station
MESACHIE LAKE
LAKE COWICHAN
to Duncan
18
Robertson Creek
to Port Renfrew
Paved Road
Logging Road
Campsite
Boat Launch
1. Lakeview Park
2. Caycuse Campsite
3. Nixon Creek Campsite
4. Heather Campsite
5. Maple Grove
6. Pine Point
7. Marine Campsite
8. Spring Beach
Map is intended for reference purposes only. Refer to topographical, provincial highway and logging road maps when travelling in area.

A left turn at the flashing amber light in Mesachie Lake will lead backroad adventurers south into the Port Renfrew area. Industrial traffic is frequent on some routes. The logging companies recommend visitors time their travels to after weekday working hours or weekends and holidays. (See Section Two: Trip 2.)

In Honeymoon Bay (around 4 km west of Mesachie Lake) turn right, on Walton Road, for Gordon Bay Provincial Park, 14 km west of Lake Cowichan. Here you can camp, swim, boat, water ski and hike. The park, a favourite family camping destination, has 130 campsites. The boat launch is suitable for larger boats. Other facilities include heated washrooms, picnic tables, a sani-station for trailers and RVs, public telephones and hot showers. Firewood is supplied and there are visitor programs over the summer. A camping fee is charged from April to October. Reserve your camping spot through the BC Parks Discover Camping Campground Reservation Service (1-800-689-9025; 689-9025 in Greater Vancouver). Gordon Bay Provincial Park is near a BC Forest Service marine park (across the bay in the shadow of Bald Mountain) and many North and South Arm fishing holes.

Cowichan Lake (6,200 ha), one of Vancouver Island's largest freshwater lakes, has year-round fishing for rainbow, brown (at the foot of the lake) and cutthroat trout, kokanee and Dolly Varden (char). Major creekmouths are the hotspots, especially in the spring and fall. Anglers work the ledges and employ gang trolls and worms; others prefer Rapala or Flatfish plugs (# 5 or # 7) on 30 m of line with no weight. Fly casters time their efforts to coincide with the many hatches that occur on lake waters during warming trends in the weather. Black ant, March Brown or shrimp imitation are good patterns to try. Some anglers use spinning gear or bait and bobber. A single salmon egg or worm lying on the lake bottom works for shorecasters. Currently (1998) a daily quota of two cutthroat trout applies (none over 50 cm) and only single, barbless hooks may be used. Bait is prohibited between November 15th and April 15th. Speed is restricted to 8 km an hour in some parts of the lake. Check the freshwater regulations carefully prior to setting out.

In Cowichan Lake's North Arm, try the Meade Creek area or the waters around Saseenos Point. The lake narrows between Gordon Bay and Bald Mountain are known to trollers, as is the Cottonwood creekmouth, west of Youbou. South Arm summer fishing can be productive in Marble Bay, around the pilings near the Boy Scout camp (south of Bald Mountain) or at the weir in the village of Lake Cowichan. Try the mouth of Robertson Creek in Bear Lake (a backwater of Cowichan Lake), the Sutton creekmouth north of Honeymoon Bay or the strike zones around Goat Island.

Reset your vehicle's trip meter to zero at the start of the gravel, west of Honeymoon Bay, and swing right. (A left at this signposted junction hooks into Gordon River Main. See Section Two: Trip 2.) Keep right at the fork (km 0.2) onto a stretch of the South Shore Road that opened in 1990. The newer section bypasses a couple of long, steep hills and a switchback in the Millar Creek Valley. A riveting viewpoint at km 1.4 looks east over Gordon Bay to the craggy rockfaces of Bald Mountain and the expanse of McKenzie Bay. On a clear day, it's possible to see down almost the full length of Cowichan Lake's slender South Arm. A second viewpoint (km 4.3) overlooks Youbou.

South Shore Road passes the TimberWest Caycuse campsite (km 10.6), a popular family camping spot with twenty-seven sites, a covered outdoor kitchen and boat launch. Anglers troll the drop-offs around the offshore islands. This seasonal campsite is monitored by TimberWest and a daily fee is charged. Gates may be locked at night. Just under the 14-km mark, the Caycuse/Gordon River Hookup (Caycuse Crossover) meets the South Shore Road. You can take this road to Gordon River Camp and Port Renfrew. (See Section Two: Trip 2.)

The route skirts the logging town of Caycuse (km 15.5). Decades ago this former logging camp was situated on floats. Roads were punched through in 1955. TimberWest closed down its active operations at Caycuse in 1992. South Shore Road heads due west to cross the Nixon Creek bridge. Directly across this span (km 17) keep right; straight ahead runs along Nixon Creek and continues south to McClure Main, the logging road to take for the Walbran Valley, within Carmanah Walbran Provincial Park. (See Section Three: Trip 3.) McClure Lake, a shallow lake about 22.5 km from South Shore Road, has a primitive campsite and contains rainbow trout.

Watch for the signpost for the BCFS Nixon Creek Recreation Site at km 18. In 1977, my brother and I canoed from Cowichan Lake's top end to this lakeside hideaway before the road had been cut in. Much has changed over the years. There is now easy road access, twenty-five user-maintained forested campsites and visitor registration upon arrival. The site is seasonally closed. There is no boat ramp here, but small cartoppers can easily be put in from the gravel beach.

The top end of Cowichan Lake is at km 23.8. Here, Nitinat Main meets the Cowichan Lake perimeter roads. Backroad adventurers journeying to Nitinat Lake, Bamfield, Port Alberni or Carmanah Walbran Provincial Park's main trailhead and campsite will turn west at this intersection. (See Section Two: Trips 5 & 6; Section Three: Trip 3.) Keep right at lakehead onto the North Shore Road to continue the loop around Cowichan Lake. The road passes a wide natural boat launch close to the TimberWest Heather Campsite. This thirty-site campground (km 24.8) is favoured by many Vancouver Island adventurers. Arrive early to secure a spot on summer weekends and

By canoe is a great way to explore Cowichan Lake.

holidays; the sites fill up by late afternoon. The campsite has a nice beach, nature trails, a covered barbecue pit and sani-station. A nightly fee is charged.

In late 1992 a rock slide blocked the North Shore Road, east of the Heather Campsite. The route wasn't reopened until June 1993. The scars of the slide are best viewed from Cowichan Lake's south side as you approach the lakehead. There are several trails in the mountains on Cowichan Lake's north side. The gates on the logging roads leading to the trailheads are usually locked, but hiking groups can make arrangements for keys through local logging companies. See *Hiking Trails II* (VITIS), for details and trail descriptions for Heather Mountain and the Shaw Creek and Cottonwood Creek valleys. Also included are trails to Mesachie and Bald mountains.

Anglers frequent four creekmouths in the western half of Cowichan Lake: Nixon, Shaw, McKay and Wardrope. Sometimes at sunset or right before dawn, large fish lurk in the shallows of Hawes Bay or the waters at lakehead. Treat Cowichan Lake, like all larger Vancouver Island lakes, with caution. Strong winds can develop without much warning, resulting in hazardous wave conditions. Be wary on the water and watch the weather.

There are a couple of side roads in the vicinity of Shaw Creek that go down to the remains of a railway trestle. At the site of the Shaw Creek logging dump, charred pilings mark what was once an important lake point where lumber was hauled to lakeside booming grounds. Logging opened up the Cowichan Lake district at the turn of the last century and remains the region's primary industry.

Some spur roads along the North Shore Road are now blocked or ditched, preventing vehicles from reaching once popular wilderness camping spots. There are two BCFS campsites on Cowichan Lake's north side. Maple Grove is at km 39; Pine Point is just under the 41-km mark. These recreation sites have thirty-eight campsites and are open seasonally. The boat ramps are suited for small trailered boats and cartoppers only. North Shore Road cuts inland to the Cottonwood Creek bridge and emerges at the parking lot behind the TimberWest Youbou mill (km 44.2). Here the pavement begins.

About 9 km from the mill, cut south onto Meades Creek Road for more backroads exploring. Meades Creek Road passes the entrance to the BC Forest Service Spring Beach Recreation Site, on Cowichan Lake's North Arm. Situated beneath a stand of stately trees, there are several walk-in campsites, picnic tables and fire rings.

Marble Bay Road (1.6 km from Youbou Road) accesses Marble Bay and the Boy Scout camp near Bald Mountain. The gate at the camp boundary line is usually locked. To make arrangements for hikes on area trails, contact Gloria Carnell at 250-749-3578. Eventually Meades Creek Road hooks into North Shore Road. Turn right for Marina Park (where there is a boat launch and public dock) and the Cowichan River bridge, the start of the Cowichan Lake Loop.

CONTACTS

- BC Forest Service (South Island Forest District): 250-724-9205
- BC Parks (South Vancouver Island District): 250-391-2300
- Cowichan Lake Research Station (Mesachie Lake): 250-749-6811
- Pacific Forest Products (Cowichan Woodlands): 250-749-3796
- TimberWest (Honeymoon Bay Operations): 250-749-6805

MAPS/GUIDES

- BC Forest Service Duncan Forest District Recreation Map
- Guide to Forest Lands of Southern Vancouver Island (Lake Cowichan Combined Fire Organization)
- Community maps of North Cowichan and South Cowichan (LRH Ventures)
- Cowichan Lake brochure (Cowichan Lake District Chamber of Commerce)
- National Topographical Series: 92C/16 Cowichan Lake (1:50,000)
- Provincial Map: 92C/NE Nitinat Lake (1:125,000)
- *Hiking Trails II* (VITIS)

NEAREST SERVICES

Honeymoon Bay; Lake Cowichan; Mesachie Lake; Youbou.

Trip 4:
The Nanaimo Lakes

IN BRIEF

A chain of lakes (First, Second, Third and Fourth) in the Nanaimo River Valley southwest of Nanaimo beckons to anglers and Vancouver Island adventurers. More remote lakes with wilderness campsites can be reached via secondary gravel roads. Fine mountain scenery along countless spur roads will intrigue backroad explorers.

ACCESS

Take the well-signposted Nanaimo Lakes cut-off on Highway 1 at Cassidy, north of the Nanaimo River Bridge. (See Section One: Trip 3.) Follow Nanaimo Lakes Road 22 km west to the start of the gravel near First Lake. Gravel mainlines from here are in good to fair condition. Secondary roads may be rough and require a 4 x 4. Deactivated roads may be impassable. Public access beyond the Second Lake gate is limited to weekends and holidays only. Entry may be restricted by active logging and fire closures.

DESCRIPTION

The Nanaimo Lakes region is a great destination for campers, paddlers and backroaders. Area lakes attract anglers of all ages. Heading in to any of the wilderness lakes is an adventure in itself. Take the Nanaimo Lakes cut-off on Highway 1 in Cassidy. (See Section One: Trip 3.) This cut-off (just south of Nanaimo) is now well known to bungee-jumping enthusiasts. At the first intersection (Nanaimo Lakes Road and South Wellington Road), reset your vehicle's trip meter to zero.

The paved road winds through hilly terrain on the Nanaimo River's north side. At km 16.5, a road to the left goes into MacMillan Bloedel territory along the South Nanaimo River Valley to the Jump Lake Reservoir, within the Nanaimo Water District. The reservoir provides Nanaimo with its water supply. Public entry is prohibited in this area.

The pavement ends just under the 22-km mark, near First Lake. The TimberWest main security gate and watchman's shack are located at km 22.5. Public access beyond the Second Lake gate is allowed between 6 a.m. and 5:30 p.m. on weekends and holidays only. These hours may vary, so

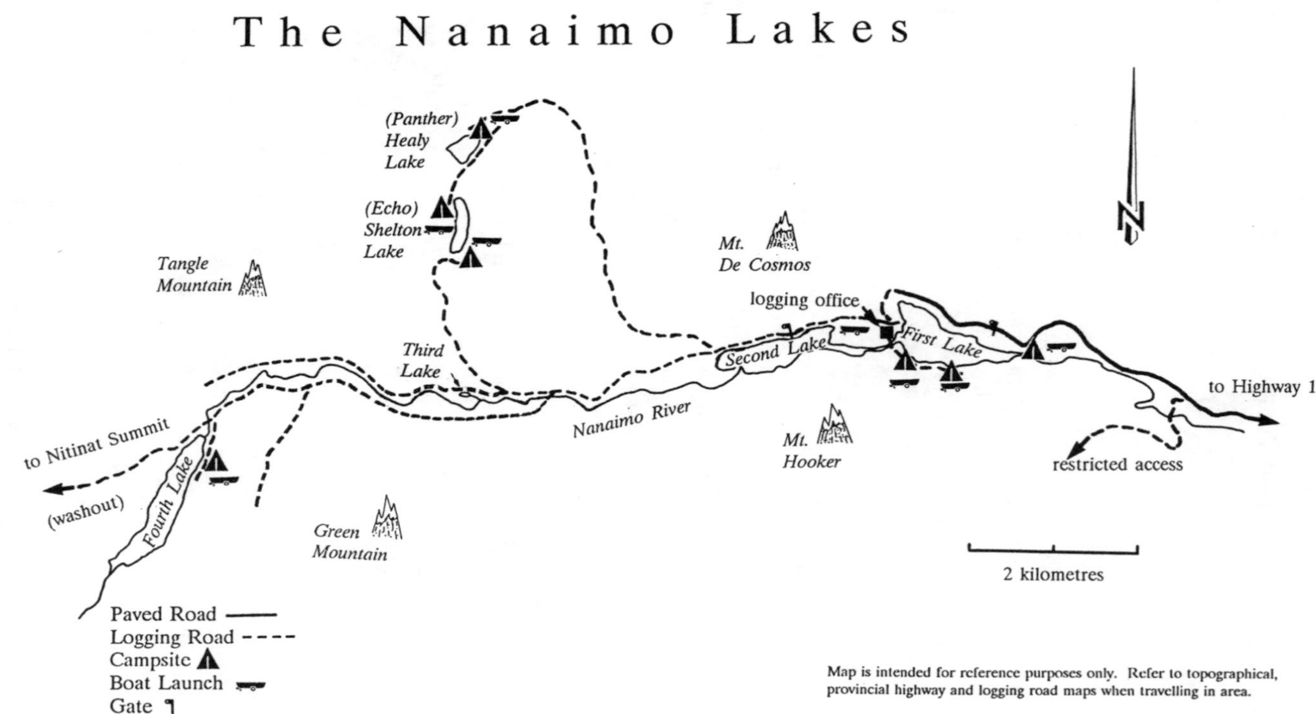
The Nanaimo Lakes
N
(Panther) Healy Lake
(Echo) Shelton Lake
Tangle Mountain
Mt. De Cosmos
logging office
Second Lake
First Lake
Third Lake
to Highway 1
Nanaimo River
to Nitinat Summit
(washout)
Fourth Lake
Mt. Hooker
restricted access
Green Mountain
2 kilometres
Paved Road
Logging Road
Campsite
Boat Launch
Gate
Map is intended for reference purposes only. Refer to topographical, provincial highway and logging road maps when travelling in area.

check with TimberWest for current updates. A $2.00-per-night fee is charged and gates are locked at night. Visitors are required to check in, giving their planned destination and length of stay. This procedure is a safeguard against theft and vandalism, which have plagued many Vancouver Island backwoods locales. An irresponsible minority continues to be a major cause for the restricted-access policies in some areas. These limitations affect responsible backwoods adventurers – the majority of whom respect the forests and practise low-impact camping.

On weekdays, stop in at the TimberWest office near First Lake and pick up an area brochure. Study your maps. There is a profusion of confusing backroads in the Nanaimo Lakes area. Just beyond the logging office, watch for the road to the wilderness campsites established by TimberWest on First Lake's south side. Cut left (km 26) and cross the Nanaimo River bridge. Turn left again for the Windy Point and Old Mill recreation sites. Covered picnic sites, natural boat launches, comfort stations and woodland trails make these campsites popular choices. A $5.00 nightly fee applies.

All the wilderness campsites in the Nanaimo Lakes region are a treat to visit, yet their atmosphere is easily tarnished. Remember to clean up your camp when you leave to ensure these user-maintained hideaways remain in as natural a state as possible. At km 27, cut left for a natural boat launch at Second Lake's east end. Second Lake is deep in places and bordered by Mount de Cosmos and Mount Hooker. The section of the Nanaimo River connecting First and Second Lake is a great paddling spot – except for the rocky shallows where the river enters First Lake. This part of the river can be productive for fly casters in the early season.

Just over the 30-km mark, near the end of Second Lake, Branch C angles off to the right and up the Dash Creek Valley. This secondary road leads to Panther (Healy) and Echo (Shelton) lakes, perched over 500 m above sea level. The roads to these rainbow trout lakes are prone to washouts in the off-season. The Echo Lake spur is 9.4 km from the mainline cut-off. To reach the lake, it's another 3 km or so along a rough secondary road. If you're heading to Panther Lake, drive 1.3 km beyond the Echo Lake turn and cut left down a sharp hill. There are natural boat ramps at both Panther (34 ha) and Echo Lake (36 ha). Panther Lake angling is limited to artificial flies, with a quota of one trout or char a day. The fishing regulations often change from year to year, so be sure to check on current restrictions.

An angling buddy and I like to fish Panther Lake whenever we can. On clear days the majestic crown of Green Mountain highlights a beautiful backdrop to our angling endeavours. We're convinced that native Panther Lake rainbow are smarter than most trout. They seem to be able to discern a hand-tied fly at ten metres – even when they do make a rare mistake, the wily fish can toss a hook or snap a leader nine times out of ten. They are also extremely adept at tangling lines around an anchor rope.

At the bridge marked by painted boulders (around the 35-km mark) the mainline cuts over to the Nanaimo River's south side. Stay on the river's north side for half a kilometre to an alternate route to Echo Lake, best suited for 4 x 4s or vehicles with good clearance. The spur climbs the east side of the Rush Creek Valley. Just under 4 km from the mainline, cut right onto somewhat confusing side roads for the water access at Echo Lake's south end. These unmaintained arteries can be rough, especially the hill down to lakeside. Third Lake, smallest of the Nanaimo Lake chain, is situated near Rush Creek. The access road is on the left, about a kilometre from the Echo Lake turn. Third Lake has a picnic site.

For Fourth Lake, cross the bridge near the 35-km mark to the Nanaimo River's south side. The wide clearing at km 40.7 is the Green Mountain junction. A left here follows Branch K and parallels Green Creek up the valley for about 5 km to Branch K30, an old spur rendered impassable to vehicles due to washouts. Green Mountain, about 3 km north of Gemini Mountain, is a beautiful alpine area for hikers and photographers.

A little over the 43-km mark, Branch L veers off to the left for Fourth Lake and a couple of wilderness campsites. Turn left, up the hill, to the dam at the lake's east end. The Fourth Lake dam was built in 1951 and provides MacBlo with a water reservoir for its Harmac mill. A spillway is located at the dam's west end, with the main outlet valve on the lake's west shore. Released water runs through a mountain tunnel to Sadie Creek.

In the fall of 1989, MacBlo lowered the level of Fourth Lake to facilitate some dam cleanup work. Floating debris and errant deadheads were removed from the dam's inside face. The drop of Fourth Lake gave visitors (and anglers who prefer trolling the shorelines) a rare opportunity to see the contours of the lake bottom that normally are submerged. Once the cleanup was completed the lake was left to fill back up naturally to its usual levels. That didn't take too long with the deluging rains that pelted the west coast later in the year.

Deteriorating conditions and washouts are prevalent along some of the old roads in the vicinity of Sadie Creek. Lack of maintenance has rendered many routes suitable only for 4 X 4s; some are impassable by vehicle. That, of course, doesn't prevent you from hiking around the area. Years ago you could follow the mainline west of Fourth Lake, climb over the Nitinat Summit, north of Mount Hooper, and drop into the Nitinat River Valley on a tortuous switchback. Several bridges have been out for years and heavy rains have ravaged the route.

The Nanaimo Lakes district is home to elk, deer, black bear and cougar.

Beaver ponds are numerous. Vancouver Island marmots (an endangered species) are found in scattered mountain meadows. In 1987, the provincial government established the Haley Lake Ecological Reserve near Green Mountain, on 93 ha of land donated by MacMillan Bloedel. In 1991, TimberWest added another 27 ha to the protected area, home to two colonies of marmots. In 1991, the Ministry of Environment designated 300 ha of alpine meadow on Green Mountain as a critical wildlife management area.

CONTACTS

- TimberWest (Nanaimo Lakes): 250-754-3206
- TimberWest (Nanaimo Lakes security gate): 250-754-3032

MAPS/GUIDES

- Guide to Forest Lands of Southern Vancouver Island (Lake Cowichan Combined Fire Organization)
- TimberWest Nanaimo Lakes Logging Road Guide
- National Topographical Series: 92G/4 Nanaimo (1:50,000); 92F/1 Nanaimo Lakes (1:50,000)
- Provincial Map: 92F/SE Port Alberni (1:125,000)
- *Hiking Trails II* (VITIS)

NEAREST SERVICES

Cassidy Area.

Trip 5:
Cowichan Lake to Port Alberni

IN BRIEF

Some of the best-known Vancouver Island backroads extend from the head of Cowichan Lake through the Nitinat Valley to Port Alberni. Paddlers travel these roads on their way to Nitinat Lake or the Nitinat Triangle lakes; hikers head to Carmanah Walbran Provincial Park and trails to giant spruce groves, or to Bamfield and the West Coast Trail's north end. The route accesses forest company campgrounds, BC Forest Service recreation sites, old trestles and many fishing lakes. And there are plenty of secondary roads to investigate.

ACCESS

Drive to the west end of Cowichan Lake on either of the two lake perimeter roads. (See Section Two: Trip 3.) The mainlines converge at the lakehead, near TimberWest's Heather Campsite boat launch. Reset your vehicle's trip meter to zero at this point and cut west onto Nitinat Main. Gravel mainlines are usually in good shape. Expect industrial traffic in some areas. Secondary roads are good to fair and subject to fire and seasonal closures; a high-slung vehicle or 4 x 4 may be required.

DESCRIPTION

A lot of people travel the backroads from Cowichan Lake's west end to Port Alberni. To reach the starting point of this 79.5-km trip, take one of two roads along Cowichan Lake and continue west to lakehead. The North Shore Road, via Youbou, has about 19 km of gravel; the South Shore Road is unpaved for 24 km, starting just west of Honeymoon Bay. Nitinat Main meets the lake perimeter roads near TimberWest's Heather Campsite boat launch. (See Section Two: Trip 3.) Reset your vehicle's trip meter to zero as you swing onto Nitinat Main.

Around the 2-km mark, a side road veers off to the right. This leads up the Nitinat River Valley. You can't travel beyond the Redbed Creek – the bridge here was blocked over a decade ago by TimberWest after the span was deemed unsafe for vehicles. The company also barricaded the bridge over the Nitinat River, effectively severing a connection to Tuck Lake. It's still worth

Cowichan Lake to Port Alberni

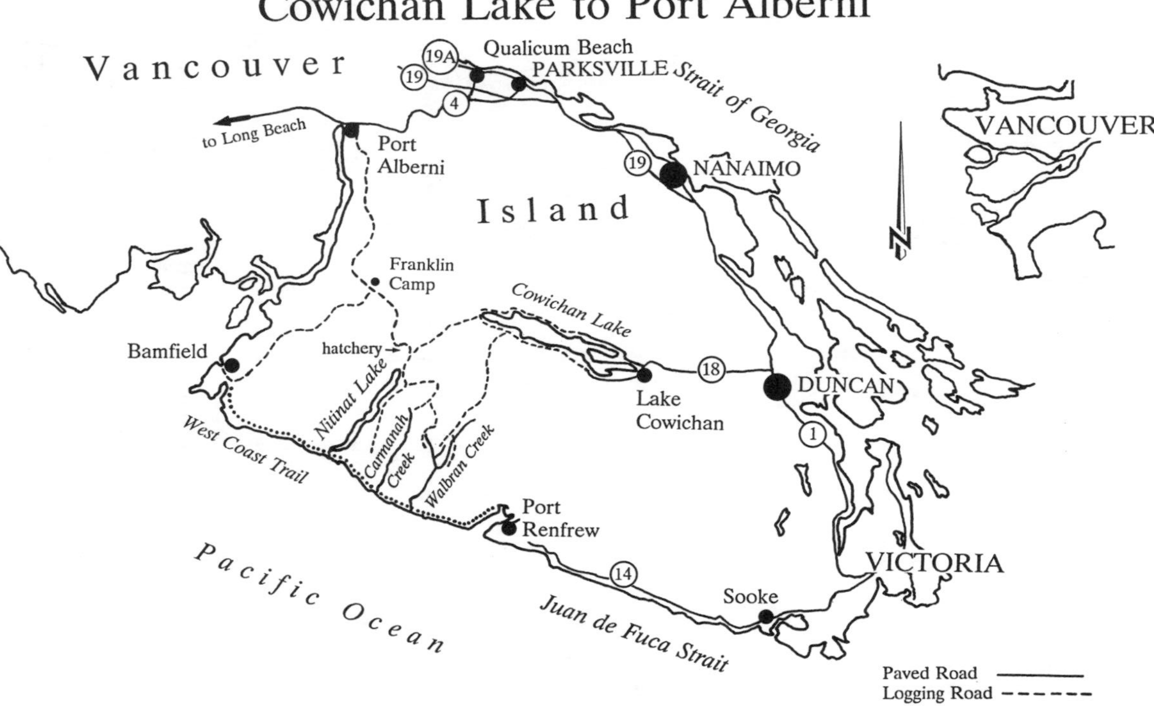
Vancouver
Qualicum Beach
19A
19
PARKSVILLE
Strait of Georgia
4
to Long Beach
Port Alberni
VANCOUVER
19
NANAIMO
Island
N
Franklin Camp
Cowichan Lake
hatchery
Bamfield
18
DUNCAN
Nitinat Lake
Lake Cowichan
West Coast Trail
Carmanah Creek
Walbran Creek
1
Port Renfrew
VICTORIA
Pacific Ocean
14
Sooke
Juan de Fuca Strait
Paved Road
Logging Road
Map is intended for reference purposes only. Refer to topographical, provincial highway and logging road maps when travelling in area.

visiting the picturesque Nitinat River waterfalls near the blocked bridge.

Take care should you explore the deteriorating spur roads in this region. Sections of these old roads are extremely rough; if it's wet out, you may have to deal with large puddles and waterholes. Climbing up even a small, slick clay hill can be tricky. It's no fun being mired in the mud on the Nitinat River flats with the river rising as a result of steady rains. If you have a 4 x 4, and the Nitinat River is low enough, you can attempt to ford the river upstream from the blocked bridge. Beware of shifting gravel beneath what first may appear to be a passable river shallows. Even 4 x 4s can get stuck, especially those not equipped with winches. If in doubt, don't try to cross.

The decaying Vernon Creek trestle (km 4.5) was built in 1933 by Industrial Timber Mills of Youbou and dates back to the days of rail logging. There are many old railway trestles along Vancouver Island backroads. Around the 12-km mark the road splits into a one-way section for a few kilometres and then parallels the Nitinat River to the Nitinat Junction (km 18.5). Here, at a T-junction near the Nitinat River bridge, South Main meets Nitinat Main. For Carmanah Walbran Provincial Park, bear left onto South Main. Cut left also for the MacMillan Bloedel/BC Forest Service Nitinat Lake Campsite, near the head of the lake, the Ditidaht First Nations Visitors' Centre and a water-taxi link to the West Coast Trail via Nitinat Narrows for pre-registered hikers. The Nitinat Lake West Coast Trail registration and information centre is open seasonally. (See Section Three: Trips 3, 4 & 5 for additional information.)

For Bamfield and Port Alberni, keep right at the Nitinat Junction, and cross the Nitinat River bridge. South Main curves 2.5 km to the Nitinat River hatchery turn, where Hitchie Main meets South Main. The DFO Nitinat hatchery is the largest chum salmon egg production hatchery in Canada and a major contributor to the commercial chum fishery. The hatchery releases more than a quarter of a million coho and over eight million chinook annually. Turn left at the hatchery cut-off for Knob Point, the usual jumping-off point for paddlers journeying to the Nitinat Triangle lakes. (See Section Three: Trip 4.) At Knob Point, about 9.2 km from the mainline, there are a handful of user-maintained campsites and a gravel boat launch for cartop boats.

Continue another 6 km on South Main to the Flora Main junction (km 27), around 8.5 km from Nitinat Junction. Flora Main and area mainlines are in places narrow with blind corners. Two-trailered off-road trucks haul on these routes. For safety reasons, public access is restricted between 6 a.m. and 6 p.m., Monday to Friday. Seasonal fire closures may prevent entry. An overgrown rail-logging trestle (near a gravel pit) spans the Little

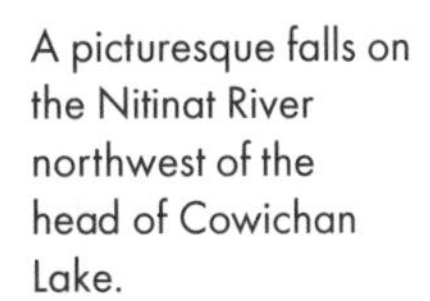

A picturesque falls on the Nitinat River northwest of the head of Cowichan Lake.

Nitinat River bridge at the Flora Main junction. Look for deep river pools beneath the trestle.

Cut left onto Flora Main for a little over 5 km to the entrance to the BCFS/MacBlo Flora Lake Recreation Site, one of the first of its kind in BC. There are several forested camping spots here and a natural boat launch, ideal for cartoppers. Flora Lake (15 ha) contains rainbow and cutthroat trout, with best fishing in the spring and fall. Always carry out all your trash and leave your campsite clean for future visitors. User-maintained sites benefit from everyone's continued efforts. The mosquitoes and no-see-ums at Flora Lake can be persistent. Don't forget insect repellent and lotion for the bites you may receive.

Stay on Flora Main and then follow Central South Main to hook into the Bamfield road near Frederick Lake. Central South Main skirts Rousseau Lake (13 ha), a rainbow trout lake with cartop boat access, and curves by Pachena Lake (59 ha) to a picnic site and boat launch on the northeast corner of Frederick Lake (41 ha). Both Pachena and Frederick lakes contain cutthroat and rainbow trout. Around the 34-km mark the road meets Sarita Main. A left heads 15 km to Bamfield; a right goes east to Franklin Camp, about 30 km away. (See *More Island Adventures*, Trip 11 for further details on this back way to Bamfield.)

From the Flora Main junction, South Main runs west to pass natural boat launches on two fishing lakes near Franklin Camp. Both Francis Lake (42 ha) and Darlington Lake (13 ha) contain rainbow trout and Dolly Varden (char). Some anglers try their luck from shore. I've had success trolling the drop-offs along each lake's north shore.

At Franklin Camp the road skirts MacBlo's Franklin Camp shop to the start of the Bamfield road (km 39.5). Cut left, adjacent to the logging yard, and follow the signs for Bamfield and Pachena Bay, the northern terminus of the West Coast Trail. (A jaunt along Bamfield Road is detailed in Section Two: Trip 6.) For Port Alberni, keep west on the mainline (now called Franklin Road) and swing right at the next signposted intersection to cross the Coleman Creek bridge (km 40). The mainline turns north and climbs into the Parsons Creek Valley. At this point the route is called the Camp B Access Road.

Turn right onto Museum Main (km 65) and then take Thistle Mine Road to Father and Son Lake (13 ha), a high-elevation destination (960 m) popular with rainbow trout anglers. The 13-km road (recommended for trucks or high-slung vehicles only) deteriorates as you approach the lake. To reach lakeside requires a one-kilometre hike along a steep, somewhat challenging trail. Great mountain scenery highlights a stay at Father and Son Lake's wilderness campsite.

The mainline to Port Alberni hugs the cliffs near several impressive viewpoints (weather permitting) of Alberni Inlet and the surrounding mountains. China Creek Park, just under the 69-km mark, features a full-service marina and campground that lures Alberni Inlet salmon anglers. This locale is packed over the summer, peak time for the annual salmon runs. Thanks to the success of the Robertson Creek hatchery and Great Central Lake's sockeye fertilization program, the waters of Barkley Sound and Alberni Inlet provide some of the finest salmon fishing in the world.

Just under the 56-km mark you'll hit pavement. At the signpost, just beyond a logging office, turn left onto Ship Creek Road for the outskirts of Port Alberni, near Anderson Road (km 79.5). Backroaders can continue northeast on the logging road to pass tiny Bainbridge Lake, a seniors-and-kids-only fishing lake. No angling from boats is allowed. The lake contains small rainbow, cutthroat and Dolly Varden. The road eventually connects with the backroads in the Cameron River Valley and Mount Arrowsmith area. (See Section One: Trip 4.)

The Alberni Economic Transportation Committee is promoting an alternate up-Island corridor (Valley Link Highway) running from Cowichan

Lake to Nitinat Lake to Franklin Camp and north to Port Alberni; from here the proposed route goes in to Comox Lake and on to Courtenay. You'll see signs marking this road link along many backroads. Somehow the idea of paved routes replacing some of Vancouver Island's most travelled gravel roads holds no appeal for many backroad adventurers. They like things just the way they are.

CONTACTS

- Alberni Forest Information Centre (Port Alberni): 250-724-7890
- BC Forest Service (South Island Forest District): 250-724-9205
- MacMillan Bloedel (Franklin Operations): 250-720-4200

MAPS/GUIDES

- BC Forest Service Port Alberni Forest District Recreation Map
- Guide to Forest Lands of Southern Vancouver Island (Lake Cowichan Combined Fire Organiztion)
- MacMillan Bloedel Recreation and Logging Road Guide to TFL 44
- National Topographical Series: 92F/2 Alberni Inlet (1:50,000); 92C/16 Cowichan Lake (1:50,000); 92C/15 Little Nitinat River (1:50,000)
- Provincial Map: Regional Map #2 Parksville/Tofino (1:125,000)
- *Backroading Vancouver Island* (Neering/Whitecap)
- *Hiking Trails II* (VITIS)

NEAREST SERVICES

Lake Cowichan Region; Port Alberni.

Trip 6: Backroads to Bamfield

IN BRIEF

Along the Bamfield road you'll find freshwater lakes for trout fishing and paddling, wilderness campsites and plenty of backroads to explore. The route accesses Poett Nook marina (a popular camping and RV park that caters to Barkley Sound saltwater anglers) and leads to the West Coast Trail's northern terminus at Pachena Bay, close to Bamfield.

ACCESS

The Bamfield road begins near MacMillan Bloedel's Franklin Camp shop, about halfway along the Cowichan Lake/Port Alberni backroads. (See Section Two: Trip 5.) Gravel mainlines are usually in good shape. There are steep hills and bumpy stretches. Secondary roads are good to fair and subject to fire and seasonal closures; a high-slung vehicle or 4 x 4 may be required on some routes. Deactivated roads may be impassable.

DESCRIPTION

Years ago, you could only reach the tiny west-coast village of Bamfield by boat or float plane. In 1963 a logging road was punched through to provide the Barkley Sound community with its first road link to other Vancouver Island centres. The Bamfield road begins at MacMillan Bloedel's Franklin Camp shop, situated along the Cowichan Lake/Port Alberni backroads. Trout anglers will encounter many diversions en route to Franklin Camp. (See Section Two: Trip 5.)

The road splits into a wide triangle junction on its approach to Franklin Camp. Watch for Bamfield signposts. For this trip we'll come in on South Main, via Nitinat Lake. (If you're on the road from Port Alberni, cross the Coleman Creek bridge and keep straight ahead up the hill when you reach a signposted intersection. This west branch of the triangle junction is about 0.2 km shorter than the east road, closer to the Franklin Camp shop.) From South Main cut left onto the Bamfield Road (the east branch of the triangle junction) adjacent to the Franklin Camp shop and reset your vehicle's trip meter to zero.

The Bamfield Road negotiates a steep grade. There's a great view as the road drops into the Sarita River Valley. Central North Main meets the Bamfield Road at km 13.4. Sarita Lake (km 14) has a couple of co-managed BC Forest Service/MacMillan Bloedel recreation sites along its shores. The Sarita Lake campsite (km 14.3) features a gravel lakefront and a handful of campsites beneath a fringe of lakeside trees. A cartop boat launch is nearby. The second recreation site (km 15.5) has water access for cartoppers and a picnic area. Both spots are user-maintained.

Sarita Lake (133 ha) contains cutthroat trout, kokanee salmon and Dolly Varden (char). Late-spring and early-fall fishing can be productive here. A boat or canoe will increase your range. The mouth of nearby Bewlay Creek is popular with shorecasters, who work the weedbeds and drop-offs with bait and bobber, small spinners and spoons. Some anglers use a sinking fly line and troll creekmouth drop-offs.

You can paddle to Sarita Lake's west end and continue a short distance down the Sarita River to where the stream drops over a ledge, creating Sarita Falls. The terrain on the lake's north side rises sharply to a height of 935 m. Winds can be funnelled through the valley, creating treacherous water conditions for anglers with smaller boats. Sarita Lake is the region's largest freshwater lake and visitors shouldn't treat it or any other wilderness lake lightly. Always keep an eye on the weather.

Backroaders with 4 x 4s or high-slung vehicles can explore countless side roads branching off the Bamfield Road. Some of these secondary spurs lead to panoramic vistas of Barkley Sound and Alberni Inlet. Pick your travel times, though; high risk of forest fires can result in closures on many routes. In the off-season, washouts or snow at higher elevations can render these backroads impassable. Some roads have been deactivated.

A right at km 22 connects with the backroad up Mount Blenheim. This jarring ride requires a high-slung vehicle or 4 x 4, but on a clear day, the outstanding seascape panorama from the summit takes in Numkamis Bay, Tzartus and Fleming islands, the Sarita River's tidal flats, Uchucklesit Inlet and a broad sweep of Alberni Inlet's lower reaches. Snow-capped peaks to the north (the most distant being part of Forbidden Plateau) and Mount Arrowsmith's rocky crown to the east complete the eagle's-eye view. It's a little under 7 km from the mainline to Mount Blenheim's summit.

The Carnation Creek watershed, close to Mount Blenheim, is the site of the world's longest-running coastal fish and forestry impact study. Initiated in 1970 by the DFO, the project was supported by the federal and provincial governments, the forest industry and others. Results of the Carnation Creek studies were the foundation for a major revision of the coastal fishery and forest guidelines in the late 1980s. The research continues today.

MacBlo logged the Carnation Creek watershed between 1976 and 1981, using both grapple yarding and high-lead techniques. Streamside logging has had positive and negative effects on fish survival and growth, depending on the species, their age and time of year. In some areas, logging destabilized the stream channel. Fine sand, deposited in the lower streambed, has deteriorated the spawning gravel. Natural factors unrelated to logging, such as climate changes and ocean survival rates of fish, were incorporated in the results.

The mainline crosses the South Sarita River bridge and heads due south before swinging west to parallel the Sarita River. Longtime backroad adventurers will recall an old route (no longer in use) to Bamfield, which ran down to the Sarita rivermouth at Numkamis Bay and then by Santa Maria Island through Sarita. Saltwater sports anglers are familiar with the Poett Nook turn at km 27.5. This well-known RV campground and marina at a tiny, protected cove on Barkley Sound's Trevor Channel fills up quickly during July and August.

Around the 30-km mark, Central South Main swings off to the left to skirt a picnic site and natural boat ramp on Frederick Lake's northeast side. You follow area backroads east to hook up with the Cowichan Lake-to-Port Alberni backroad at the Flora Main junction, 13 km south of Franklin Camp. (See Section Two: Trip 5.) This 34-km alternative route passes Rousseau, Crown and Flora lakes and runs through parts of three river valleys – South Sarita, Klanawa and the Little Nitinat. Flora Lake has a BCFS/MacBlo wilderness campsite. MacBlo has been active in this region, so it's best to travel after normal working hours to avoid abrupt confrontations with industrial traffic on the narrow, twisting corners. The hulking off-road logging trucks are in radio contact with each other; most backroaders aren't, so arrange your journeys accordingly.

Keep right at the km-30 junction for Bamfield. The road passes Frederick Lake (41 ha), then Pachena Lake (59 ha). Watch for an overgrown spur on the left that peters out at Pachena Lake. Last time I was there, after a period of heavy rains, mud bogs and waterholes on the access road forced me to walk in using my gumboots. Anglers casting from shore for rainbow and cutthroat trout have to endeavour to avoid snagging deadheads and fallen trees at both lakes. You can follow the rough logging road at km 39 (on the left) to the 3-km trail (on an old logging road) to Black Lake (60 ha). Cutthroat-trout fishing is good right through the summer here, although the best times are in the spring and fall.

The entrance to the West Coast Trail's northern trailhead is at km 40.7. Pachena Bay on the open Pacific is only a short walk away from the parking lot. Many visitors spend a day on the expansive sandy beach; others set out on day hikes to the Pachena Point lighthouse. (For details on Parks Canada regulations and registration requirements for the West Coast Trail, see Section Three: Trip 5.)

The road reaches Bamfield just over the 45-km mark. Half of the village straddles Mills Peninsula, on Bamfield Inlet's west side, and can only be reached by boat or float plane. A water-taxi service is available to visitors. Bamfield's post office, school, coast guard station and general store are all located in Bamfield West. A wooden boardwalk weaves along the waterfront. A short trail winds to beautiful Brady's Beach, fronting Barkley Sound's Imperial Eagle Channel. Bamfield East was once the western North American terminus of the trans-Pacific telegraph cable. Today, the Bamfield Marine Science Research Station occupies the site of the old cable station. At the end of Imperial Eagle Road in Bamfield, a low-tide trail skirts the flats at the head of Bamfield Inlet to the often muddy paths for Keeha Bay and Cape Beale, within Pacific Rim National Park Reserve.

Bamfield Inlet serves as Bamfield's main street and bustles with activity most days. Canoes, kayaks, rowboats, power craft and sailboats of all sizes mingle with sea planes and larger fish boats. The M.V. *Lady Rose*, out of Port Alberni, makes regular stops. And then there are the sport anglers, who base at private fishing resorts in and around Bamfield. There has been talk of connecting both sections of Bamfield with a bridge or causeway. Such a link would erode the feeling of isolation that has always been one of Bamfield's intangible charms.

CONTACTS

- BC Forest Service (South Island Forest District): 250-724-9205
- MacMillan Bloedel (Franklin Operations): 250-720-4200

MAPS/GUIDES

- BC Forest Service Port Alberni District Recreation Map
- MacMillan Bloedel Recreation and Logging Road Guide to TFL 44
- National Topographical Series: 92C/14 Barkley Sound (1:50,000); 92C/15 Little Nitinat River (1:50,000)
- Provincial Map: Regional Map #2 Parksville/Tofino (1:125,000)
- *Adventuring in British Columbia* (Nanton/Simpson/Douglas & McIntyre)
- *Pacific Rim Explorer* (Obee/Whitecap)
- *The West Coast Trail and Nitinat Lakes* (Sierra Club of BC)

NEAREST SERVICES

Port Alberni; Bamfield.

Trip 7:
The Nahmint Lake Loop

IN BRIEF

I always enjoy loop tours along Vancouver Island backroads, and one of my favourites is the 75-km Nahmint Lake Loop through the mountains west of Port Alberni. The route accesses several freshwater trout lakes, wilderness camping spots and some great paddling destinations. Deer, Roosevelt elk, cougar and black bear roam area forests.

ACCESS

Stay on Highway 4 (River Road) and head west from Port Alberni to the Somass River bridge. Cross the bridge and make an immediate left onto Mission Road. (See Section One: Trip 5.) Continue past MacMillan Bloedel's Sproat Operations office and climb the hill to Cous Creek Road (Cous Main) junction, 3 km from the highway. Gravel mainlines are in good to fair condition. Watch for sharp rocks. There are several steep grades. Secondary roads may be rough. Active logging and fire closures may restrict public access. Deactivated roads may be impassable.

DESCRIPTION

To reach the starting point for the Nahmint Lake Loop (the intersection of Cous Creek Road and Stirling Arm Main), drive through Port Alberni and take Highway 4 (River Road) to the Somass River bridge. Cross the river and turn left onto Mission Road. (See Section One: Trip 5.) Drive beyond the entrance to the J.V. Clyne Bird Sanctuary (a wintering area for trumpeter swans) and the MacMillan Bloedel Sproat Operations office. Its *Recreation and Logging Road Guide to TFL 44* includes the logging roads for the Nahmint Lake Loop. Prior to your trip, pick up a copy at the Port Alberni Forest Information Centre at Harbour Quay.

Keep right at the fork, 2.7 km from the highway, and climb the short hill to the signposted turn for Cous Creek Road. (See Section Two: Trip 8.) Turn left onto Cous Creek Road and reset your vehicle's trip meter to zero. Just over the 7-km mark, swing left onto Branch 1100 (Canal Main) and cross the Cous Creek bridge. Straight ahead, Cous Creek Road stays on the north side of Cous Creek to hook up with Kanyon Main.

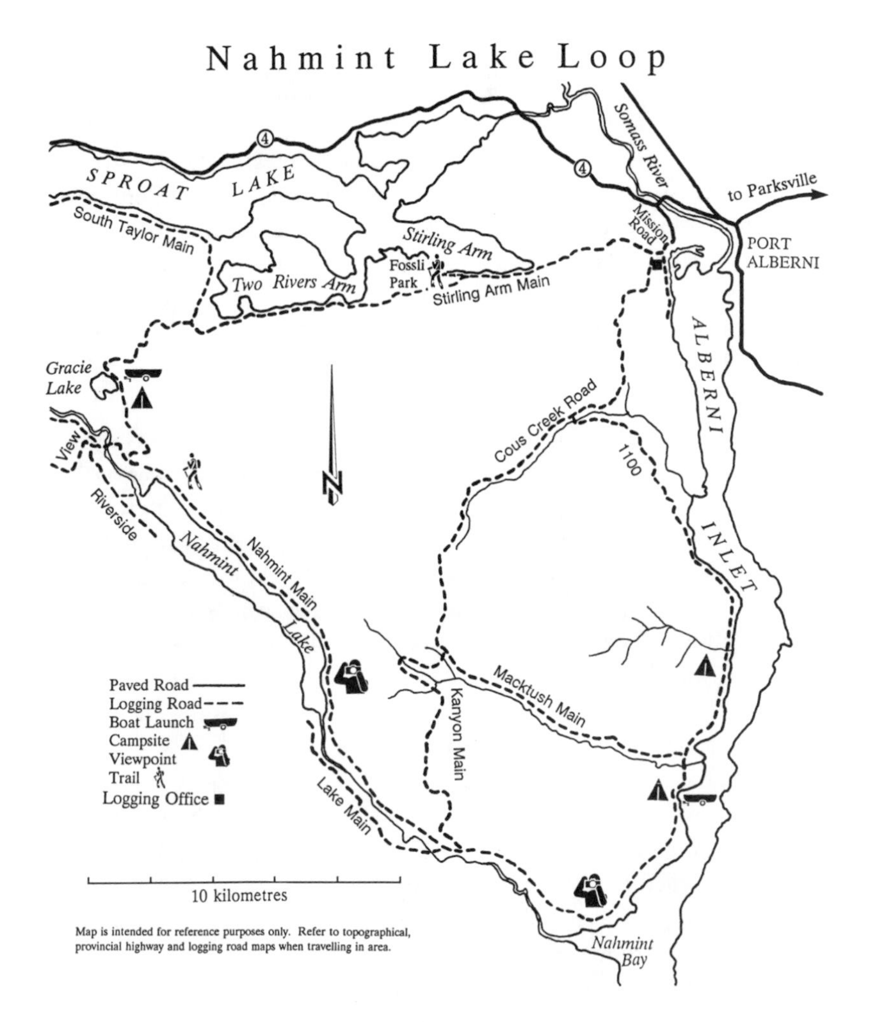
Nahmint Lake Loop
SPROAT LAKE
South Taylor Main
Two Rivers Arm
Stirling Arm
Fossli Park
Stirling Arm Main
Somass River
Mission Road
to Parksville
PORT ALBERNI
ALBERNI INLET
Gracie Lake
View
Riverside
Nahmint Lake
Nahmint Main
Cous Creek Road
1100
Macktush Main
Kanyon Main
Lake Main
Nahmint Bay
Paved Road
Logging Road
Boat Launch
Campsite
Viewpoint
Trail
Logging Office
10 kilometres
Map is intended for reference purposes only. Refer to topographical, provincial highway and logging road maps when travelling in area.

You'll see Alberni Inlet a couple of times before the road drops to sea level. At km 17.4, a steep side road (on the left) accesses the BC Forest Service Arden Creek campsite, with seven user-maintained forested campsites. A short path leads to a picnic area with a spectacular view. There is no boat ramp here, but cartoppers can be carried down to the water. Alberni Inlet has many moods. Sometimes only a slight swell disturbs its calm. When the wind is up, inlet waters are alive with chop and whitecaps, creating tricky conditions that are easily magnified when tidal currents battle contrary gusts. Be wary out on the water.

The mainline, now called Macktush Access, crosses the Macktush Creek bridge to the Bill Motyka Recreation Area (km 22.3), located on private MacMillan Bloedel property. RVs and campers line the waterfront at the peak of the summer salmon season. You can also set up a tent in a forested fringe near the water. The mainline (Nahmint Main) continues beyond the recreation area and runs southwest to Nahmint Bay, a coastal indentation on Alberni Inlet's west side where the Nahmint River meets the sea. Alberni Pacific Lumber logged the lower Nahmint Valley in the late 1920s. A logging railway extended along the river's northeast side almost right to Nahmint Lake. There is a great Nahmint Bay viewpoint, just over the km-28 mark.

The DFO has imposed a fishing closure in Nahmint Bay from August 1st to October 31st each year in an effort to rebuild dwindling chinook salmon stock. Four other species of salmon return seasonally to the lower Nahmint River. Their upstream migration (and that of sea-run cutthroat trout and winter steelhead) is blocked by a 4-m waterfall in the Nahmint Canyon, just under 5 km from tidewater. Only a small number of summer steelhead are able to negotiate the natural barrier.

Torrential rainfall and fast runoff can deluge area creeks and rivers. Overnight water rises of over 3 m have been recorded at Nahmint Lake. Sometimes waterfalls tumble down right at roadside. These backroads were literally chiselled out of rock – blasting was the only way to punch the arteries through. Area mainlines are in good to fair shape and receive regular maintenance, though washboard hills, sharp rocks and muffler-grabbing gravel ridges may be encountered.

Kanyon Main (km 33.5) cuts off to the right and hooks into Cous Creek Road. Lake Main (on the left just over the 34-km mark) crosses a wooden bridge over the Nahmint River and eventually deadends in old-growth timber. The road doesn't reach Nahmint Lake, but you can see the lake's south end.

Nahmint Main runs high along Nahmint Lake's east side to two viewpoints, one a little over the km-40 mark, the other at km 42. Nahmint Lake

(710 ha in size and 8 km in length) is habitat to large rainbow and cutthroat trout, Dolly Varden (char) and kokanee salmon. Several angling restrictions apply to Nahmint area waters. In the lake, all wild rainbow trout over 50 cm in length must be released. Only single barbless hooks may be used and an outboard motor restriction of 7.5 hp applies. A bait ban pertains to both the lake and river. The Nahmint River and its tributaries above Nahmint Lake are designated as trout and char catch-and-release waters, restricted to fly-fishing only. The river below the lake is closed to all angling from November 1st to April 30th. Check current fishing regulations carefully.

Around the 50-km mark, watch for the Nahmint Lake Trail signpost (if it is still there and readable). Known to locals as the Anderson Trail, the path is near Anderson Creek and its clamorous 20-m waterfall. The somewhat steep route drops from the logging road to Nahmint Lake's northeast shore. Determined anglers will lug a canoe or cartop boat through stands of towering old growth to lakeside.

Nahmint Main cuts left at a T-junction (km 51) to drop down a grade and cross a bridge over the Nahmint River. The deep, jade pools and mini-canyon near this crossing are spectacular. Keep left, on the west side of the bridge, for Riverside and View mainlines. Nahmint Main parallels the Nahmint River to active logging areas. MacBlo has established riparian buffer zones along the Nahmint River and key tributaries to lessen logging's impact on fish and wildlife habitat.

It was in this region that I came upon a perplexing signpost. The names of most junctions along Vancouver Island backroads are derived from local geographic features like rivers, mountains or lakes. This particular sign didn't follow that pattern. Later, the enigma was cleared up by a MacBlo engineer. Apparently, one hauler, carrying logs out from Riverside Main, made the wrong turn on Nahmint Main and discovered his error some distance up the Nahmint River Valley. The truck had to be unloaded, turned around and then reloaded. As a private joke, fellow loggers renamed the intersection after the driver to commemorate the episode.

Four-wheelers can explore View Main to several spurs offering great Nahmint Lake vistas. Follow Riverside Main a short distance down the lake's west side to a tanker-truck access route, constructed by MacBlo in co-operation with the BCFS. This spur ends at a steep bank on the Nahmint River, where it enters the lake. This water access was situated upstream from a shallow gravel bar to deter large boat launching.

Canoeists and kayakers can put-in here and head out to several secluded rocky beaches along Nahmint Lake. Watch out for sudden winds and waves. With a combination of paddling, lining and portaging you can work upriver about 2 km to the green pool, near the logging road bridge. This is a bit like paddling the lower San Juan River near Port Renfrew, or the more remote Tahsish River, on northern Vancouver Island. The latter destination requires an ocean inlet crossing. (See Section Three: Trip 11.)

Turn right at the km-51 T-junction to continue the Nahmint Lake Loop. The switchback up to Gracie Lake is probably the worst hill on the route. Halfway up the grade is an exceptional look up the Nahmint River Valley. The Gibson/Klitsa Plateau, near the headwaters of the Nahmint River, is under consideration by the BCFS as a designated wilderness area. Nearly 6,000 ha in size, this sub-alpine region of small lakes, meadows and forest can be accessed via an unimproved trail near Sproat Lake's west end.

Gracie Lake (38 ha and up at the 335-m level) is a popular rainbow trout fishing destination in the spring and fall. A secondary spur (km 55) accesses a BCFS five-site wilderness campsite at Gracie Lake's north end and a natural boat launch. Prior to the road access, determined anglers slid down a tricky slope on the lake's eastern fringe.

From Gracie Lake, the road makes an abrupt descent of the Gracie Creek Valley (which includes an eagle's-eye look at Sproat Lake's Two Rivers Arm). At km 59 you'll reach Sproat Lake's south-shore logging roads. A left onto South Taylor Main leads west to Highway 4. Turn right onto Stirling Arm Main and head east for Port Alberni. Hikers can follow an overgrown side road (on the left at km 68.7) to Fossli Provincial Park. (See Section Two: Trip 8.) Just under the 75-km mark is our starting point – the junction of Cous Creek Road and Stirling Arm Main.

CONTACTS

- Alberni Forest Information Centre (Port Alberni): 250-724-7890
- BC Forest Service (South Island Forest District): 250-724-9205
- MacMillan Bloedel (Sproat Operations): 250-720-4100

MAPS/GUIDES

- BC Forest Service Port Alberni Forest District Recreation Map
- MacMillan Bloedel Recreation and Logging Road Guide to TFL 44
- National Topographical Series: 92F/2 Alberni Inlet (1:50,000); 92F/3 Effingham River (1:50,000); 92F/6 Great Central Lake (1:50,000); 92F/7 Horne Lake (1:50,000)
- Provincial Map: Regional Map #2 Parksville/Tofino (1:125,000)

NEAREST SERVICES

Port Alberni.

Trip 8:
The Sproat Lake Loop

IN BRIEF

The 75-km Sproat Lake Loop (like the Cowichan Lake Loop) follows gravel roads and paved highways. Starting just west of Port Alberni, logging mainlines on Sproat Lake's south shore pass wilderness campsites, boat launches and challenging roads to more remote angling and camping spots. The return route to Port Alberni via Highway 4 (Pacific Rim Highway) runs near a tiny Taylor Arm user-maintained campsite on Sproat Lake's north side, near the Taylor River's mouth. Sproat Lake Provincial Park is just off the highway, closer to Port Alberni.

ACCESS

Stay on Highway 4 through Port Alberni and head west on River Road to the Somass River bridge. On the south side of the bridge turn left onto Mission Road. (See Section One: Trip 5.) Gravel mainlines are in good to fair shape. Watch for industrial traffic. Secondary logging roads may require a 4 x 4 or high-slung vehicle.

DESCRIPTION

The Port Alberni region, known for its salmon fishing, also has good trout waters. Some of the most accessible are found along Sproat Lake backroads. Named in 1864 after Gilbert Malcolm Sproat, a principal member of the Vancouver Island Exploring Expedition, Sproat Lake's aboriginal name, *Kleecoot*, means "wide-open." There are over 160 km of shoreline along Sproat Lake (3,775 ha) and its four spidery arms: Kleecoot, Stirling, Two Rivers and Taylor. The lake is connected to Alberni Inlet by the Sproat and Somass rivers.

The start of the Sproat Lake Loop is just west of Port Alberni. Follow the Tofino signposts through Port Alberni. At the foot of Johnston Street take River Road 3 km west and cross the Somass River bridge. (See Section One: Trip 5.) On the span's south side, cut left onto Mission Road and reset your vehicle's trip meter to zero.

Mount Arrowsmith stands guard over the Alberni Valley and is visible along the first stretch of this run. The entrance for the J.V. Clyne bird

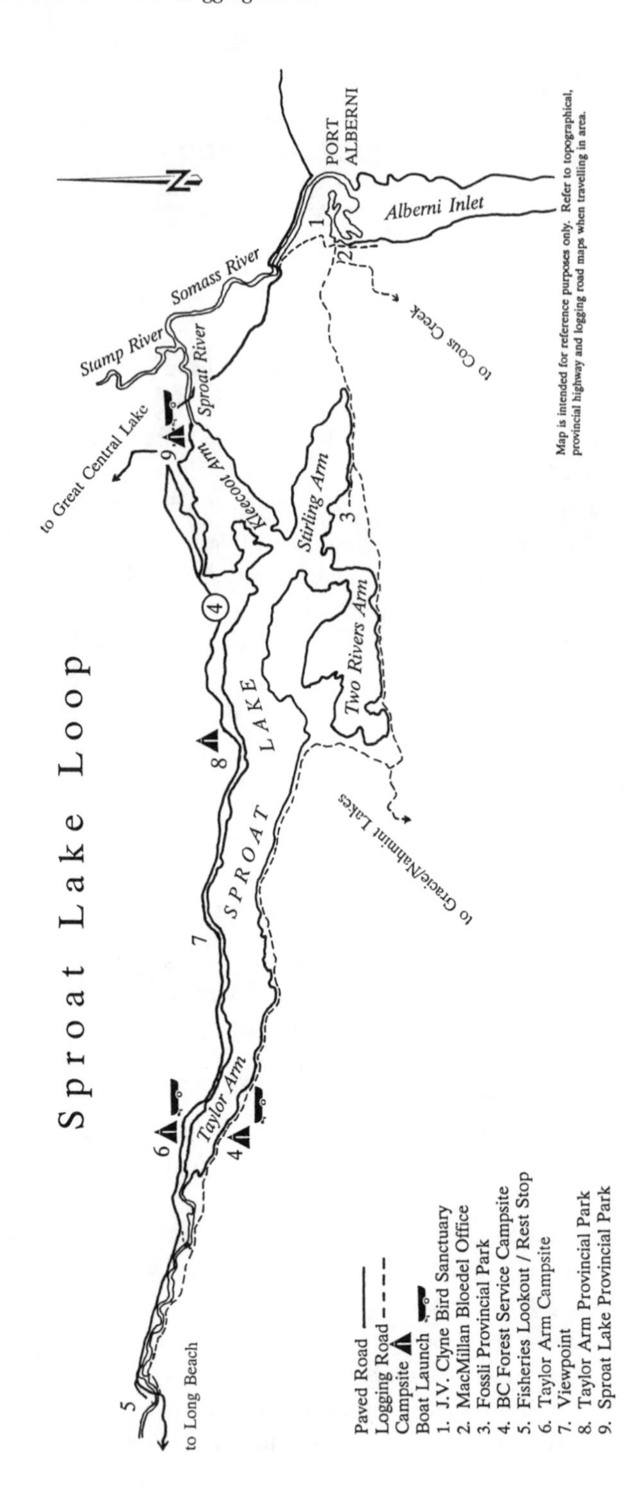

Sproat Lake Loop
PORT ALBERNI
Alberni Inlet
Somass River
Stamp River
Sproat River
to Great Central Lake
Stirling Arm
Two Rivers Arm
SPROAT LAKE
Taylor Arm
to Cous Creek
to Gracie/Nahmint Lakes
to Long Beach
Map is intended for reference purposes only. Refer to topographical, provincial highway and logging road maps when travelling in area.
Paved Road
Logging Road
Campsite
Boat Launch
1. J.V. Clyne Bird Sanctuary
2. MacMillan Bloedel Office
3. Fossli Provincial Park
4. BC Forest Service Campsite
5. Fisheries Lookout / Rest Stop
6. Taylor Arm Campsite
7. Viewpoint
8. Taylor Arm Provincial Park
9. Sproat Lake Provincial Park

sanctuary is at km 1.7. Here visitors may view the trumpeter swan, Canada's largest waterfowl, in its natural habitat. The birds winter in the estuary from November to March. A 1971 study of the tidal flats, undertaken by the Canadian Wildlife Service, focused on winter feeding habits and ecology of the area's trumpeters. MacMillan Bloedel subsequently donated over 32 ha as a refuge for migratory birds. Dedicated in 1972, it was named after J.V. Clyne, former chairman and chief executive officer of MacMillan Bloedel (1958-1972).

The road curves by MacBlo's Sproat Operations headquarters. The Alberni Forest Information Centre (at Alberni Harbour Quay in Port Alberni) distributes area logging road maps and has information on seasonal mill and logging tours. Pop in and pick up a copy of MacBlo's *Recreation and Logging Road Guide to TFL 44*. You can also get updates on area logging operations. When you share backroads with industrial traffic, it's nice to know if, where and when active hauling is taking place. Remember to travel with your headlights on. If you encounter any industrial traffic, pull well off to the side of the road and stop. You won't win an argument with a loaded logging truck. Drive with caution and respect any posted notices.

At km 2.7 the road splits. Keep right for Sproat Lake. At a second junction (km 3) keep right onto Stirling Arm Road. A left onto Cous Main is the start of the Nahmint Lake Loop that leads to several BC Forest Service wilderness campsites, Alberni Inlet saltwater access points and great fishing and paddling at Nahmint and Gracie lakes. (See Section Two: Trip 7.) Stirling Arm Road passes Devil's Den Lake, a roadside pond, and heads west to Branch 301 (on the right at km 9.3). This spur leads to trails into Fossli Provincial Park. Fossli is a Norwegian word meaning "waterfalls," and there are many here. St. Andrews Creek intersects the park and features a number of scenic cascades as it tumbles to lakeside. The park has a picnic area with fire pits, hiking trails and a developed beach. You can also reach the site by boat.

The mainline skirts Two Rivers Arm. A little over the 13-km mark is a small pull-off providing a panoramic view. Watch for the Gracie Lake/ Nahmint Lake turn, on the left, just under the 19-km mark. This steep and often bumpy mainline climbs to Gracie Lake, a high-elevation rainbow trout fishing destination. The road carries on beyond Gracie Lake to make an equally sharp descent to Nahmint Lake.

From the Gracie/Nahmint cut-off the Sproat Lake Loop continues on South Taylor Main. There are some blind corners and steep cliffs in this stretch. At km 32.7 you'll cross the Snow Creek bridge. Watch for a nearby side road, on the right, that accesses the co-managed BCFS/MacBlo Snow Creek Recreation Site, on Taylor Arm. A natural boat launch for cartoppers

Two young anglers set up for some shoreline casting.

is close to a handful of roadside pull-ins. Kids and grownups alike will enjoy shorecasting here. You can also hike to the deep pool at the base of the waterfall on Snow Creek.

Cut right at the Taylor River bridge (km 37.3) and head east for about 3 km to a Taylor Arm wilderness campsite. This tiny hideaway has a cartop boat launch close to the Taylor River mouth. Spring fishing can be excellent here. South Taylor Main continues west through a region that was devastated by the Tay Fire of 1967. The blaze was accidentally started during road construction and eventually ravaged over 2,500 ha of forest – half of which was prime timber. Seventy percent of the scorched trees were salvaged and the area was successfully replanted. Grim evidence of the fire's passage still remains on the mountainsides, where you'll see burned tree trunks on the steep slopes.

The route follows the Taylor River, Sproat Lake's largest tributary with a watershed of forty square kilometres. The river was named after Charles Taylor, the Port Alberni district's first settler (1864). The mainline emerges at Highway 4, near the Taylor River rest area. Rough trails parallel the river and one steep path overlooks a deep pool. It's not uncommon to detect the shadowy shape of a resident fish lurking amid the river's sunken rocks.

Two species of salmon spawn in the Taylor River. Coho begin their runs in September, with the peak in October. Sockeye appear in early July through late September. Steelhead, the sea-going rainbow trout, spawn in the winter and spring. Kokanee, rainbow and cutthroat are also present in Sproat

Lake. Cutthroat remain in the lake and spawn in local streams in late spring. They are among the largest known cutthroat trout in BC, averaging 58 cm in length and weighing between 2.2 and 6.8 kg. Snorkel surveys by the Ministry of Environment reflect a decline in cutthroat migration over the last decade and a dominant rainbow population. Through creel surveys and swim counts, officials hope to learn more about these fish and their Sproat Lake wanderings. Check the current freshwater fishing regulations carefully before fishing area waters.

Reset your vehicle's trip meter to zero at the Highway 4 rest stop and take the paved road east to Port Alberni. At km 5.8 you can cut right onto the backroad to the Taylor Arm user-maintained campsite. At km 14.4 the highway rest stop offers an expansive view east over Sproat Lake. At km 23.5 Lakeshore Road (west) meets the highway. This alternate route passes several private campgrounds and resorts and is close to the Martin Mars water bomber base. Lakeshore Road (east) meets Highway 4 near Sproat Lake Provincial Park. From here Highway 4 winds about 11 km to Mission Road, the start of the Sproat Lake Loop. (See Section One: Trip 5 for more detailed information on the many points of interest along this stretch of Highway 4.)

CONTACTS

- Alberni Forest Information Centre: 250-724-7890
- BC Forest Service (South Island Forest District): 250-724-9205
- MacMillan Bloedel (Sproat Operations): 250-720-4100

MAPS/GUIDES

- BC Forest Service Port Alberni Forest District Recreation Map
- MacMillan Bloedel Recreation and Logging Road Guide to TFL 44
- National Topographical Series: 92F/2 Alberni Inlet (1:50,000); 92F/3 Effingham River (1:50,000); 92F/6 Great Central Lake (1:50,000); 92F/7 Horne Lake (1:50,000)
- Provincial Map: Regional Map # 2 Parksville/Tofino (1:125,000)

NEAREST SERVICES

Port Alberni area.

Trip 9: Clayoquot Sound Backroads

IN BRIEF

If you are planning on spending some time in the Long Beach area, consider adding a few days to your itinerary to include some backroad adventuring. Two logging mainlines meet Highway 4 close to Kennedy Lake. One route accesses Toquart Bay and the BC Forest Service Toquart Bay Recreation Site (a jumping-off point for the Broken Islands, part of Pacific Rim National Park Reserve). A second mainline leads to the forests between Tofino Inlet and Kennedy Lake's Clayoquot Arm. Some visitors base at the BCFS Clayoquot Arm Beach Recreation Site. Close by are fishing and paddling waters, short hiking trails, two waterfalls and all sorts of intriguing secondary roads.

ACCESS

Take Highway 4 (Pacific Rim Highway) west from Port Alberni: 76 km for the Toquart Bay turn; 86 km for the West Main junction. (See Section One: Trip 5.) Gravel mainlines along Highway 4 are in good to fair shape. Some secondary roads are best suited for a high-slung vehicle or 4 x 4. Logging may restrict access in certain areas.

DESCRIPTION

There is more to the Long Beach area than whale watching, pounding surf and spectacular beach walking. While you need a boat to visit much of Clayoquot Sound, several backroads near Kennedy Lake connect with Highway 4 and stretch into the region's southern forests.

After Highway 4 negotiates the Kennedy Lake switchbacks it drops down to lakeside and levels off. Watch for the signposted Maggie Lake Forest Service Road (Toquart Road), about 76 km west of Port Alberni. (See Section One: Trip 5.) This is the start of a 16-km backroad route to the BC Forest Service wilderness campsite on Toquart Bay. Reset your vehicle's trip meter to zero when you swing left onto the gravel and backtrack up the washboard hill for Toquart Bay.

The road to Toquart Bay is a well-travelled gravel mainline with several one-lane bridges. On weekdays you may encounter industrial traffic, so drive

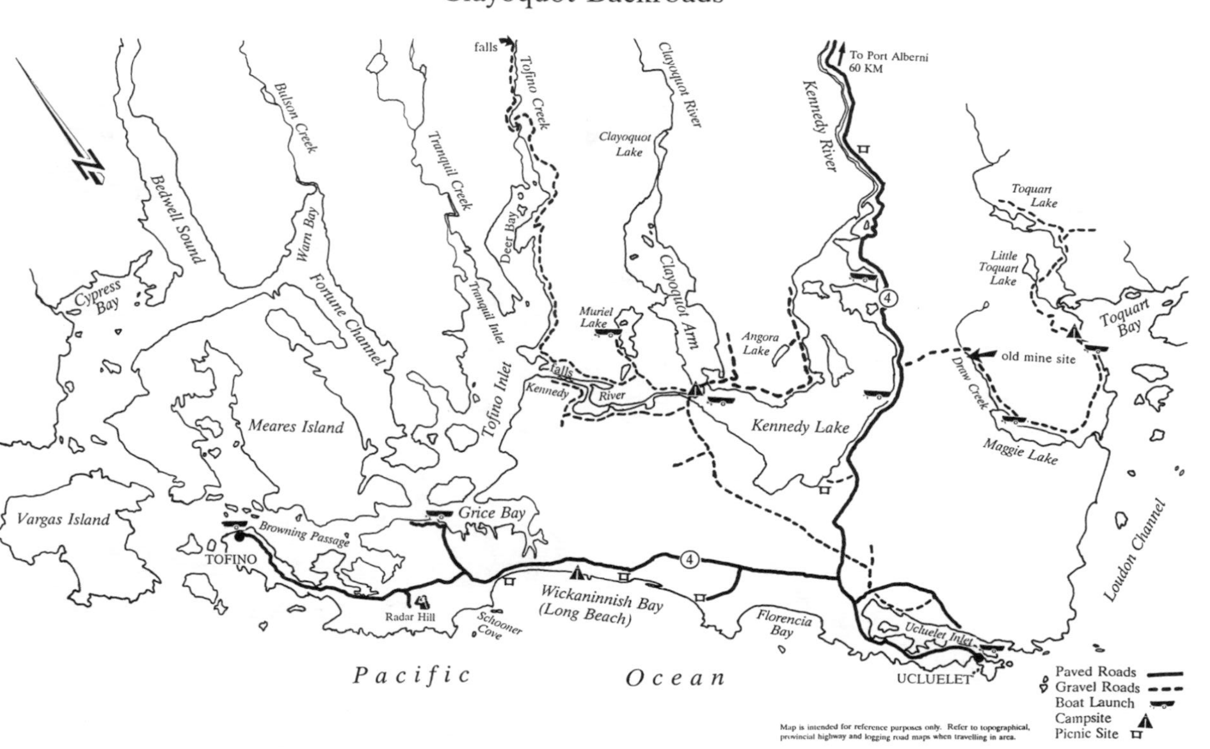

Clayoquot Backroads
falls
Tofino Creek
Clayoquot River
To Port Alberni 60 KM
Kennedy River
Bulson Creek
Tranquil Creek
Clayoquot Lake
Bedwell Sound
Warn Bay
Deer Bay
Toquart Lake
Little Toquart Lake
Cypress Bay
Fortune Channel
Tranquil Inlet
Clayoquot Arm
Muriel Lake
Angora Lake
Toquart Bay
4
old mine site
Draw Creek
falls
Kennedy River
Tofino Inlet
Meares Island
Kennedy Lake
Maggie Lake
Vargas Island
Grice Bay
Browning Passage
TOFINO
Loudon Channel
Wickaninnish Bay (Long Beach)
Radar Hill
Schooner Cove
Florencia Bay
Ucluelet Inlet
UCLUELET
Pacific Ocean
Paved Roads
Gravel Roads
Boat Launch
Campsite
Picnic Site
Map is intended for reference purposes only. Refer to topographical, provincial highway and logging road maps when travelling in area.

with caution and watch out for potholes. At the 3.5-km mark the road skirts a pond that was once an open pit mine. This area had attracted the attention of geologists as far back as 1902 when magnetic anomalies were noted in the Draw Creek Valley. Nearby Maggie Lake and River are said to be named after these magnetic irregularities, which still affect compass readings and can pose problems for boaters negotiating area waters in fog.

By the early 1960s, logging road extensions coupled with Japan's increased demand for iron concentrate led to the development of the Brynnor Mine. In an early example of environmental concerns, rather than subject Maggie Lake to possible siltation from mine tailings, the company punched through a road link to Toquart Bay. Here a small mill and concentrator were built; ore was loaded directly into ocean-going ships and mine tailings were disposed of in the tidal flats. Mining operations had ceased by 1969. Over the decades, sea action has created Toquart Bay's beautiful beach.

Maggie Lake (249 ha) holds cutthroat trout and Dolly Varden. Watch for a tiny pull-off on the right (km 8.2) near a natural boat ramp. After heavy rains in January 1996, slides from unstable slopes and flooding creeks severed the Toquart Bay Road in several places. The bridge at km 9.3 has since been raised substantially. Sharp rocks make up the short but steep incline to the new bridge deck. Until the approaches are smoothed out a little, take care negotiating the span, particularly if you are travelling in a larger RV or pulling a trailered boat.

The BCFS Toquart Bay Recreational Site (km 16) remains a summer favourite with RVers and campers. The BCFS estimates twenty to forty thousand people visit the site annually. A concrete boat launch accommodates year-round saltwater anglers and there are walk-in tent sites. Parks Canada says about half the kayakers and canoeists heading to the Broken Islands begin at Toquart Bay and cross the relatively sheltered waters to the Barkley Sound archipelago. Another forty percent come in on the M.V. *Lady Rose* out of Port Alberni. Officials are unsure where the rest launch from. Contact the Pacific Rim National Park Reserve office (Ucluelet) at 250-726-7721 for current information on Broken Islands access regulations and overnight camping fees.

A rugged logging road extends beyond the Toquart Bay campsite, skirts a Coulson Forest Products industrial site and runs close to Little Toquart Lake (a primitive trail leads in to the lakeside) and Toquart Lake. Call ahead for hauling updates before you venture on these sometimes restricted-access arteries.

MacMillan Bloedel's West Main, the second backroad gateway to Clayoquot Sound, crosses the highway 10.5 km west of the Toquart Bay cut-off, near the Walk in The Forest interpretative trail. Look for a Forest

Renewal BC signpost at the junction. The Ministry of Environment and the BCFS are assessing fish habitat in area streams and rivers. You'll see many of their stream markers along the logging roads. MacBlo shut down its Kennedy Lake Division in early 1998.

Reset your vehicle's trip meter to zero, swing north on West Main and avoid any secondary roads. The road crosses the Kennedy River on a wooden bridge (km 11.3) that was the site of numerous logging blockades. On the east side of the river, the road splits. A left at this junction goes to Berryman Point and passes the secondary road leading to Muriel Lake. Muriel Lake (145 ha) contains cutthroat trout and has good summer fishing May to October. Lake access is via a steep hill adjacent to a gravel pit. Large logs block the waterfront, precluding trailered boats, but you can easily put in a cartopper or canoe. On one trip there, a fishing buddy and I discovered how long the battery for his new electric motor would last and rediscovered how much we dislike rowing against a strong headwind.

Just over 5 km from the bridge junction watch for an overgrown road, on the left. A ten-minute walk along the old artery leads to a short trail that drops through a cedar forest to the boisterous rapids and chutes that are the Kennedy River Falls. Downstream, the Kennedy River enters the saltchuck at Kennedy Cove on Tofino Inlet. The closest boat launch is the public ramp on Grice Bay or facilities in Tofino. These waters provide good coho fishing at the end of August and early September. Check with DFO for updates on seasonal closures. If you have a 4 x 4, your backroading can extend beyond Berryman Point and northeast along Tofino Inlet to Deer Bay. When the roads are passable, you can continue up the Tofino Creek Valley to Virgin Falls.

Keep right at the junction near the Kennedy River bridge, and travel less than a kilometre to the BCFS Clayoquot Arm Recreation Site, co-managed with MacBlo. Situated just before a second bridge over Clayoquot Arm, the user-maintained site has limited camping and a natural boat launch. A nature trail winds through a pocket mature forest of Sitka spruce, twisted red cedars and shoreline pine to a beach and cove on Clayoquot Arm. The trail was named for Norm Godfrey, a regional MacBlo forester.

Kennedy Lake can provide good cutthroat trout fishing if you have the patience to seek them out. Area trout prefer three-spined stickleback and sculpins, and the stickleback and sculpins hang out in the weed beds. Successful anglers troll baitfish imitations along likely shoreline drop-offs or creekmouths. You'll soon discover that the shallows in some parts of the lake extend quite a distance offshore. Beware of sudden winds on Kennedy Lake and Clayoquot Arm, as gusts surge in from the Pacific and are funnelled by sheer topography.

Since 1992, the Clayoquot Biosphere Project has compiled scientific research on coastal ecosystems within Clayoquot Sound. Representatives from First Nations communities in Clayoquot Sound work with the CBP's Central Region Board in the year-round operation of three field stations. Terrestrial studies began in 1992 at Clayoquot Lake. A marine station opened in 1994 on Flores Island. The newest research post is involved with estuary studies at the head of Sidney Inlet.

MacBlo's *Recreation and Logging Road Guide to TFL 44* is the best reference map to carry with you on area backroad explorations. You can pick up a copy at the Alberni Forest Information Centre in Port Alberni.

CONTACTS

- Alberni Forest Information Centre (Port Alberni): 250-724-7890
- BC Forest Service (South Island Forest District): 250-724-9205
- BC Parks (Strathcona District): 250-954-4600
- Coulson Forest Products (Port Alberni): 250-723-8118
- Pacific Rim National Park Reserve (Ucluelet): 250-726-7721
- Rainforest Interpretative Centre (Tofino): 250-725-2560

MAPS/GUIDES

- BC Forest Service Port Alberni Forest District Recreation Map
- MacMillan Bloedel Recreation and Logging Road Guide to TFL 44
- National Topographical Series: 92F/3 Effingham River (1:50,000); 92F/4 Tofino (1:50,000)
- Provincial Map: Regional Map #2 Parksville/Tofino (1:125,000)
- *Four-Wheeling On Southern Vancouver Island* (Lee/Thirkell/Harbour)
- *Hiking Trails III* (VITIS)
- *Island Paddling* (Snowden/Orca)
- *Pacific Rim Explorer* (Obee/Whitecap)

NEAREST SERVICES

Tofino; Ucluelet.

Trip 10:
Port Alberni to Courtenay

IN BRIEF

The backroads that connect Port Alberni with Courtenay pass through a paradise of lakes, forests and mountains. The 59.5-km logging-road route cuts into the Ash River Valley and skirts Comox Lake's west side to emerge in the Courtenay area. Anglers, paddlers and boaters will find countless lakes, many with shoreline wilderness campsites. Myriad side roads will appeal to off-road explorers.

ACCESS

Drive through Port Alberni and head west on Highway 4 (Pacific Rim Highway). Turn right onto Great Central Road, about 7 km beyond the Somass River bridge. This cut-off is near the entrance to Sproat Lake Provincial Park. (See Section One: Trip 5.) From here it's 7.5 km to the foot of Great Central Lake. Mainlines are usually in good to fair condition; secondary spurs (and a few washboard hills on the mainlines) could require a truck or 4 x 4. Deactivated roads may be impassable. Industrial traffic may be frequent in some areas. Best travel times are after 6 p.m. on weekdays and on weekends and holidays. Fire closures, seasonal snows and active logging may restrict public entry on some roads.

DESCRIPTION

The backroads from Port Alberni to Courtenay are well known to many Vancouver Islanders. You can day-trip to fishing and paddling lakes or stay overnight at a wilderness campsite. Many visitors base at serviced sites, such as Stamp Falls or Sproat Lake provincial parks, just outside of Port Alberni.

Take Highway 4 west from Port Alberni. About 7 km beyond the Somass River bridge, turn right onto Great Central Road. (See Section One: Trip 5.) It's about 7.5 km to the lake. A kilometre before the start of the logging road near the Ark Resort is the Robertson Creek coho and chinook salmon hatchery. Seasonal tours are available. The hatchery's steelhead enhancement program has benefited the Stamp/Somass river systems.

At the foot of Great Central Lake (at 5,085 ha, one of Vancouver Island's largest) many outdoorsmen launch their boats to test the fishing.

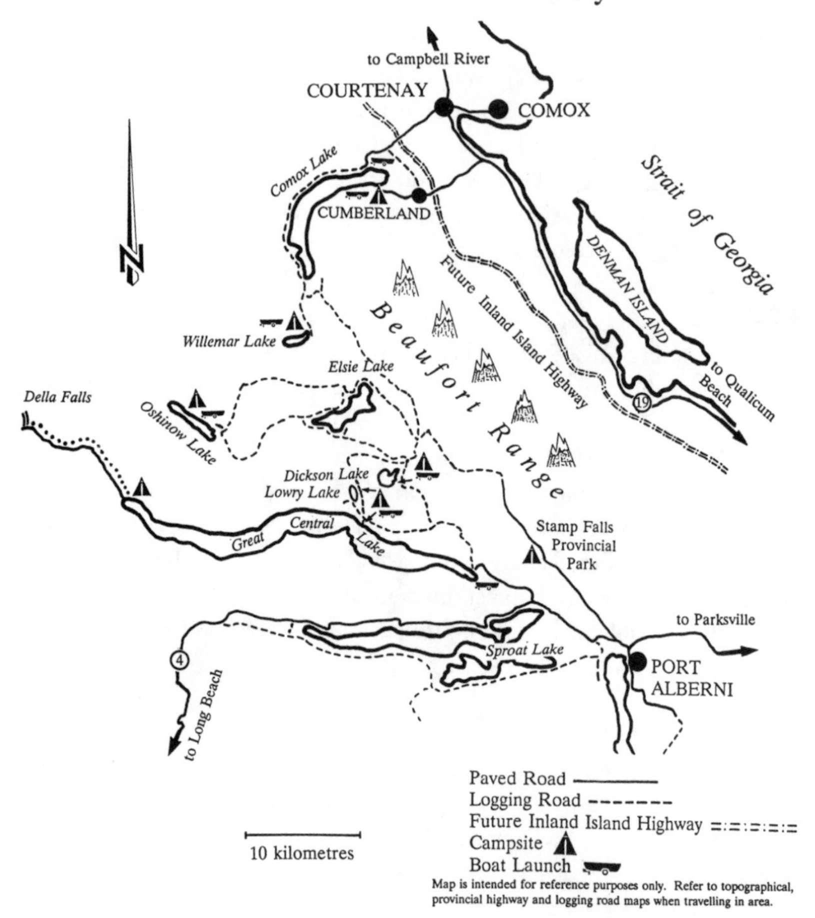
Port Alberni to Courtenay
to Campbell River
COURTENAY
COMOX
Strait of Georgia
Comox Lake
CUMBERLAND
DENMAN ISLAND
Future Inland Island Highway
Beaufort Range
Willemar Lake
Elsie Lake
Della Falls
Oshinow Lake
to Qualicum Beach
19
Dickson Lake
Lowry Lake
Great Central Lake
Stamp Falls Provincial Park
to Parksville
Sproat Lake
4
PORT ALBERNI
to Long Beach
Paved Road
Logging Road
Future Inland Island Highway
Campsite
Boat Launch
10 kilometres
Map is intended for reference purposes only. Refer to topographical, provincial highway and logging road maps when travelling in area.

The lake contains cutthroat trout, stocked steelhead, Dolly Varden (char) and sockeye salmon. A left at the Ark Resort goes by some floating cabins to a public boat ramp. For a small fee you can launch at the resort's private dock. This is the starting point for paddlers venturing to lakehead to tackle the 16-km trail up the Drinkwater Creek Valley to Della Falls. This cascade, Canada's tallest, tumbles a total of 440 m down from Della Lake. (The amphibious journey from Great Central Lake to Della Falls is described in Section Three: Trip 6.)

Near the Ark Resort, a dam regulates water flow in the Stamp River and creates water storage for area mills. As a result, Great Central Lake's shoreline harbours sunken stumps and deadheads. When paddling the lake always stay within a safe range of shore. Blustery winds can come up suddenly, creating heavy chop.

To begin the backroads run to Courtenay, turn right (north) as you reach Great Central Lake. Reset your vehicle's trip meter to zero, and cross the Stamp River bridge on MacMillan Bloedel's Ash River Road. Several secondary roads in this first stretch can be explored, though a 4 x 4 may be required. A trail winds in to Patterson Lake. Area spurs run to Sumner Lake, marshy Moran Lake and a beautiful riverbend on the Ash River. (See *More Island Adventures*, Trip 15.)

Branch 83 (on the left at km 6.5) is the road to an alternate put-in spot for boaters and Della Falls paddlers who want to cut down their lake travel time. Take Branch 83 for 9.3 km to a junction with a secondary spur (83D), just south of Lowry Lake. Turn left for 1.5 km to the BC Forest Service Scout Beach Recreation Site on Great Central Lake's north side. There are wilderness campsites, picnic tables and a steep, natural boat launch.

Back now to Ash River Road. At km 11.7 park your vehicle on the shoulder of the mainline (make sure you're well off to the side of the road) and hike a short way up an old road to a trail that drops down to the Ash River and Dickson Falls. The waterfall looks like a grand staircase when the Ash River is running high.

You can't miss Dickson Lake, visible on the left as the mainline crosses the Ash River bridge, just under the 13-km mark. Take the first left on the far side of the wooden span for a wilderness campsite at lakeside and a natural boat launch for cartoppers and paddlers. This location, on private property, has no comfort stations, garbage cans, picnic tables or amenities of any sort. Visitors can help ensure continued public access. Tidy up your site before you leave, follow seasonal fire restrictions and don't cut trees for firewood.

Dickson Lake (199 ha) cutthroat trout action picks up in the spring and fall. The lake also contains Dolly Varden and wild steelhead. A bait ban applies at Dickson Lake, and remember to use only single, barbless hooks. No

A rest stop on the Ash River.

trout or char over 50 cm may be kept. Check the current regulations carefully. Each of the lake's spidery arms offers anglers a variety of casting hideaways. Try working the drop-offs or trolling or casting in lake narrows and near creekmouths. Some of the smaller streams are hard to see; these must be located by a steady gurgle and a subtle change in lakeside vegetation.

At a major junction (km 15), backroad adventurers have several choices. Option One: Anglers looking for rainbow and cutthroat trout waters with cartop boat access swing left to stay on Ash River Road. Cross the Ash River to a deteriorated spur (on the left at km 15.5) that runs to the southeast end of Ash Lake (65 ha) and a rough water access point. Like many area lakes, Ash Lake has been stocked with rainbow and cutthroat trout. You'll find Dolly Varden (char) in some lakes as well. From here Branch 105 cuts along Ash Lake's east side. Shorecasters must climb down a steep bank to lakeside. By km 20 McLaughlin Lake (41 ha) will be visible through the trees. Just under the 21-km mark, bear left up a hill. This secondary road ends at a wilderness picnic site at McLaughlin Lake.

Beyond the McLaughlin Lake cut-off, the road winds down to the access for the BCFS Lowry Lake Recreation Site (km 25.4). This location, co-managed with MacBlo, has a few wilderness campsites and a natural boat launch. Over the summer, the fish may have soft flesh, less than ideal for eating. Prime fishing seasons are the spring and fall. Trumpeter swans winter at Lowry Lake (46 ha). The sloping shoreline, unlike the rocky, muddy bottoms of other area lakes, is good for wading and swimming. From Lowry

Lake the backroad runs south for just under 1.5 km to intersect Branch 83. Straight ahead (on 83D) goes to Great Central Lake and the BCFS Scout Beach Recreation Site; a left onto Branch 83 will bring you back to the 6.5-km mark on Ash River Road.

Option Two: Turn left at the km-15 junction and proceed along Ash River Road to pass Turnbull Lake (23 ha), a long, slender and relatively shallow fly-casting destination. There are steep, washboard grades beyond Turnbull Lake. At the crest of one hill, a spectacular viewpoint looks out over McLaughlin Lake, Lois Lake, Lowry Lake and a distant sliver of Great Central Lake. What looks like a giant snake or worm is actually the penstock that carries water from Elsie Lake over hilly terrain to the BC Hydro generating station on Great Central Lake. About 10.5 km from the km-15 junction the mainline again crosses the boisterous Ash River, near Elsie Lake. Elsie Lake (1,107 ha) is 320 m above sea level and has natural boat launches on its north and south shores. To reach them, you first negotiate old spur roads down to lakeside. You can venture along the lake's north side on Branch 114 to the Long Lake Road and loop back to the km-15 junction along the east side of the Ash River Valley.

Option Three: If you really want an isolated fishing and backroad destination, stay on the Ash River Road beyond Elsie Lake and continue for approximately 11 km along the upper Ash River to Oshinow (Deep) Lake in the southeast corner of Strathcona Provincial Park. The road is best suited for trucks or 4 x 4s. Oshinow Lake (264 ha) contains rainbow and cutthroat trout. Perched at an elevation of 426 m, the lake is bordered by steep mountains. Its chilling waters originate from the headwaters of the Ash River, southwest of the Cliffe Glacier. The mountain vistas at the wilderness campsite at Oshinow Lake's east end are superb. From a rough boat ramp you can launch a small cartopper.

Beyond Oshinow Lake, the road deteriorates as it heads northeast to Toy (10 ha) and Junior (4.2 ha) lakes. (Toy Lake is limited to artificial flies.) Hauling has been sporadic in this region so there is little road maintenance. The condition of some bridges becomes more tenuous each year. Expect rough sections, potholes, puddles, washouts and fallen trees. First-time visitors may find area logging roads a little confusing. Make sure you consult MacBlo's *Recreation and Logging Road Guide to TFL 44* and regional topographical maps. Many backroads are closed during the fire season. Higher-elevation roads may be blocked by snow over the winter.

Let's return now to the km-15 junction on Ash River Road, and continue on the backroads to Courtenay. Keep straight ahead on Long Lake Road. At km 17.5 turn left at a triangle junction; a right follows the signs back to Port Alberni. At the next intersection (km 18) Long Lake Road veers off to the left and climbs up to Elsie Lake. Keep right and then make an immediate left onto Toad Lake Road, the section of the proposed Valley Link Highway that goes to Comox Lake. This turn is indicated by a white Comox marker.

The route leaves MacBlo territory and descends into TimberWest's Oyster River Operations, where the road becomes Toma Main Line. There are plenty of potholes to dodge and a couple of older bridges to cross, so take it slow. Near the south end of Comox Lake (km 34.5) swing west and cross the Toma Creek and Puntledge River bridges to a T-junction (km 36). Culvert and bridge replacements were made near these streams in 1997. This area can be very muddy. At the T-junction cut left for about 3 km to Willemar Lake. (See Section Three: Trip: 7.)

Turn right at the T-junction for Courtenay. This is TimberWest's CoLake Road (short for Comox Lake Road), the mainline that follows a serpentine course along the rugged west and north shores of Comox Lake. Like many of the arteries back in MacBlo's forest lands, this route is not recommended for trailered boats. Sharp rocks are prevalent on the washboards hills. Many visitors prefer to drive a high-slung vehicle or 4 x 4 rather than the family car.

At km 41 you'll reach a high bridge over the Cruickshank River. The spur road on the left, just before the bridge, drops down to the river. Bear right at the bottom of the hill for Old Camp Point and access to Comox Lake (1,620 ha). In the 1930s, Old Camp Point was the site of a logging camp with an extensive lake booming ground. Logs were once driven down the Cruickshank River. In its operating days the camp had a schoolhouse and housing for the loggers, their wives and children. The Cruickshank rivermouth is popular with anglers trying for Dolly Varden (char), rainbow and cutthroat trout. Locals consistently bring in large fish. Their secret? Home-carved plugs.

Go left at the base of the hill near the Cruickshank River bridge and head west along the river to South Main, an inactive logging road that climbs the Comox Creek Valley. Via this artery, hikers and climbers can access a number of trails, including one to the Comox Glacier. *Hiking Trails III* (VITIS), gives a comprehensive description of these backpacking destinations. Road conditions are rough and in many spots passable only in a 4 x 4. Deteriorating bridges, road deactivation, seasonal washouts and slides can preclude vehicular access.

Comox Lake Road cuts inland through hilly terrain. Look for lake access at km 47.5, a picnic site near Pierce Creek. At Boston Bay the route again goes inland to negotiate a series of hills. At km 55 the road passes the BC Hydro dam that regulates water flow from Comox Lake into the

Puntledge River. The DFO maintains two hatcheries on the Puntledge River, above and below the confluence with Browns River. Visitors are welcome at either location to learn more about the efforts to increase area salmon and winter steelhead runs.

Cross the causeway (near the lake outlet) to where the pavement begins, just under the 56-km mark. At km 58 you'll reach an intersection. Turn right and follow the signs for Cumberland and a boat launch, on Comox Lake's east side, and a seasonally open private campground. For Courtenay keep straight ahead at the km-58 junction to a second crossroads (just over the 59-km mark). Turn right and stay on Lake Trail Road into Courtenay.

CONTACTS

- Alberni Forest Information Centre (Port Alberni): 250-724-7890
- Ark Resort: 250-723-2657
- BC Forest Service (South Island Forest District): 250-724-9205
- MacMillan Bloedel (Sproat Operations): 250-720-4100
- TimberWest (Oyster River Operations): 250-287-7979

MAPS/GUIDES

- BC Forest Service Port Alberni Forest District Recreation Map
- Comox Valley Map (Comox Valley Chamber of Commerce/Comox Valley Ground Search and Rescue Association)
- MacMillan Bloedel Recreation and Logging Road Guide to TFL 44
- TimberWest Oyster River Operations Courtenay Logging Road Guide
- National Topographical Series: 92F/ll Forbidden Plateau (1:50,000); 92F/6 Great Central Lake (1:50,000); 92F/7 Horne Lake (1:50,000)
- Provincial Maps: 92F/SE Port Alberni (1:125,000); 92F/SW Kennedy Lake; 92F/NW Buttle Lake (1:125,000)
- *Hiking Trails III* (VITIS)

NEAREST SERVICES

Port Alberni; Courtenay.

Trip 11:
Courtenay to Campbell River

IN BRIEF

A backroads run on the logging roads east of Highway 19 from Courtenay to Campbell River is a popular choice for backroad adventurers. The first part of the route is travelled by skiers over the winter and hikers in the summer, on their way to the alpine meadows and trails on Mount Washington. Local anglers haunt area mainlines almost year round, on trips to numerous lakes. Some fishing spots are close to the main roads; others are accessed via secondary roads.

ACCESS

In Courtenay, where Highway 19 turns right at 17th Street to cross the Puntledge River, stay on Cliffe Avenue to First Street and turn right. At the bottom of the hill, make a left onto Condensory Road. Continue to Piercy Road, turn left and follow the Mount Washington signposts about 4.5 km to where Duncan Bay Main meets the paved road. Straight ahead (Forbidden Plateau Road) goes to the Forbidden Plateau Ski Area. Cut right onto Duncan Bay Main. Mainlines are in good shape. Secondary roads may be rough and could require a 4 x 4. Most area backroads are restricted-access routes and are closed to public travel on weekdays due to heavy industrial traffic. Snow may block higher-elevation routes over the winter.

DESCRIPTION

The backroads from Courtenay to Campbell River start at the intersection of Piercy Road and TimberWest's Duncan Bay Main. Straight ahead, Forbidden Plateau Road climbs up to the Forbidden Plateau ski lodge and area trailheads. Turn right (north) onto Duncan Bay Main, reset your vehicle's trip meter to zero and cross the bridge over Browns River, a major tributary of the Puntledge River. This steelhead stream is also known for its beautiful Browns River Falls. It's a little over 5 km to the intersection with the Mount Washington Road. (You can reach this intersection via Headquarters Road.) A left onto Mount Washington Road leads up the mountain to the Forbidden Plateau trailheads, which begin at the nordic ski hut. (See Section Three: Trip 8.)

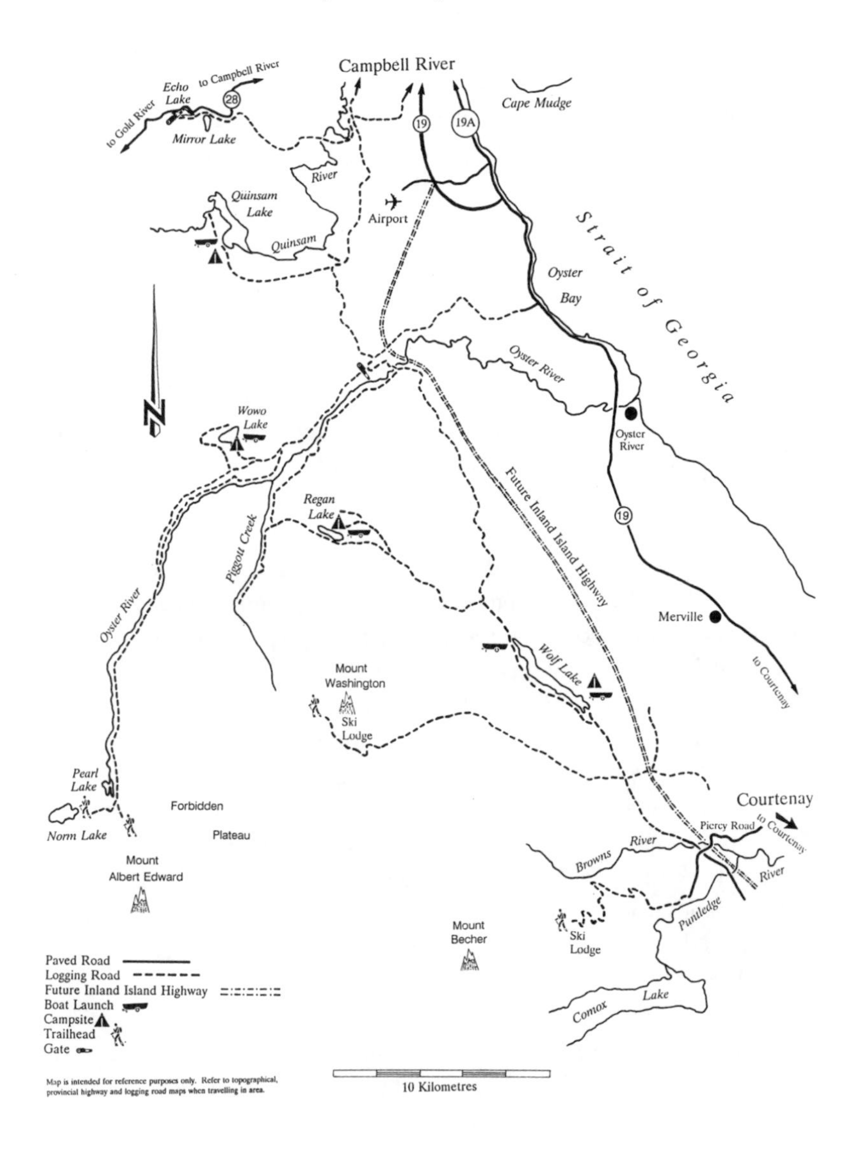
Courtenay to Campbell River
Campbell River
Echo Lake
to Campbell River
to Gold River
28
Mirror Lake
19
19A
Cape Mudge
River
Quinsam Lake
Quinsam
Airport
Strait of Georgia
Oyster Bay
Oyster River
Wowo Lake
Oyster River
Regan Lake
Piggott Creek
Future Inland Island Highway
19
Merville
to Courtenay
Oyster River
Wolf Lake
Mount Washington
Ski Lodge
Pearl Lake
Forbidden
Plateau
Norm Lake
Mount Albert Edward
Courtenay
Piercy Road
to Courtenay
Browns
River
Punteledge
River
Ski Lodge
Mount Becher
Comox
Lake
Paved Road
Logging Road
Future Inland Island Highway
Boat Launch
Campsite
Trailhead
Gate
Map is intended for reference purposes only. Refer to topographical, provincial highway and logging road maps when travelling in area.
10 Kilometres

From the Mount Washington Road junction north to the Campbell River area, Duncan Bay Main is a restricted-access artery. Public entry is not allowed between 6 a.m. and 6 p.m. on weekdays due to active hauling. These hours may vary. Prior to your trip, call TimberWest for updates.

Just over the 8-km mark, watch for a narrow side road, on the right, that goes to Wolf Lake (156 ha). Even in drier weather, the road can be challenging for those with regular passenger vehicles. There are dips and dives, potholes and branches to avoid. Turning around at the cartop boat launch can be a problem as well. A few years ago, after several days of heavy rains, a friend and I went on a day trip to Wolf Lake. We encountered a high lake level that inundated the road. We didn't have pontoons with us, so we left our vehicle on higher ground and gingerly hiked around the impeding waterholes with the help of gumboots.

The road ends at a tiny dam on Wolf Lake's southeast shoreline, near the outlet of Headquarters Creek. The shorecasting in this vicinity can be good – so good at times that anglers often line the lakeside, throwing out everything from bait and bobber to spinning lures in eager attempts to entice the resident cutthroat and rainbow trout. The lake has been regularly stocked with cutthroat trout.

The Wolf Lake access road is washed out beyond the dam, but you can proceed farther on foot. The old spur climbs the east slope of Constitution Hill. When Wolf Lake waters recede, the decaying timbers of a weathered railway trestle can be seen near the dam. Rail logging was the forerunner to today's truck logging, and many logging mainlines follow the old railbeds.

Around the 14-km mark, watch for a branch road on the right. This goes down to lakeside at Wolf Lake's top end. It's a great put-in spot for canoes and cartop boats. Some travellers camp overnight here. If you do so, keep in mind that fire-season regulations do not permit open fires between April 15th and October 15th. Such closures should be observed wherever you travel on Island backroads. The northwest corner of Wolf Lake can become choked with deadheads when a southeast wind is steady. While on the water, paddlers and boaters should watch the weather carefully. Even a relatively small lake like Wolf can turn ugly in blustery conditions.

At km 16, Rossiter Main cuts off to the left. You can follow this TimberWest logging road to the Regan Lake (22 ha) access or continue on up the rugged Piggott Creek Valley. The overgrown spur to Regan Lake is similar to the Wolf Lake road – bumpy and with tricky mudholes in rainy weather. It traverses somewhat swampy terrain to a primitive lakeside campsite. Farther down Rossiter Main you'll reach a four-way junction. Here you can turn right onto the logging road that parallels the Oyster River's south side to the bridge along Duncan Bay Main. Straight ahead skirts the yawning chasm of the Piggott Creek Valley.

Between the Rossiter Main turn and the Oyster River bridge, Duncan Bay Main passes rough spur roads that lead to four little lakes: Helldiver, Lost, Little Lost and Blue Grouse. There is a wilderness campsite and cartop boat launch at Blue Grouse (67 ha). These lakes have been stocked with cutthroat and/or rainbow trout. A few of the smaller lakes in the forests between Courtenay and Campbell River can be difficult to reach. Many are accessed via unmaintained secondary spurs. Getting through road washouts, quagmires and water holes may require a 4 x 4 or high-slung vehicle. If in doubt about any of the larger puddles, it's always a good idea to check the depth before slogging through.

Duncan Bay Main crosses the Oyster River bridge. Be sure to park well off on the shoulder of the road should you stop to look at this picturesque stream on foot. Just before the bridge, Oyster Main South swings left to hook up with Rossiter Main at the four-way intersection near Regan Lake.

At the 31.3-km mark is a three-road junction and a MacMillan Bloedel security checkpoint on the left. Keep right for Campbell River; the two other roads at this intersection (Oyster River Main and Caribou Main) extend into part of MacBlo's Menzies Operations. Some anglers seek out Wowo Lake, which has been stocked with rainbow trout. Visitors will find a wilderness campsite and natural boat launch here. Current freshwater regulations limit the catch to two fish daily (trout or char) and anglers are limited to artificial flies; electric motors only.

You can stay on Oyster River Main (to pass an impressive Oyster River waterfall on the way) to Norm Lake. Roads in the upper valley are best suited for a high-slung vehicle or 4 x 4. Just south of Norm Lake a spur road leads to the Gem Lake trailhead. This beautiful alpine lake lies just north of Mount Albert Edward, within Strathcona Provincial Park. The trail has been marked by the Comox District Mountaineering Club. At the end of the mainline, another trail leads up to Pearl Lake. Both Pearl and Gem lakes have received rainbow trout stocking, making them ideal destinations for backpackers who carry along collapsible fly rods or spinning tackle.

Explore the Oyster Main on weekends or after normal working hours. That way you won't have to tangle with loaded logging trucks as you're climbing the sometimes steep and narrow twists of road in the upper valley. Sometimes you may be asked to follow a truck up the mainline. Active logging and seasonal fire closures may also restrict public travel. Anyone venturing into the area must first report to the security station; even the logging crews check in and out.

Keep left for Campbell River at km 31.6; the right fork is MacBlo's Iron River Main, a restricted-access hauling road going east. Duncan Bay

Main winds north for about 5 km to the junction with Gilson Main (Lower Quinsam Road). Turn left onto this secondary backroad for the primitive campsite on the shoreline of (Lower) Quinsam Lake (105 ha), known for good rainbow and cutthroat trout fishing right through the summer. Dolly Varden (char) also inhabit the lake. It's not uncommon to see anglers with float tubes working potential Quinsam Lake hotspots.

Duncan Bay Main skirts the Campbell River airport to the intersection (km 44.8) with TimberWest's Elk River Main, a restricted-access, active hauling road. Continue straight ahead on Duncan Bay Main for the outskirts of Campbell River.

CONTACTS

- BC Forest Service (Campbell River): 250-286-9300
- MacMillan Bloedel (Menzies Operations): 250-287-5000
- TimberWest (Oyster River Operations): 250-287-7979

MAPS/GUIDES

- BC Forest Service Campbell River District Recreation Map
- Comox Valley Map (Comox Valley Chamber of Commerce/Comox Valley Ground Search and Rescue Association)
- Logging and Highway Road Map (Campbell River Search and Rescue Society)
- MacMillan Bloedel Campbell River/Sayward Recreation and Logging Road Guide
- TimberWest Courtenay and Campbell River Logging Road Guides
- National Topographical Series: 92F/11 Forbidden Plateau (1:50,000); 92F/14 Oyster River (1:50,000); 92K/3 Quadra Island (1:50,000)
- Provincial Map: 92F/NW Buttle Lake (1:125,000)
- *Hiking Trails III* (VITIS)

NEAREST SERVICES

Campbell River; Courtenay.

Trip 12:
The Sayward Forest Loop

IN BRIEF

The Sayward Forest northwest of Campbell River is intersected by logging roads and filled with fishable lakes. Campsites (including provincial parks, BC Forest Service and logging company recreation sites) almost outnumber the lakes. You can visit a new lake every night. Scattered throughout the area are remnants from the days of rail logging. Watch for pilings from logging rail lines and overgrown trestles that span shadowy ravines. More recent are the dams, spillways, water diversions and flumes, part of the BC Hydro Campbell River Development.

ACCESS

Drive through Campbell River to the junction of Highway 19, Highway 19A and Highway 28 (near the Campbell River bridge). (See Section One: Trip 6.) Mainlines accessed along Highway 19 and Highway 28 are in good to fair shape. Expect frequent industrial traffic on some routes. Secondary spurs are rougher and not suitable for large trailered boats or RVs. Older roads may require a 4 x 4. Active logging and fire closures could restrict access.

DESCRIPTION

There are several ways to get to the Sayward Forest, and travellers will find countless lakes, many with wilderness campsites. Area backroads snake through second-growth forests. Extensive rail logging decades ago extracted a great deal of the old trees. The disastrous Campbell River fire of 1938 razed 30,375 ha of prime timber. The following year BC's first reforestation program was launched.

Drive through Campbell River to the junction of highways 19, 19A and 28. To reach one gateway to the Sayward Forest, bear north on Highway 19 and cross the Campbell River bridge. Continue 14.5 km to MacMillan Bloedel's Menzies (Salmon River) Main, near Menzies Bay. (See Section One: Trip 8.) Turn left onto the mainline, reset your vehicle's trip meter to zero and head west.

The Morton Lake Provincial Park access road is just over the km-9.5

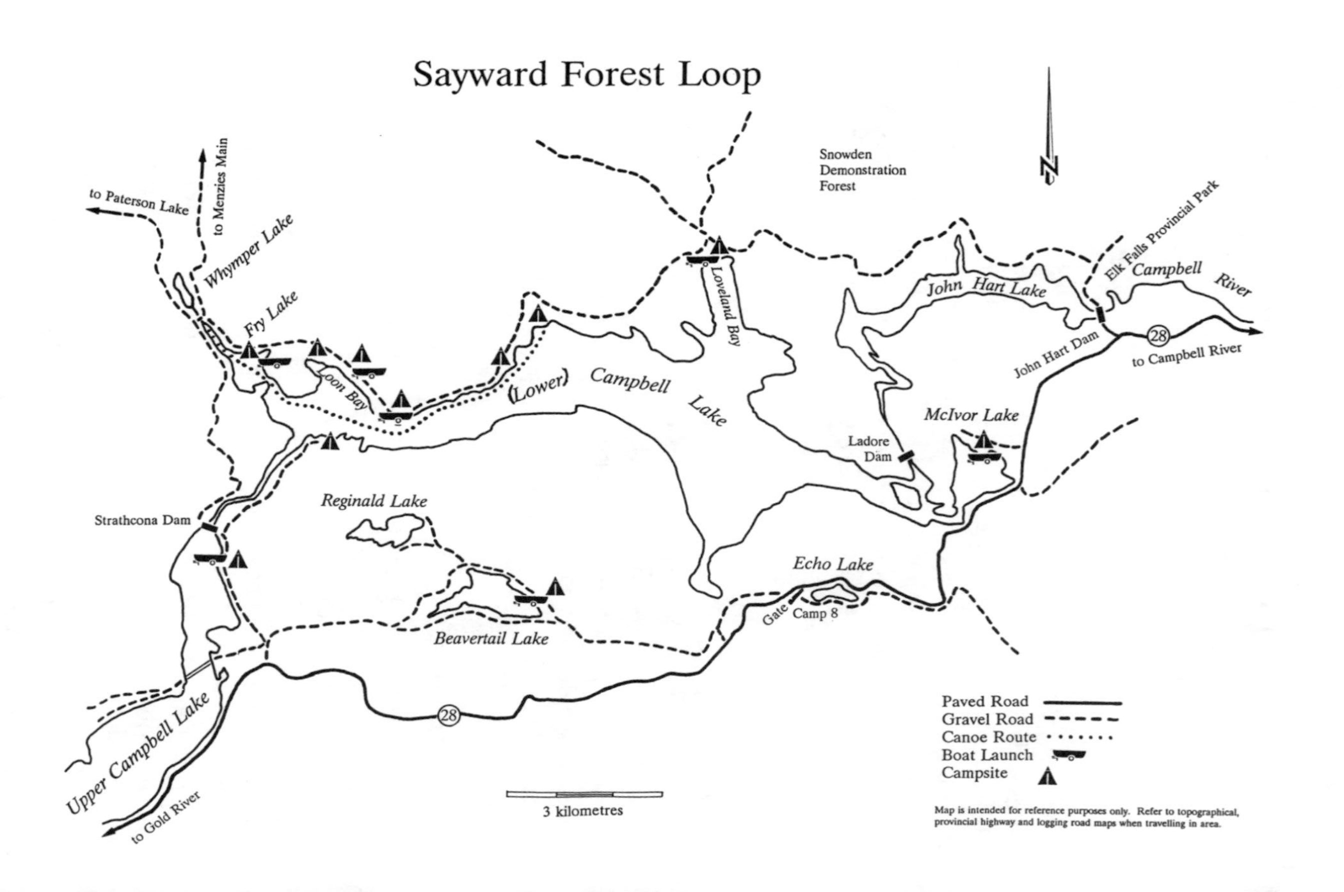
Sayward Forest Loop
Snowden Demonstration Forest
to Paterson Lake
to Menzies Main
Whymper Lake
Fry Lake
Loon Bay
(Lower) Campbell Lake
Loveland Bay
John Hart Lake
Elk Falls Provincial Park
Campbell River
28
to Campbell River
John Hart Dam
McIvor Lake
Ladore Dam
Strathcona Dam
Reginald Lake
Echo Lake
Gate
Camp 8
Beavertail Lake
Upper Campbell Lake
to Gold River
3 kilometres
Paved Road
Gravel Road
Canoe Route
Boat Launch
Campsite
Map is intended for reference purposes only. Refer to topographical, provincial highway and logging road maps when travelling in area.

mark. Cut right onto the sometimes bumpy Morton Lake Road for another 6.5 km to the park. There are twenty-four vehicle/tent camping spots, a boat launch, large picnic area and provided firewood. Best of all is the inviting sandy beach on 10-ha Morton Lake. In the spring and fall the lake is a popular destination for cutthroat trout anglers. A forested trail (great for day hikes with the kids) extends from the campground to Andrew Lake. Mohun Lake (part of the Sayward Forest Canoe Route) is close to the Morton Lake campsite. Mohun Lake (621 ha) holds rainbow and cutthroat trout and Dolly Varden (char). The Mohun Lake boat launch at adjacent Morton Lake is the BCFS-recommended water access point for canoe route paddlers. (See Section Three: Trip 9.)

Menzies Main passes the two-site BCFS Mohun Lake Recreation Site, near the Sayward Forest Canoe Route portage trail to Lawier Lake. This small user-maintained campsite has a concrete boat ramp. Mohun West Road meets Menzies Main at km 13.3. Swing right for a boat launch and wilderness campsite on Mohun Lake's southwest tip. Just over the 15-km mark, Long Lake Main (a link to Highway 19) hooks into the mainline. Cut right and travel north to parallel Brewster Lake's east shore. About 6 km from the mainline, a secondary spur runs 2.5 km to the BCFS Amor Lake Recreation Site. These backroads are not suitable for trailered boats or RVs and may be seasonally impassable. Continue north to skirt Blackwater Lake and then swing east to the Cedar Lake BCFS campsite. This somewhat bumpy route emerges on Highway 19, just south of Roberts Lake. (See Section One: Trip 8 for further details.)

There are two BCFS recreation sites (just off Menzies Main) close to Brewster Lake's southern fringe. A narrow access spur leads to the Brewster Lake campsite with nine primitive sites and a sandy beach. No vehicles are allowed on the beach. The Apple Point location has six campsites and a gravel boat launch. The open camping spots here can be breezy. Brewster Lake (413 ha), one of the larger Sayward Forest lakes, contains rainbow and cutthroat trout and Dolly Varden (char). You can fish through the summer, but the prime seasons are the spring and fall. Like many area angling destinations, Brewster Lake is stocked. Beware of sudden winds when out on the water.

At km 17 Menzies Main meets Gray Lake Road, near the bridge at Brewster Lake's south end. In the 1940s, a logging camp with bunkhouses and a large cookhouse was located nearby. It was inhabited by Chinese railroad maintenance men who worked on area logging rail lines and spent most of their off-hours in the camp. Straight ahead, over the bridge, leads to logging roads in the Salmon River Valley.

Stay on Salmon River Main to access the Gold Lake trailhead, situated

River diversions are found throughout the Sayward Forest.

along a rough spur road, about 13 km from Brewster Lake. Sections of the 5-km trail are prone to flooding. Beware of the quick-rising river waters. Snows may block the route as late as June. Gold Lake (within Strathcona Provincial Park) lies northwest of Horseshoe Mountain. If you carry in a collapsible fishing rod, be sure to use only single, barbless hooks. A bait ban applies and you can't keep any wild rainbow trout over 50 cm.

At km 17 turn south on Gray Lake Road for 3 km to the Gray Lake BCFS Recreation Site, with five camping spots, a natural boat launch and a small dock. Gray Lake, known for its cutthroat trout, is a treat for canoeists. You can paddle down to the old logging trestle or explore the lake's slender top end. Gray Lake (like Brewster Lake) is part of the Sayward Forest Canoe Route. About 2 km south of Gray Lake, Gray Lake Road joins (Lower) Campbell Lake Road, close to Fry Lake's northern end. We'll return to this intersection later and proceed east along Campbell Lake's north shore to Highway 28; first let's return to the junction of highways 19, 19A and 28 and take a look at a second way in to the Gray Lake Road/Campbell Lake Road junction.

Take Highway 28 (Gold River Highway) and reset your vehicle's trip meter to zero. (See Section One: Trip 7.) At the top of the steep hill (km 4.5) cut right for the day-use section of Elk Falls Provincial Park, close to the John Hart Dam. You can cross the dam and hook into Camp 5 (Brewster Lake) Road, then (Lower) Campbell Lake Road, to access a string of BCFS wilderness campsites along Campbell Lake's north side. This is the quickest route to Loveland Bay Provincial Park (around 12.5 km from Highway 28) and the best road to take with RVs or trailered boats.

Near the TimberWest Oyster River Operations logging yard (Camp 8) at Echo Lake's west end, Elk River Main crosses the highway, a little under 16 km from the start of Highway 28. Turn right onto the mainline and reset your vehicle's trip meter to zero. The side road (on the right at km 5.4) leads along the north shore of Beavertail Lake (103 ha) to a couple of TimberWest user-maintained wilderness campsites and a cartop boat launch. The lake contains rainbow and cutthroat trout, Dolly Varden (char) and kokanee salmon.

Elk River Main skirts Beavertail Lake's south side to a major intersection at km 11.6. A left goes back to Highway 28. Elk River Main continues west to cross an Upper Campbell Lake narrows over to the lake's west shore. Anyone thinking of exploring the backroads on Upper Campbell Lake's west side should first contact TimberWest's Oyster River Operations office for updates on hauling and safest travel times; it's prudent to wait until logging truck traffic has slowed a little before tackling these often-busy mainlines.

Turn right at the 11.6-km junction for Strathcona Dam. The road follows Upper Campbell Lake's east side to some TimberWest recreation sites and cartop boat water accesses. Upper Campbell Lake (2,400 ha) holds rainbow and cutthroat trout and Dolly Varden (char). Watch out for strong winds and resultant rough water. A little over the 14-km mark, you'll reach the sluiceway and dam. Only during periods of heavy rains does the lake overflow the spillway. As you cross Strathcona Dam the view south takes in Upper Campbell Lake's top end and the TimberWest logging road bridge that spans the lake narrows. The tiny island nearby is really a high point of land that escaped the flooding following the dam's completion in the late 1950s.

The BC Hydro generating station, easily identified by the hum of its generators, lies beneath the dam's north side. From here the Campbell River flows into Lower Campbell Lake. Cross the dam and drop down a hill. At km 15.3, keep left onto the Greenstone Forestry Road, a bumpy, narrow, winding route that precludes trailered boats; a right goes to the hydro facility. The road crosses the Greenstone Creek bridge and (by km 20) runs by Fry Lake (with stands of dead trees out in the water). A narrow channel links Fry Lake with Campbell Lake. Fry Lake (and Campbell Lake) are part of the Sayward Forest Canoe Route.

At km 20.5, be sure to cut right onto Campbell Lake Road and cross the bridge near Fry Lake's northwest tip. This will bring you to the T-junction (km 20.7) where Gray Lake Road meets Campbell Lake Road. (Straight ahead at km 20.5 follows a sometimes rough road to Paterson Lake.) Reset your vehicle's trip meter to zero at the Gray Lake Road/ Campbell Lake Road T-junction and head east along Campbell Lake's north shore to various BCFS recreation sites and Loveland Bay Provincial Park, about 14 km away. Not all the BCFS campsites are suitable for large RVs and some of the access roads are rough and narrow. If you own a larger boat or trailer, contact the BCFS Campbell River office for information on suitable boat launching and camping facilities or consult its recreation map.

Area Hydro developments divert the waters of the Salmon and Quinsam rivers into Campbell Lake (2,250 ha). The Ladore Dam at the lake's east end, completed in 1949, raised the water level substantially. Periodic hydro surges from Strathcona Dam result in fluctuations to Campbell Lake water levels. This can make the bite somewhat tentative, but the lake is still a popular rainbow and cutthroat trout destination. Dolly Varden (char) are also present. Boaters and paddlers should watch out for submerged stumps and roots in lake shallows. The water approaches to the many BCFS campsites pose no real problems: they were "grubbed" (underwater trunks and stumps were cut short or removed entirely) by BC Hydro years ago.

Off-season visitors may find area campsites vacant. Over the summer many locations fill up, especially if word has spread that the fishing action has warmed up in neighbouring lakes. Arrive early in the day to secure a spot. Firewood is scarce near campsite areas. Often a short walk on the overgrown railbeds yields fallen branches for campfires. Obey seasonal fire restrictions and don't cut any trees.

Loveland Bay Provincial Park is open all year, with a fee charged over the summer. There are twenty-two campsites, comfort stations and a picnic area. Swimming, water skiing, boating and picnicking are popular pastimes. The Snowden Demonstration Forest is close by. Two self-guided forestry tours through this forest are described in the *Trees and Trestles* and *Elk Habitat Management* pamphlets, available at the BCFS Campbell River office. Its latest brochure, *Snowden Demonstration Forest*, highlights a number of interpretative trails ideal for hiking and mountain biking. From Loveland Bay take Camp 5 (Brewster Lake) Road and head east to Elk Falls Provincial Park. The backroad runs through second-growth forest north of John Hart Lake (the restricted-access domestic water supply reservoir for Campbell River) and crosses John Hart Dam, at the lake's east end, to reach Highway 28, about 12.5 km from Loveland Bay.

The BCFS in Campbell River reports a twenty-five percent increase in visitors to the Sayward Forest in recent years. When current campsites are enlarged or newer sites developed, the Forest Service works closely with the Ministry of Environment and area logging companies to ensure that any improvements will not affect area fishing or contribute to overcrowding. The wilderness campsites are well maintained by their users. The only problem is that the recreation sites are *too* nice, leading some people to overextend their visits. Current regulations allow a maximum two-week stay.

CONTACTS

- BC Forest Service (Campbell River): 250-286-9300
- TimberWest (Oyster River Operations): 250-287-7979
- MacMillan Bloedel (Menzies Operations): 250-287-5000

MAPS/GUIDES

- BC Forest Service Campbell River Forest District Recreation Map
- BC Forest Service Sayward Forest Canoe Route Recreation Map
- Campbell River Search and Rescue Society Logging and Highway Road Map
- MacMillan Bloedel Campbell River/Sayward Recreation and Logging Road Guide
- TimberWest Campbell River Logging Road Guide
- National Topographical Series: 92K/4 Brewster Lake (1:50,000); 92F/14 Oyster River (1:50,000); 92K/3 Quadra Island (1:50,000); 92F/13 Upper Campbell Lake (1:50,000)
- Provincial Map: 92F/NW Buttle Lake (1:125,000)
- *Backroading Vancouver Island* (Neering/Whitecap)
- *Hiking Trails III* (VITIS)

NEAREST SERVICES

Campbell River.

Trip 13:
Gold River to Woss

IN BRIEF

Until Highway 19 was completed in the late 1970s, the only way to drive all the way to northern Vancouver Island was on logging roads from Gold River to Woss Camp. Today, the rugged 82-km gravel route is used by industrial traffic and backroad adventurers. Several lakes have wilderness campsites along their shores (Muchalat, Vernon, Klaklakama, Little Klaklakama and Woss) and there are plenty of backroads to explore.

ACCESS

Starting in Campbell River, follow Highway 28 for 87 km to Gold River. (See Section One: Trip 7.) Expect industrial traffic along the logging roads from Gold River to Woss. Mainlines are in good to fair shape with rough sections. Secondary roads may require a high-slung vehicle or 4 x 4. Deactivated roads may be impassable.

DESCRIPTION

The gravel backroads between Gold River and Woss once provided the only road link with northern Vancouver Island. Though the majority of travellers now take Highway 19, some backroad adventurers can't get enough of the logging roads. To reach their starting point, take Highway 28 from Campbell River to Gold River. (See Section One: Trip 7.) Reset your vehicle's trip meter to zero when you reach the gravel, just outside Gold River. On weekdays, travellers must stay alert for any industrial traffic on the mainlines. Don't forget to use your headlights, particularly when the roads are dry and dusty.

At km 3 you'll reach the Gold River bridge. Keep right just before the bridge, onto the branch road to Antler Lake (20 ha), a local picnic site and cutthroat trout fishing destination. The lake has a boat launch. No power boats are permitted. A nature trail connects Antler Lake with nearby Scout Lake. Cross the Gold River bridge to the west side and a signposted T-junction.

If you're heading for Tahsis, keep left at the T-junction. Remember to watch out for industrial traffic and be cautious on the steep, washboard hills. The road passes several lakes: Upana (45 ha), Malaspina (13 ha) and Perry. Upana Lake is known for its rainbow trout fishing. A short trail leads to the Upana Caves. Perry Lake angling is limited to artificial flies with a one-fish/char daily quota. There is a wilderness campsite along the Conuma River, at the confluence with Leagh Creek. A DFO fish hatchery is situated nearby. The road skirts Moutcha and Head bays at the top of Tlupana Inlet and swings northwest up the Sucwoa River Valley. Some travellers set up at the BC Forest Service Leiner River wilderness campsite, close to the Tahsis townsite. There are eight campsites at this riverside location.

Tahsis is a mill town, a deep-sea port and jumping-off point for Nootka Island boaters and paddlers. The M.V. *Uchuck III* stops here and area waters offer good salmon fishing. The Great Walk, an annual walkathon, follows the 62-km logging-road route from Gold River to Tahsis to raise money for various charities.

Back now to the T-junction at the Gold River bridge. Cut right on Gold River Main and head north for Woss. Watch for the entrance to the BCFS Muchalat Lake Recreation Site, around the 14-km mark. It's on the left and easy to miss. A second, steeper spur angles down to the boat launch a little farther along. The thirty campsites here can be full on summer weekends and holidays. There are picnic tables, fire rings and a large dock, used for boat mooring and as a float-plane terminus. Many sites are suitable for large trailers.

Muchalat Lake (642 ha) is an excellent paddling lake, but be wary of afternoon winds. A mirror-smooth lake can turn lumpy in minutes. The lake contains both rainbow and cutthroat trout, with the best fishing in the spring and fall. Trolling the strike zones at the mouth of the Oktwanch River, to the northwest of the campsite, can be productive.

About 42 km from Gold River is an intersection. Several spurs to the right lead to Canadian Forest Products restricted-access Vernon industrial reload area. The largest logging railway in North America runs north from Vernon to Woss and Beaver Cove. (See Section One: Trips 9 & 10 for additional information.) A left onto Vernon Lake Road heads to the east shore of Vernon Lake. Keep straight ahead on Nimpkish Road for Woss.

Approximately 50 km from Gold River, you'll reach the Klaklakama lakes junction. Keep right to cross the Nimpkish River bridge and the rail line for the Klaklakama lakes and Highway 19. It's 17.3 km to the highway junction, near Croman Lake. Not too far from the highway, both Klaklakama Lake (252 ha) and Little Klaklakama Lake (100 ha) have a tiny wilderness campsite and natural boat launch on their rocky shores. Most Woss-area forest campsites are co-managed by Canfor and the BCFS. The lakes contain cutthroat trout and Dolly Varden (char).

Keep left at the Klaklakama junction for Woss. Just before the Sebalhall Creek bridge watch for the signposted left turn for Canfor's Vernon Lake campsite, 2 km away. There is a boat launch, twenty-four camping spots and a sandy beach. Vernon Lake (780 ha) contains both rainbow and cutthroat trout. The mainline crosses Sebalhall Creek (which drains Vernon Lake into the Nimpkish River) and swings north to Kiyu Creek. At the confluence of Kiyu Creek and the Nimpkish River, an island of old-growth timber has been preserved as an ecological reserve. Most of the trees here (Douglas fir, western red cedar and western hemlock) are around 350 years old. The Nimpkish Island trees are a remaining remnant of the old-growth forest that once dominated the Nimpkish Valley.

The mainline (now called Rona Road) runs north to follow the Nimpkish River's west side. Near Frost Lake, 10.7 km from Kiyu Creek, Duncan Road cuts off to the right. This secondary spur follows the Davie River, east to the Klaklakama lakes road. Stay on Rona Road; then take the Rona cutoff to a major junction near the Nimpkish River bridge, just outside Woss. Turn right and cross the high Nimpkish River bridge to Woss (Canfor headquarters) and the Highway 19 junction, 1.5 km away. There is a beautiful waterfall to the right as you cross the river. Kayakers often use this stretch of the Nimpkish River when water levels are right. One of the river takeout spots is just before the falls.

Instead of crossing the Nimpkish River bridge, bear left and follow the signs about 3 km to Canfor's Woss Lake campsite. Just before the campsite entrance, an industrial road cuts off to the right to cross the Woss River bridge. When the route is passable, you can travel 24 km along the south side of Nimpkish River to Zeballos Road. (See Section One: Trip 10.) Anglers can seek out numerous river casting spots. Inquire locally before venturing on this route; some bridges may be closed.

The Woss Lake campsite, nestled in a forested grove at Woss Lake's north end, has two dozen sites, picnic tables and fire pits. Trails wind through the surrounding forest. The sandy beach is ideal for summer wading or swimming. The campsite is close to the Woss River, the outlet stream that empties Woss Lake into the Nimpkish River. (Note the rainbow trout release restriction for Woss River.) A developed launch ramp helps fishermen with trailered boats and cartoppers access the lake. There's also a seaplane dock.

Woss Lake contains cutthroat and rainbow trout as well as Dolly Varden (char). You can fish right through the summer, but the best seasons are the spring and fall. Woss Lake (1,366 ha), one of northern Vancouver Island's largest lakes, is susceptible to strong winds and changeable water conditions. Boaters and paddlers should be cautious.

Logging roads extend along both sides of Woss Lake, but only halfway down. From the Woss Lake campsite you can take logging roads another 7 km down Woss Lake's eastern shore to a couple of lake access points. Space is tight here, but you can set up a wilderness camp. Remember to carry out your trash and follow seasonal fire restrictions.

Experienced big-lake paddlers can journey to the head of the lake and Woss Lake Provincial Park. Rugged Mountain (1,875 m), part of the Haithe Range, stands guard over Woss Lake's southern end, where at least eight streams enter the lake. An old aboriginal trail followed one watershed south, up over the divide to the Tahsis River Valley. Woss Lake is long and narrow and knifes deep into the mountains. The lake's 9 km of wilderness shoreline have limited landing spots, and even fewer rough campsites. Be prepared and watch the weather. (For a more detailed account of a canoe trip down Woss Lake, see *More Island Adventures*, Trip 22.)

CONTACTS

- BC Forest Service (Campbell River): 250-286-9300
- BC Forest Service (Port McNeill): 250-956-5000
- Canadian Forest Products (Woss): 250-281-2300
- North Island Forestry Centre (Beaver Cove): 250-956-3844
- Pacific Forest Products (Gold River): 250-283-2221

MAPS/GUIDES

- BC Forest Service Campbell River Forest District Recreation Map
- BC Forest Service Port McNeill Forest District Recreation Map
- Canadian Forest Products Englewood Logging Division (TFL 37) Recreation Map
- Pacific Forest Products Recreation and Logging Road Guide to the Forest Lands of West Vancouver Island
- National Topographical Series: 92E/16 Gold River (1:50,000); 92L/1 Schoen Lake (1:50,000); 92L/2 Woss Lake (1:50,000); 92E/15 Zeballos (1:50,000)
- Provincial Maps: 92L Alert Bay (1:250,000); 92E Nootka Sound (1:250,000)
- *Hiking the Ancient Forests of British Columbia and Washington* (Stoltmann/Lone Pine)
- *Hiking Trails III* (VITIS)
- *Whitewater Trips for Kayakers, Canoeists and Rafters on Vancouver Island* (Pratt-Johnson/Soules)

NEAREST SERVICES

Gold River; Woss.

Trip 14: Port McNeill Backroads

IN BRIEF

A 65-km loop on the logging roads near Port McNeill will appeal to hikers, anglers, paddlers and backroad adventurers. There is a plethora of fishing lakes, both large and small, with boat launches, picnic sites and user-maintained wilderness campsites. Hikers can choose between the Skidder Lakes Trail, the Trout Lake (Lac Truite) Trail or the more strenuous climb up the Merry Widow Mountain Trail. Geological features known as karst formations are common in this region. Water action on limestone bedrock has resulted in many unusual points of interest with equally unusual names. Our route passes the Devil's Bath and the Eternal Fountain. Similar stops of interest are accessed along area backroads.

ACCESS

Near MacMillan Bloedel's Port McNeill headquarters on Highway 19, turn southwest onto West Main. (See Section One: Trip 10.) Gravel mainlines are in good to fair shape. Rougher secondary roads may require a 4 x 4. When heavy hauling occurs on area mainlines, MacBlo and Western Forest Products recommend you limit your travels to after weekday working hours or weekends and holidays.

DESCRIPTION

A jaunt along Port McNeill backroads starts on Highway 19 near MacMillan Bloedel's Port McNeill Division, 3.7 km north of the Port McNeill cut-off. (See Section One: Trip 10.) The world's largest burl, at the entrance to the logging office, was discovered in the Benson River area in 1976. The burl and its host spruce trunk were later relocated to their current location. You can pick up a copy of MacBlo's *Port McNeill/Port Hardy Recreation and Logging Road Guide* during weekday office hours. The map is also available at the North Island Forestry Information Centre on Highway 19 (at the Beaver Cove cut-off). This office is open seasonally from June through August.

To begin the Port McNeill backroads run, swing southwest from Highway 19 onto West Main and reset your vehicle's trip meter to zero. Cabin Main, on the left at km 0.5, heads east to become Kilpala Road near the

There are several user-maintained wilderness campsites in the Port McNeill area.

Nimpkish River bridge, where the river drains out of Nimpkish Lake. At km 3.4, West Main continues (naturally enough) west for 7.5 km to O'Connor Lake and a Western Forest Products day-use recreation site. This mainline eventually hooks up with Port Hardy Main, near the Port Alice Highway. (See Section One: Trip 11.) Swing left onto Benson Main at the km-3.4 junction.

At km 7.7, you'll reach C Main, the mainline to the Skidder Lakes Trail. Be forewarned. The trail is poorly marked and it's easy to wander from the rugged 3-km path that leads to three small lakes.

Keep right on Benson Main. The road skirts Keogh Lake (80 ha) to a rough boat access at km 10.6. Keogh Lake contains rainbow and cutthroat trout. Next comes a cutthroat trout lake chain that includes Angler, Three Isle (22 ha) and Maynard (84 ha) lakes, linked by Three Lakes Creek. There are small boat launches and picnic sites at Three Isle Lake (km 19.2) and Maynard Lake (km 25.3). These sites and others in the area are co-managed by MacBlo and the BC Forest Service. Maynard Lake is dammed at its south end. Watch out for drifting deadheads. The mainline passes Iron Lake to a fork at km 29, where R Main cuts off to the left. Keep right and cross the Raging River bridge. A spur road (on the right, near Lac Truite's northern tip) accesses the Iron Lake boat launch. At km 31.2 watch for the trailhead to Lac Truite.

The road crosses the Benson River bridge to a T-junction at km 31.5. B Main, to the left, branches into J Main. The latter is the backroad to the Vanishing River. Keep right at the T-junction for the Devil's Bath and Benson Lake. Branch M 1080, the rough spur at km 32.7, snakes up to the Merry Widow Mountain trailhead. A steep climb rewards hikers with a panoramic view of the region.

Many Benson Lake (77 ha) anglers launch at the private boat launch (km 37) for good spring and fall fishing. The lake holds cutthroat and rainbow trout and Dolly Varden (char). On my last visit to Benson Lake, the first test for my newly acquired breathable raingear turned out to be a deluge that pelted the area. A friend and I were across the lake from the camper when the skies opened. The raingear passed the audition.

At km 38, Wady Main cuts off to the right. Take this turn for Kathleen Lake's east end and a wilderness campsite and cartop boat launch. Kathleen Lake (127 ha) has good cutthroat and rainbow trout fishing. Dolly Varden (char) are also present. Canoeists can paddle down to the Benson River lake outlet. My brother and I once saw two black bears romping in the logging slash in this vicinity. The north-shore cliffs at Kathleen Lake display the remains of a narrow-gauge rail line that ran to the long-defunct Old Sport Mine.

Keep left at km 38 for the Devil's Bath. The road climbs a series of switchbacks and at km 43 you'll find the roadside pull-off for the Devil's Bath. A short walk from the mainline leads visitors to a high bank overlooking a small pond, choked with fallen trees and surrounded on all sides by sheer rock walls.

At km 48 you'll reach an important junction. WFP's Southeast Main is to the left. Keep right on Alice Lake Main and cross the Benson River bridge. Several wilderness campsites on Alice Lake can be accessed along Alice Lake Main. (See Section One: Trip 11 for more details.) On the Benson River's north side, watch for Branch 41 (km 48.4), an overgrown spur that winds in to the Eternal Fountain, a boisterous creek that pours over a limestone ledge and reverses direction to disappear back into the ground. It's easy to get lost in this area, as the older roads are not well marked. Branch 41 meets Port Hardy Main at km 50.2. Turn left and follow Port Hardy Main about 15 km out to the Port Alice Highway.

CONTACTS

- BC Forest Service (Port McNeill): 250-956-5000
- MacMillan Bloedel (Port McNeill Division): 250-956-5200
- North Island Forestry Centre: 250-956-3844
- Regional District of Mount Waddington (Port McNeill): 250-956-3301

MAPS/GUIDES

- BC Forest Service Port McNeill Forest District Recreation Map
- MacMillan Bloedel Port McNeill/Port Hardy Recreation and Logging Road Guide

- National Topographical Series: 92L/6 Alice Lake (1:50,000); 92L/11 Port McNeill (1:50,000)
- Provincial Map: 92L Alert Bay (1:250,000)

NEAREST SERVICES

Port Alice; Port McNeill.

Trip 15: The Mahatta River Region

IN BRIEF

Mahatta River, west of Port Alice on northern Vancouver Island, was once an isolated logging community, accessible only by boat or float plane. In 1985, Western Forest Products punched through a hauling road that connected the area with Port Alice. The 58-km run from the Port Alice mill to Mahatta River leads to saltwater and freshwater fishing destinations. Several logging roads wind over to striking west coast vistas of Brooks Bay, Quatsino Sound and the Pacific Ocean.

ACCESS

Take the Port Alice turn on Highway 19, about halfway between Port McNeill and Port Hardy. (See Section One: Trip 10.) Drive through Port Alice and head south to the mill. (See Section One: Trip 11.) Marine Drive mainline begins nearby. There are narrow sections and some long, steep switchbacks. Gravel mainlines are in seasonally good to fair shape. Secondary roads can be rough or overgrown and suitable only for 4 x 4s. Deactivated roads may be impassable. Active logging or fire closures may restrict public access on area mainlines, including Restless Main, North Main and Klaskino Main.

DESCRIPTION

Beyond Port Alice, challenging backroads extend out to the coast. Active hauling on area mainlines often involves the wide, off-road logging trucks, and although the roads are in good shape, they can be narrow with many blind corners. For safety reasons, Western Forest Products recommends public weekday travel be limited to between 6 a.m. and 6 p.m. Monday to Friday. Best travel times are on weekends and holidays. Anyone contemplating a run to the Mahatta River region should stop at WFP's Port Alice office near Jeune Landing (on Quarry Main, just north of Port Alice). Pick up an updated copy of its northern Vancouver Island logging road guide (also available from its office in Port McNeill and the seasonally open North Island Forest Centre on Highway 19 at the Beaver Cove turn). You can watch the often-bustling dryland sort operations on a tidal flat below the

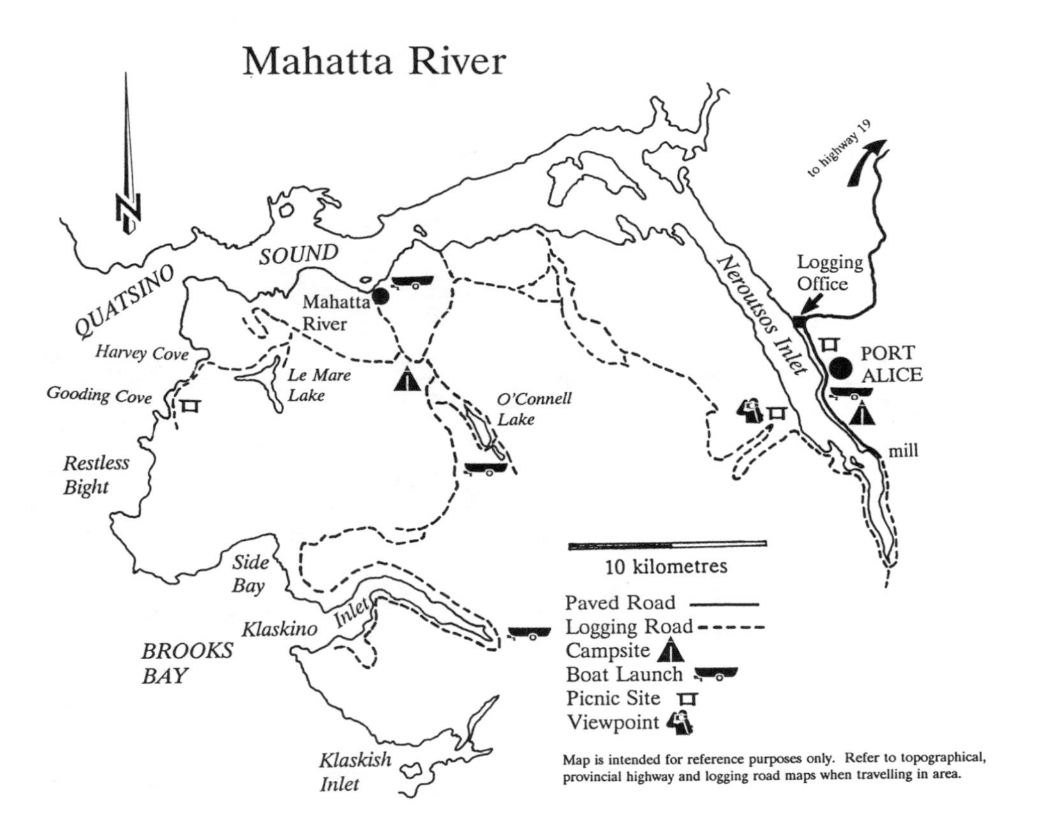
Mahatta River
to highway 19
QUATSINO
SOUND
Mahatta River
Logging Office
Neroutsos Inlet
PORT ALICE
mill
Harvey Cove
Le Mare Lake
Gooding Cove
O'Connell Lake
Restless Bight
Side Bay
Klaskino Inlet
BROOKS BAY
Klaskish Inlet
10 kilometres
Paved Road
Logging Road
Campsite
Boat Launch
Picnic Site
Viewpoint
Map is intended for reference purposes only. Refer to topographical, provincial highway and logging road maps when travelling in area.

logging office. Pick up any last-minute groceries and top up the gas tank in Port Alice; there are no services along the backroads.

We'll begin our Mahatta River run at the Port Alice mill. Reset your vehicle's trip meter to zero at the start of the gravel. The mainline, known as Marine Drive, heads southeast to the head of Neroutsos Inlet. There are several log dumps along the inlet where logs are trucked in for booming. The route swings north near the Colonial Creek salmon hatchery. In 1990, nearby Cayeghle Creek was the site of a habitat-improvement project sponsored by the DFO, WFP, the Sport Fishing Institute and other organizations. The creek's side channels were dug out and restored, creating winter habitat for coho salmon.

The mainline follows Neroutsos Inlet's west side and cuts inland on Teeta Main to a series of steep switchbacks. WFP's Neroutsos Inlet Lookout and Recreation Area (km 23.5) is a great viewpoint looking over Neroutsos Inlet, the Port Alice townsite and the mill that provides the lifeblood of the town. The road levels out in a clearcut near McKay Summit, over 720 m above sea level. This peak is part of the McKay Ridge, a high plateau on Mount Pickering. The road then dives into the Klootchlimmis River Valley.

At km 36.7, keep left on K Main; East Main, to the right, ends at a log dump on Quatsino Sound. At a junction just under the 42-km mark, K Main swings off to the right. Keep left onto I Main for Mahatta River. Watch for glimpses of Quatsino Sound. I Main hooks into J Main, near Kewquodie Creek. J Main turns south via a major haul road for area log dumps. Most junctions are clearly marked.

Around the 52.5-km mark is a major intersection called The Crossroads. Here, two mainlines merge to create a ditched, double-wide artery. To the left is B Main, the turn cutthroat-trout anglers take to reach the cut-offs for M Main and B11, the backroads that extend down both sides of O'Connell Lake. A couple of older roads merge near a weathered timber bridge spanning a narrow neck at the lake's south end. You can't drive across anymore – large rocks and a deep ditch block the route. On the west shore is a small boat launch and wooden dock near a picnic area, complete with tables and comfort stations. This site (co-managed by the BC Forest Service and WFP) is about 5.5 km from the Crossroads. With a 4 x 4 you can explore parts of the backroads south of O'Connell Lake.

B Main also leads to panoramic seascapes at Side Bay (a coastal indentation in the northern reaches of Brooks Bay) and Klaskino Inlet, to the southeast. B Main becomes North Main in the Buck Creek watershed. A little over 10 km from The Crossroads is the Klaskino Main cut-off. (Straight ahead, North Main has been deactivated.) Turn left onto Klaskino Main and drive through logged patches to Side Bay. The route bends south to the

An old bridge spans O'Connell Lake near a picnic site.

mouth of Klaskino Inlet and then parallels the fjord to a gravel boat launch tucked away at the inlet's east end, about 22 km from the Klaskino Main cut-off. Kayakers launch here for paddling adventures in Brooks Bay.

For Mahatta River, keep right at The Crossroads (km 52.5) onto Mahatta Mainline and look for the sign (km 53) marking the entrance to a small, scenic campsite on the banks of the Mahatta River. The site is co-managed by the BCFS and WFP. Of ten user-maintained sites here, several have been closed due to severe erosion from the river. At this central location, many visitors set up a base camp and day-trip to other locales.

Restless Main (km 54) snakes 16 km out to Gooding Cove. The road skirts high above Le Mare Lake and then cuts west at Culleet Creek. The breathtaking view of the open Pacific Ocean and Quatsino Sound from high along the cliffs near Harvey Cove takes in pristine pocket beaches below precipitous Mount Bury and the Gillam Islands. The road cuts inland near Gooding Cove. Some visitors hike out over the rocks to the surf-pounded sandy beach. Gooding Cove is a BCFS wilderness picnic site.

Beyond the Restless Main cut-off, Mahatta Mainline passes a clearing on the right that once served as an airstrip. Next is a logging yard, close to the old Mahatta River townsite. Some travellers pull boat trailers into Mahatta River and launch at the boat ramp for salmon fishing in Quatsino Sound. Anglers should be aware of current regulations, as some restrictions apply to the waters east of Cliffe Point. Beyond the dock, where boats and float planes once moored, the road terminates at a log dump.

The bay at the Mahatta River camp is normally protected from wind and waves, but not always. High winds once tore apart a covered dock; heavy surf flipped a float plane. The *Mahatta 4* (known as the *Silver Slug* by the loggers) was the camp's main supply vessel. It carried supplies, groceries, machinery, visitors and loggers. If the workers missed the boat, they missed their shift. One enterprising fellow kayaked from Port Alice to Mahatta River to avoid being fired. The journey took all night.

Years ago, a visiting writer from a well-known magazine went to Mahatta River to research an article on logging-camp life. The loggers' exaggerations (excellent working conditions, exorbitant salaries – even tall tales about drinking whiskey from caulked boots) all appeared in print. In the weeks that followed, the logging company was swamped with requests from job applicants in British Columbia, Alberta and the northwest United States. These people all hoped to reap the benefits of becoming a lumberjack in the BC wilderness.

The logging-camp buildings in Mahatta River were dismantled with the pullout of the WFP workforce in the late 1980s. Such was the fate of the White Bunkhouse, renowned for its rooftop barbecues. Only a clearing marks the former townsite. Some who once lived in camp talk of Mahatta River's isolation with fondness, recalling a pure sense of community spirit and togetherness. One former resident remarked, "The best time of my life was living in Mahatta River...before the roads came. Then everything changed."

CONTACTS

- BC Forest Service (Port McNeill): 250-956-5000
- North Island Forest Centre (Beaver Cove): 250-956-3844
- Western Forest Products (Port Alice): 250-284-3395
- Western Forest Products (Port McNeill): 250-956-3391

MAPS/GUIDES

- BC Forest Service Port McNeill Forest District Recreation Map
- MacMillan Bloedel Port McNeill/Port Hardy Recreation and Logging Road Guide
- Western Forest Products Visitors' Guide to Northern Vancouver Island
- National Topographical Series: 92L/6 Alice Lake (1:50,000); 92L/5 Mahatta Creek (1:50,000)
- Provincial Map: 92L Alert Bay (1:250,000)

NEAREST SERVICES

Port Alice.

Trip 16:
Port Hardy to Cape Scott

IN BRIEF

It's about 500 km from Victoria to Port Hardy via Highway 1 and Highway 19. Logging roads lead farther west to Holberg and the boundaries of Raft Cove and Cape Scott provincial parks. Visitors will discover BC Forest Service and logging company campsites, fishing lakes and notable historical points of interest. One route leads to the fishing community of Winter Harbour. There are many secondary roads to explore.

ACCESS

The Holberg Road begins 2 km south of Port Hardy. (See Section One: Trip 10.) Reset your vehicle's trip meter to zero at this turnoff along Highway 19. Gravel mainlines are usually in good to fair shape. Watch for potholes and sharp rocks. Secondary roads may require a high-slung vehicle or 4 x 4. Deactivated roads may be impassable. During weekday working hours (usually 6 a.m. to 6 p.m.) access on some routes, particularly those closer to Holberg, may be restricted due to active logging, fire closure and for public safety. Check with Western Forest Products in Holberg or Port McNeill for current hauling and area road conditions.

DESCRIPTION

To reach Cape Scott Provincial Park, drive to Port Hardy (500 km from Victoria; 390 km from Nanaimo). On the way, stop in at the North Island Forestry Centre on Highway 19, near the Beaver Cove turn, for area logging road maps and information on a variety of forest tours. This office is open from June to August. About 2 km south of Port Hardy, take the Holberg/Cape Scott/Winter Harbour cut-off on Highway 19 and reset your vehicle's trip meter to zero. (See Section One: Trip 10.) Expect industrial vehicles and logging trucks on the 64-km stretch of gravel road from Port Hardy to Cape Scott Park. Exercise caution and always drive with your headlights on.

Turn right at km 7 for the BC Forest Service Georgie Lake Recreation Site with five camping spots, a rough boat launch and a small, sandy beach. Georgie Lake (472 ha) contains cutthroat and rainbow trout. A challenging

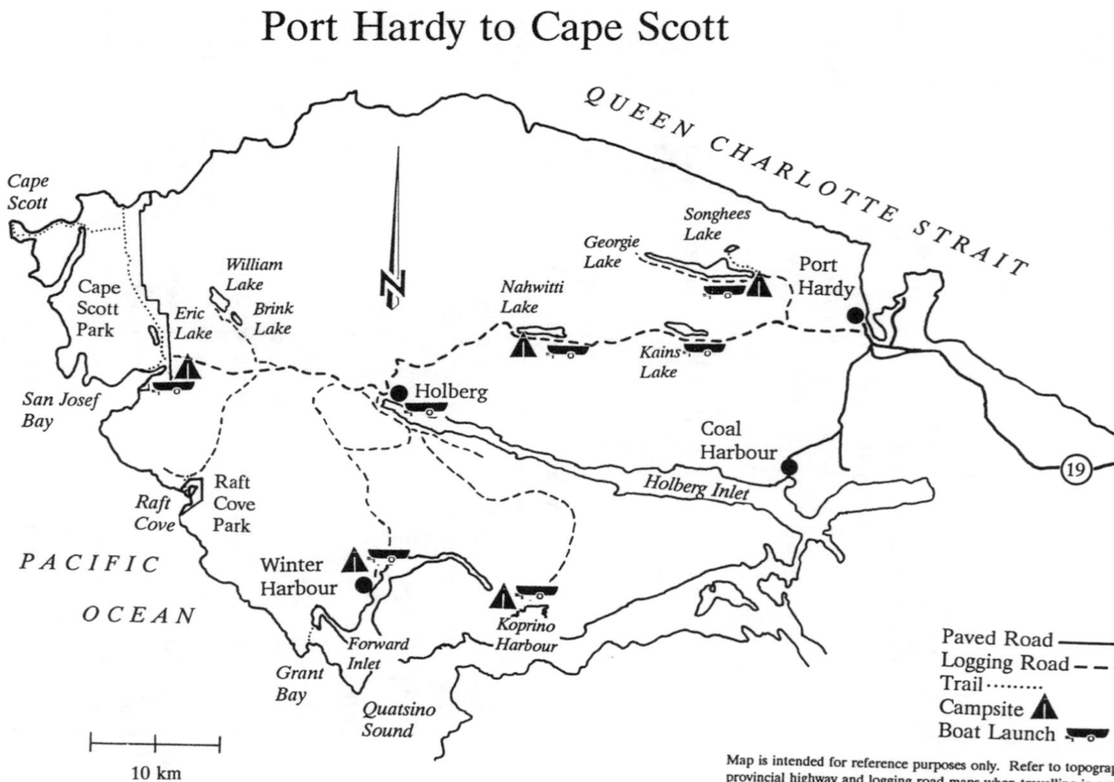

Port Hardy to Cape Scott
QUEEN CHARLOTTE STRAIT
PACIFIC OCEAN
Cape Scott
Cape Scott Park
Eric Lake
William Lake
Brink Lake
San Josef Bay
Nahwitti Lake
Georgie Lake
Songhees Lake
Port Hardy
Kains Lake
Holberg
Coal Harbour
Holberg Inlet
19
Raft Cove
Raft Cove Park
Winter Harbour
Koprino Harbour
Forward Inlet
Grant Bay
Quatsino Sound
10 km
Paved Road
Logging Road
Trail
Campsite
Boat Launch
Map is intended for reference purposes only. Refer to topographical, provincial highway and logging road maps when travelling in area.

trail winds 3 km from Georgie Lake to Songhees Lake. This well-marked route is seasonally maintained. Kains Lake (km 13.5) has resident cutthroat trout and a gravel boat access that accommodates cartop boats or canoes. Anglers will sometimes find good shorecasting right at the launch point or at numerous spots reached on foot via a lakeside path. Sunken deadheads and fallen trees make a practised cast invaluable when working parts of the shoreline.

Nahwitti Lake, known for its cutthroat-trout fishing, also holds kokanee and rainbow. There is a boat launch on the lake's south side and a BCFS recreation site (Helper Creek) at km 27.7. Camping space is limited, but you can squeeze in five small camper units. Fire pits are provided. Some anglers prefer to hike to the sand and gravel bar where the Nahwitti River enters the east end of the lake. This path is a delightful walk through a stand of old-growth spruce. Conservation-minded anglers follow a catch-and-release ethic when fishing for the wild trout inhabiting area lakes and rivers.

The route from Port Hardy to Nahwitti Lake is a public BC Forest Service road. Once beyond Nahwitti, it enters Western Forest Products territory and climbs a long grade. At the top, a deteriorated signpost reads "Be Prepared for the Unexpected." The sign is attached to a giant butt log. Beneath the huge stump sits an old squashed car. Remember to use caution when driving these roads.

There are several steep hills to negotiate before the road drops to tidewater at Holberg (km 44.8). This region was initially settled by Danes relocating from thwarted attempts at colonizing the Cape Scott region around the turn of the last century. (See Section Three: Trip 13.) Holberg, once the site of a floating logging camp, is the headquarters for WFP's Holberg Division. The community sits at the head of Holberg Inlet, a long, narrow waterway knifing inland almost 29 km. The inlet is one of the fjord-like arms of Quatsino Sound. Holberg's Scarlet Ibis pub and restaurant is much appreciated by weary hikers returning from lengthy Cape Scott treks.

In Holberg, close to the pub, South Main meets Holberg Road at a signposted junction (km 45.7). Winter Harbour and Koprino Harbour travellers will turn left here. Follow the road by the log sort and around the head of Holberg Inlet to a T-junction. San Josef Main is to the right. Keep left on South Main and follow the signs. At Koprino Harbour, a large bay on Quatsino Sound, you'll find the Spencer Cove Recreation Site, co-managed by the BCFS and WFP. There is a boat ramp, docking area and eleven user-maintained campsites. Many saltwater anglers launch from here to try their luck in Quatsino Sound waters. From the South Main turnoff in Holberg, it's 33 km to the Koprino Harbour campsite, 25 km to Winter Harbour.

Winter Harbour is located at the top end of Forward Inlet. It's protected waters are a haven for commercial fishermen waiting out Pacific storms. The waterfront of the logging and fishing hamlet features a wooden boardwalk, dating back to the days when Winter Harbour could only be visited by water. Gravel roads were punched through in the 1970s. Telephone and hydro lines only reached the community in 1990. The Kwaksistah campground, operated by the Regional District of Mount Waddington, is one kilometre north of town. The twelve sites here (some with wooden tent platforms) are utilized by saltwater anglers and those base camping for area hiking forays. The boat launch nearby is best used at high tide. (For a more detailed look at backroading this part of the North Island see *More Island Adventures*, Trips 28 & 29.)

Grant Bay, a wild west-coast beach, is worth the effort to visit. It can be reached by water from Winter Harbour and Browning Inlet, then via a trail. You can take West Main, then a spur road to a more strenuous land route that connects with the Grant Bay Trail at the head of Browning Inlet. *Hiking Trails III*, published by VITIS, has a chapter on the Grant Bay Trail.

Let's backtrack to Holberg and the Winter Harbour turn at km 45.7. Keep straight ahead and cross the Goodspeed River. The route parallels the river to the intersection with San Josef Main (km 49.6). This junction of two active hauling roads is known as the Elephant Crossing. Years ago the intersection was marked by a railway-crossing signpost adorned with two elephants: one pink, the other red.

At the Elephant Crossing, swing right onto San Josef Main and follow the Cape Scott Park signs. A little over the 52-km mark, SJ 40 cuts off to the left. This road hooks up with South Main and provides travellers with an alternate route to Winter Harbour. You'll hit SJ 100 at km 55.7. This branch road swings off to the right and runs up to Brink and William lakes, two picturesque bodies of water nestled in the hills north of the San Josef River. There is a picnic site on William Lake.

Ronning Main, on the left at km 58, heads to Raft Cove Provincial Park, and its sandy beach and spit at the mouth of the Macjack River. With daypacks the hike to the beach usually takes under an hour. Note that the trail is a flagged route through deadfall and mudholes. Wet weather will slow down your pace. Raft Cove's sandy strand tapers to a beach spit at the mouth of the Macjack River. Directly across this tidal waterway is Willie Hecht's old trapping cabin. Hecht was an early pioneer of the region. (See Section Three: Trip 12.) Ronning Main also accesses Coast Main, along which you can reach five walk-in wilderness campsites at WFP's Palmerston Recreation Site, northwest of Raft Cove.

At km 59 watch for the side road (on the right) that leads to the Ronning Garden and part of the Cape Scott wagon road. Today, most of the historic route has been reclaimed by the Quatsino rainforest; other sections have been obliterated by logging. An Anglican cemetery lies east of a small parking area, but the path is somewhat overgrown. A short hike west goes to the homestead of Bernt Ronning, who settled the area in 1910 and lived there until the 1960s. In recent years, the local caretakers of the site have cleared extensive brush from Ronning's exotic garden to allow the beautiful 2-ha site to reestablish itself. Among the intriguing specimens are two magnificent monkey puzzle trees. A derelict steam donkey engine, just west of the Ronning homestead, marks the spot where work halted on the wagon-road link to Cape Scott. Contact the Port Hardy Chamber of Commerce for information on seasonal tours of the Ronning Garden.

WFP's San Josef River campsite (just over the 64-km mark) features eleven user-maintained campsites and a rough boat launch on the San Josef River. A privately owned campsite with river access is closer to the eastern boundary of Cape Scott Provincial Park, just over a kilometre away. The meandering twists of the San Josef River conceal cutthroat trout, Dolly Varden (char) and seasonal coho and steelhead. With a cartopper, canoe or kayak you can float the river to its mouth. Be wary of rip currents and standing waves that develop at San Josef Bay. DFO reminds anglers that the tidal waters of the San Josef and those near the mouth of the Fisherman River at Hansen Lagoon require a saltwater sports fishing license.

The Cape Scott Park parking lot is as far as you can drive on the backroads from Port Hardy, but if you've come this far, you're probably planning to continue farther on foot, hiking one of the many trails in the rugged Cape Scott region. Many visitors base camp for day hikes to San Josef Bay or Eric Lake. (See Section Three: Trip 13 for more information on Cape Scott Provincial Park.) Don't forget your raingear!

CONTACTS

- BC Forest Service (Port McNeill): 250-956-5000
- BC Parks (Strathcona District): 250-954-4600
- North Island Forestry Centre (Beaver Cove): 250-956-3844
- Regional District of Mount Waddington (Port McNeill): 250-956-3301
- Western Forest Products (Holberg): 250-288-3362
- Western Forest Products (Port McNeill): 250-956-3391

MAPS/GUIDES

- BC Forest Service Port McNeill Forest District Recreation Map
- Western Forest Products Visitors' Guide to Northern Vancouver Island

- National Topographical Series: 92L/11 Port McNeill (1:50,000); 92L/12 Quatsino (1:50,000); 102I/9 San Josef (1:50,000)
- Provincial Map: 92L Alert Bay (1:250,000)
- *Canadian Tide and Current Tables: Vol. 6* (Canadian Hydrographic Service)
- *Hiking Trails III* (VITIS)

NEAREST SERVICES

Holberg; Winter Harbour.

Section Three: Hiking and Paddling Destinations

Trip 1: The Juan de Fuca Marine Trail

IN BRIEF:

The Juan de Fuca Marine Trail, within Juan de Fuca Provincial Park, extends 47 km along Vancouver Island's west coast from China Creek Provincial Park to Botanical Beach. There are four trailheads along Highway 14 (the West Coast Road). Hikers can test their skills on a range of trails. Generally, the south end has the roughest sections; the north end is easier. The Juan de Fuca Marine Trail does not connect with the West Coast Trail.

ACCESS

The Juan de Fuca Marine Trail has four access points located on Highway 14 (the West Coast Road). (See Section One: Trip 1 for information on how to reach the China Beach, Sombrio Beach, Parkinson Creek and Botanical Beach trailheads. Botanical Beach itself is featured in Section Three: Trip 2.)

DESCRIPTION

If you have ever been to Botanical, Mystic or Sombrio beaches you've been on part of the Juan de Fuca Marine Trail. All these west-coast shorelines are now linked by a challenging 47-km hiking route that stretches from China Beach (west of Jordan River) to Botanical Beach, near Port Renfrew. Hikers have a choice of four trailhead starting points along the West Coast Road (Highway 14). These are located at China Beach, just west of Jordan River, Sombrio Beach, Parkinson Creek and Botanical Beach, closer to Port Renfrew. (See Section One: Trip 1 for details on getting to the trailheads.) Each has a parking area, pit toilets and an information signpost. Botanical Beach also has a picnic area. Overnight camping fees are collected through self-registration at the trailheads. Pit toilets are located at most designated wilderness campsites along the trail.

The trail extends 29 km northwest from China Beach to Sombrio Beach.

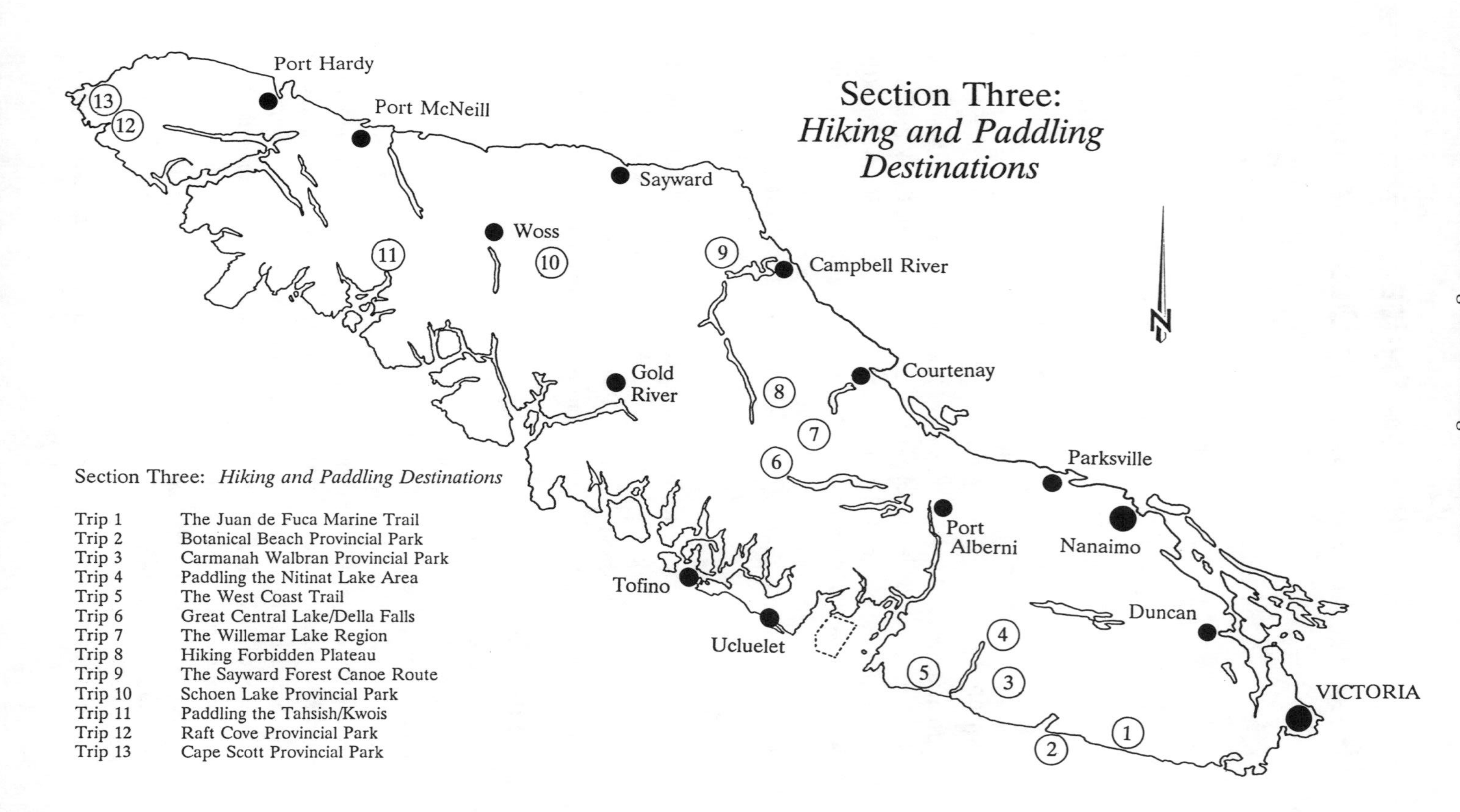
Section Three:
Hiking and Paddling
Destinations
N
Port Hardy
Port McNeill
Sayward
Woss
Campbell River
Gold River
Courtenay
Parksville
Port Alberni
Nanaimo
Tofino
Ucluelet
Duncan
VICTORIA
1
2
3
4
5
6
7
8
9
10
11
12
13
Section Three: Hiking and Paddling Destinations
Trip 1 The Juan de Fuca Marine Trail
Trip 2 Botanical Beach Provincial Park
Trip 3 Carmanah Walbran Provincial Park
Trip 4 Paddling the Nitinat Lake Area
Trip 5 The West Coast Trail
Trip 6 Great Central Lake/Della Falls
Trip 7 The Willemar Lake Region
Trip 8 Hiking Forbidden Plateau
Trip 9 The Sayward Forest Canoe Route
Trip 10 Schoen Lake Provincial Park
Trip 11 Paddling the Tahsish/Kwois
Trip 12 Raft Cove Provincial Park
Trip 13 Cape Scott Provincial Park

The first campsite is at Mystic Beach, about 2 km from the China Beach trailhead. The next camping spot is 7 km away at Bear Beach. Expect moderate hiking in this section. The shoreline route, southeast of Bear Beach, is impassable at high tide. Similar coastal walks near China Beach and Sombrio Beach may be severed by high tides or stormy conditions. If you time it wrong, delays are unavoidable. Tidal predictions are available in the *Canadian Tide and Current Tables: Vol.* 6 published by the Canadian Hydrographic Service. BC Parks posts crucial tidal information at the trailheads. To access the trail from the beaches, watch for fluorescent orange balls dangling in the shoreline trees.

The 20-km route from Bear Beach to Sombrio Beach is considered by many the toughest part of the Juan de Fuca Marine Trail. Elevation changes are frequent, the signage is still incomplete and trail conditions between Newmarch and Loss creeks are usually muddy and wet. Take care at the numerous creek crossings. This part of Vancouver Island has fast runoff. Only a few hours of coastal rains can flood streams and creeks and turn stretches of the trail into quagmires. Camping is possible at Chin Beach, where there is an emergency shelter. The Loss Creek suspension bridge is a trail highlight.

Sombrio Beach, popular with surfers, has a cave and waterfall. Camping is allowed at the beach's southeast end. The creation of the Juan de Fuca Marine Trail forced well-established Sombrio Beach squatters out. With them went some of the Sombrio area's unique character. Between the Sombrio Beach trailhead and Parkinson Creek (a distance of 8 km) the going is a lot easier although there are muddy sections. The campsite is halfway along at Little Kuitshe Creek. From the Parkinson Creek trailhead it's a little under 4 km along a bumpy logging road back up to the West Coast Road.

The final 10 km (from the Parkinson Creek access north to Botanical Beach) is the best section of the trail from which to view marine mammals. The designated campsite in this area is at Pazants Creek, about a kilometre away from Providence Cove. Some sections of the route may be muddy. The Juan de Fuca Marine Trail's northwest terminus is 7 km from Pazants Creek, at Botanical Beach. The intertidal life within Botanical Beach's tidepools is a big feature of the area. (See Section Three: Trip 2.)

Many visitors try the less difficult trails at Botanical Beach first. Anyone planning an overnighter at the designated campsites should be self-sufficient. Wear sturdy footwear and gear up for wet conditions. Hikers should be able to gauge changeable weather conditions and their own limitations. As a safeguard, give your departure and return times to someone reliable back home. Remember the Juan de Fuca Marine Trail is a wilderness environment.

Surfers are a familiar sight in the waters near Jordan River and Sombrio Point.

Consult the BC Parks *Juan de Fuca Marine Trail* brochure carefully prior to a hike and contact BC Parks (South Vancouver Island District) at 250-391-2300 for current regulations, camping fees and information on trail upgrades and improved signage. Check also the trailhead information signposts. Should you encounter any work crews, be sure they know you are hiking through. BC Parks can also provide schedules and phone numbers for the Pacheedaht First Nations bus service that takes hikers to and from the trailhead of their choice.

CONTACTS

- BC Parks (South Vancouver Island District): 250-391-2300

MAPS/GUIDES

- BC Parks Juan de Fuca Marine Trail brochure
- Guide to Forest Lands of Southern Vancouver Island (Lake Cowichan Combined Fire Organization)
- National Topographical Series: 92C/8 Jordan River (1:50,000); 92C/9 Port Renfrew (1:50,000)
- Provincial Map: 92C/NE Nitinat Lake (1:125,000)
- *Canadian Tide and Current Tables: Vol. 6* (Canadian Hydrographic Service)

NEAREST SERVICES

Port Renfrew; Sooke.

Trip 2: Botanical Beach Provincial Park

IN BRIEF

If you're near Port Renfrew, be sure to stop at Botanical Beach Provincial Park, renowned for its tidepools. At low tide, a wide sandstone shelf is exposed to reveal a profusion of intertidal life within wave-gouged tidepools. You can loop-hike to the beach, explore the shoreline, rock-scramble or just take in the great seascapes. The Juan de Fuca Marine Trail starts at Botanical Beach and stretches 47 km along the coast to China Beach, just west of Jordan River. (See Section Three: Trip One.)

ACCESS

From Victoria take the West Coast Road (Highway 14) through Sooke and west to Port Renfrew. (See Section One: Trip 1.) Turn left onto Cerantes Road (near the Port Renfrew Hotel and the government wharf) and continue about 3 km to the parking area. Cerantes Road is gravel with washboard sections from heavy traffic.

DESCRIPTION

A must-see for Port Renfrew visitors are the low-tide tidepools on the sandstone shelf at Botanical Beach Provincial Park. The relative ease with which visitors can see a variety of sea life within sea-carved bathtubs is a big feature of the area. Botanical Beach is the northern terminus of the Juan de Fuca Marine Trail. (See Section Three: Trip 1.)

To get to Botanical Beach Provincial Park, drive to Port Renfrew on the West Coast Road (Highway 14). (See Section One: Trip 1.) Continue to Cerantes Road, close to the Port Renfrew Hotel and government dock. Walk out onto the wharf for a look at Port San Juan and Snuggery Cove, the adjacent small bay. For Botanical Beach turn left onto Cerantes Road and head south-west toward San Juan Point. In misty weather you may hear the drone of the foghorn, near Cerantes Rock.

Two washed-out hills along Cerantes Road were problem spots in the off-season. Visitors without 4 x 4s had to park and hike into the beach. Improved road access makes it a lot easier to drive to the parking area, although the increased traffic has created a washboard effect on the roadway.

The tidepools are a big feature at Botanical Beach Provincial Park.

Just over 2 km along, hikers can take the 650-m Mill Bay Trail to a pocket cove on Port San Juan. Cerantes Road ends at the parking area (km 3). From the park information signpost, two trails descend via old roads to the mostly rocky shoreline. You can hike a 2.7-km loop back to either trailhead via the Shoreline Trail.

The University of Minnesota operated a marine biology laboratory on Botany Bay from 1901 to 1906. It was the first of its kind in North America. The seaside station was headed by Doctor Josephine Tilden, a marine biologist from the University of Minnesota. Up to eighty people could be housed at the site. Students and scientists came from all over the world to research Botanical Beach's wealth of marine life. The station operated for six years. Supplies were brought in on the *Queen City*, a small steamer often delayed by capricious seas. Landed goods were lugged along a rugged trail to the laboratories. A lack of funding eventually forced the station's closure. During the Second World War, a gun emplacement was constructed on the beach. It was never needed and later was torn down. Several universities have studied marine life at Botanical Beach over the years, including the University of BC and the University of Victoria.

Within Botanical Beach's many seaweed-shrouded tidepools (one is called the Devil's Billiard Table), starfish, sea anemones, plant life and small fish are easily and safely observed at low tide. You might be fortunate enough to catch a rare glimpse of an octopus trapped in one of the deeper pools.

Visitors can explore the sandstone headland or watch passing fishing boats and freighters.

Botanical Beach's shoreline is rocky and slippery, so wear suitable footwear. Beware of rogue waves. Keep children away from the surf zone. You can't camp or build a fire within park boundaries. The closest wilderness campsite is located a fair distance along the Juan de Fuca Marine Trail. Visitors must know the tides. Tidal information is listed in the *Canadian Tide and Current Tables: Vol. 6* (Canadian Hydrographic Service). The prime time to visit Botanical Beach is during the lowest tides of the month. The lowest tides of the year usually occur in late May or June.

CONTACTS

- BC Parks (South Vancouver Island District): 250-391-2300

MAPS/GUIDES

- BC Parks Botanical Beach pamphlet
- National Topographical Series: 92C/9 Port Renfrew (1:50,000)
- Provincial Map: 92C/NE Nitinat Lake (1:125,000
- *Adventuring Around Vancouver Island* (Lebrecht/Noppe/Greystone)
- *Canadian Tide and Current Tables: Vol. 6* (Canadian Hydrographic Service)
- *Hiking Trails I* (VITIS)
- *Parks of British Columbia and The Yukon* (Paquet/Maia)

NEAREST SERVICES

Port Renfrew.

Trip 3:
Carmanah Walbran Provincial Park

IN BRIEF

A challenging wilderness hiking destination on southern Vancouver Island is Carmanah Walbran Provincial Park. From the small campsite at the end of Rosander Main, trails lead through an ancient forest of cedar, hemlock and fir and stands of giant Sitka spruce.

ACCESS

From Port Alberni or Lake Cowichan, take the logging roads to the top end of Nitinat Lake. (See Section Two: Trip 5.) At the Nitinat Junction, head west on South Main and then take Rosander Main and follow the signs about 38 km to the trailhead. Gravel mainlines are in good to fair shape. Expect industrial traffic in some areas. The roads to the Carmanah Valley have several steep grades. Watch for sharp rocks and gravel ridges along rougher sections. Secondary spurs may require a 4 x 4. Many intersections are confusing; not all are signposted.

DESCRIPTION

Carmanah Walbran Provincial Park was first created as Carmanah Pacific Provincial Park in June 1990. It was renamed Carmanah Walbran in 1995, after the addition of the lower Walbran Valley and the upper Carmanah Valley. The park preserves an exceptional old-growth forest on Vancouver Island's west coast. Valley slopes harbour giant spruce, large western hemlock and twisted cedars, many over 1,000 years old.

The Walbran Valley, one valley to the east, consists of an ancient forest of cedar, spruce, hemlock and Douglas fir. There are several small lakes, river canyons and waterfalls. Walbran Valley and its tributary watersheds are habitat for bear, cougar, elk and deer. Among its varied bird life are hawks, eagles and marbled murrelets; the latter are robin-sized seabirds that nest in old-growth forests between May and late July.

From the Nitinat Junction near Nitinat Lake's top end it's just under 38 km to the parking area and park campsite at the end of MacMillan Bloedel's Rosander Main. You can reach the Nitinat Junction along well-travelled logging mainlines that start from the Cowichan Lake area or Port

Alberni. (See Section Two: Trip 5.)

If you come in via Cowichan Lake, take one of its perimeter logging roads and travel to the west end. (See Section Two: Trip 3.) Cut west on Nitinat Main for 18.5 km to the Nitinat Junction, where South Main comes in from Port Alberni. (See Section Two: Trip 5.) Reset your vehicle's trip meter to zero at the signposted Nitinat Junction and head west on South Main. A little over the 5-km mark, cut right for 1.5 km to the Ditidaht First Nations grocery store and cafe, gas station and motel. Nearby is the Parks Canada Nitinat Lake West Coast Trail information and registration centre. (See Section Three: Trip 5.)

For the Carmanah Valley trailhead keep left and stay on South Main to climb a hill. The turn for the Nitinat Lake Campsite (co-managed by the BC Forest Service and MacMillan Bloedel) is on the right, just under the 8-km mark. It's about a kilometre from the mainline to the campsite entrance. Some visitors base camp at Nitinat Lake and day-trip to the park. This user-maintained facility is a windsurfing hotspot, and it's easy to see why. Daily winds out on Nitinat Lake provide ideal conditions for sailboarding. The campsites are canopied by a pocket stand of old-growth forest. You can hike a trail down to the Caycuse rivermouth. Vacant spots are rare over the summer, particularly on long weekends. If you savour the Nitinat Valley's solitude, time your backroad travels to the off-season.

Up until the 1980s, the Caycuse River bridge (km 9) was the farthest you could go before active logging areas restricted public entry to non-weekday working hours. Today the roads to the Carmanah Valley are open at all times. Road improvements don't make the off-road logging trucks any less formidable. If you're leery of sharing the narrow logging roads with industrial traffic, tackle the hauling roads after the logging crews have quit for the day (usually by 6 p.m.). Most people prefer to journey on weekends and holidays.

Cross the Caycuse River bridge to a T-junction. A left on South Main goes to cutblocks northeast of Mount Walbran. Turn right onto Rosander Main for Carmanah Walbran Provincial Park. Should you encounter a logging checkpoint, follow any given directions closely. Over the centuries Hooper Creek has etched a sheer canyon in area limestone. If you stop for a look be sure to park safely on the road's shoulder. Rosander Main cuts back toward Nitinat Lake. Logging in this region has opened up the forest and Nitinat Lake is visible at several points. Prior to the clearcutting, tall Douglas fir and cedar lined the roadside.

At km 14.5 the mainline switchbacks up the northeast slope of Mount Rosander. Near the top of the grade (just under the 16-km mark) is a spectacular vista of Nitinat Lake's top end. Continue through a narrow pass near Rosander Lake. A rough side road (on the left) splits into washed-out spurs extending up a west slope on Mount Rosander. A steep hike up the old roads goes to a panorama of Nitinat Lake, west to the Pacific Ocean.

Rosander Main soon drops into the Marchand Creek drainage. Be cautious at bridge crossings and when negotiating blind corners. You may be confused (or intrigued) by all the side roads and crossroads intersections in some areas. Ignore these diversions and keep straight ahead on Rosander Main. There are two exceptions. The first, on the right around the 24-km mark, leads to a remote Nitinat Lake water access point where a now-dismantled Malloch and Moseley logging camp once straddled the shoreline. The second spur, one kilometre away, hooks up with the road that skirts Doobah Lake's east side. This secondary road ends at the boundary of Pacific Rim National Park Reserve, near a logged-off area. The park's largest known western red cedars grow nearby, on Cheewhat Lake's east side. Randy Stoltmann's *Hiking the Ancient Forests of British Columbia and Washington* describes the Cheewhat area. The Doobah Lake Cedar, on that lake's northern fringe, is accessed along a rugged trail.

Rosander Main runs south, through a series of cutblocks separated by pocket old-growth forest. The junction with gated Bonilla Main is at km 35. From here, the road swings east to the Carmanah Walbran parking lot (km 37.5) and the seasonal BC Parks information office. Close by, BC Parks has established twelve campsites with tent pads, tables and fire rings. No fires are allowed anywhere else in the park. You may short-term vehicle camp in the parking lot. Piped well water is close by. Be sure to boil or treat any water obtained from Carmanah Creek or area streams. From the parking lot, trails and boardwalks switchback through pristine forest to the cathedral-like atmosphere of the valley bottom near groves of ancient trees and beautiful Carmanah Creek viewpoints. Less than an hour's hike away is a wilderness campsite near the Three Sisters grove. Two other designated camping areas are farther upstream. Camping locations are primitive. Camp only on Carmanah Creek's gravel bars, but beware; water levels can rise quickly in heavy rains to flood these and other low-lying regions.

Carmanah Walbran Provincial Park visitors should expect muddy, slippery trails with some rough sections. Those planning on extended upstream hikes should be in good shape and experienced with wilderness travel. Carry enough food, raingear and warm clothing and expect changeable weather conditions. Annual rainfall increases substantially near Vancouver Island's west coast. While Duncan averages 89 cm, the Carmanah and Walbran valleys average a torrential 508 cm! Rugged water-resistant footwear is essential. Leave no litter, practise low-impact camping and avoid tenting in the spruce groves. Stay on the trails and boardwalks to minimize vegetation damage. Black bears may sometimes be encountered. The animals will normally shy away from people, but they can be unpredictable and dangerous. Give them a wide berth.

You can hike downstream to a ford. Beyond this point the trail is closed. BC Parks has imposed this restriction for public safety reasons (the routes are not constructed to park standards) and to protect the fragile root systems of lower valley trees and the Carmanah Giant (a towering spruce 95 m high) from the boots of too many hikers. Thousands visit Carmanah Walbran Provincial Park annually. Equally impressive spruce trees, such as those at the Randy Stoltmann Commemorative Grove, the Three Sisters grove and Heaven grove, grow in less sensitive areas and are more accessible to Carmanah Valley visitors.

CONTACTS

- BC Forest Service (South Island Forest District): 250-724-9205
- BC Parks (South Vancouver Island District): 250-391-2300
- MacMillan Bloedel (Franklin Operations): 250-720-4200
- TimberWest (Honeymoon Bay Operations): 250-749-6805

MAPS/GUIDES

- BC Parks Carmanah Walbran Provincial Park brochure
- BC Forest Service Port Alberni Forest District Recreation Map
- Guide to Forest Lands of Southern Vancouver Island (Lake Cowichan Combined Fire Organization)
- MacMillan Bloedel Recreation and Logging Road Guide to TFL 44
- West Coast Trail Map (ITMB Publishing)
- National Topographical Series: 92F/2 Alberni Inlet (1:50,000); 92C/14 Barkley Sound (1:50,000); 92C/10 Carmanah Creek (1:50,000); 92C/16 Cowichan Lake (1:50,000); 92C/15 Little Nitinat River (1:50,000)
- Provincial Map: Regional Map #2 Parksville/Tofino (1:125,000)
- *Backroading Vancouver Island* (Neering/Whitecap)
- *Four-Wheeling on Southern Vancouver Island* (Lee/Thirkell/Harbour)
- *Hiking the Ancient Forests of British Columbia and Washington* (Stoltmann/Lone Pine)
- *Parks of British Columbia and The Yukon* (Pacquet/Maia)

NEAREST SERVICES

Lake Cowichan area; Port Alberni. There is an emergency telephone at the Ditidaht Reserve.

Trip 4:
Paddling the Nitinat Lake Area

IN BRIEF

Perhaps the most demanding of Vancouver Island's bigger lakes is the 20-km-long Nitinat Lake, connected to the Pacific Ocean by Nitinat Narrows. Experienced wilderness paddlers can explore Nitinat Lake and camp at secluded shoreline beaches. Some visitors make it down to the Nitinat Narrows. Paddlers can also venture to the Nitinat Triangle, northwest of Nitinat Lake. This series of lakes (Hobiton, Squalicum, Tsuquadra and Tsusiat) is linked by rugged portage trails. Both lower Nitinat Lake and the Nitinat Triangle are within Pacific Rim National Park Reserve and a free park permit is required.

ACCESS

Launch Points: BC Forest Service/MacMillan Bloedel Nitinat Lake Campsite: Take the logging roads from Port Alberni or Cowichan Lake to the Nitinat Junction, near the Nitinat River bridge. (See Section Two: Trip 5.) Head south toward Carmanah Walbran Provincial Park for about 8 km and watch for a side road (on the right) that leads to the Nitinat Lake Campsite. This turn on the mainline may not be signposted. (See Section Three: Trip 3.) Knob Point: The access road (Hitchie Main) cuts off the Cowichan Lake/Port Alberni backroads about 2.5 km from the Nitinat Junction. This is also the turn for the Nitinat hatchery. (See Section Two: Trip 5.) The road runs just over 9 km along Nitinat Lake's northwest shore to Knob Point. Gravel mainlines are in seasonally good to fair shape. Active hauling may be frequent on some routes.

DESCRIPTION

The waters of Nitinat Lake and the Nitinat Triangle (a lake chain that includes Hobiton, Squalicum, Tsuquadra and Tsusiat) are challenging paddling destinations for overnight trips or extended wilderness excursions. Nitinat Lake's north shore (from Hobiton Creek to the narrows), south shore (west of Doobah Lake to the narrows) and the Nitinat Triangle are within Pacific Rim National Park Reserve. Paddlers must obtain a free park permit prior to their trip. These are available from the seasonal West Coast

Trail registration offices at either Pachena Bay (close to Bamfield) or Nitinat Lake (near the Ditidaht Reserve). Contact Pacific Rim National Park Reserve (Ucluelet) at 250-726-7721 for details.

You can reach Nitinat Lake from the Cowichan/Port Alberni logging roads. (See Section Two: Trip 5.) Expect industrial traffic on some sections of mainline. There are two main launch points on Nitinat Lake: the BC Forest Service/MacMillan Bloedel Nitinat Campsite on the lake's southeast shore, and the BCFS Knob Point Recreation Site on the north side. The latter is the start for paddlers heading for the Nitinat Triangle.

Nitinat Lake, the only tidal lake on Vancouver Island, should be called Nitinat Inlet. Fed by numerous watersheds (notably the Nitinat, Caycuse and Hobiton river systems), the lake is connected to the Pacific by the treacherous tidal flows at Nitinat Narrows. Nitinat Lake reacts to frequent winds that spring up by late morning and blow all day. The lake's steep shoreline contributes to confused sea conditions, dangerous chop and white-caps. Be wary when tides battle contrary winds. Danger zones are near shoreline cliffs where safe landings are impossible and rebound waves numerous. Getting an early start will usually avoid the rougher water. Be prepared. The weather can turn ugly in minutes; you may be forced to shore to wait until the winds die down.

Travel on Nitinat Lake in the early morning, before the daily winds and waves develop. As you skim into quiet bays you could startle a blue heron. The hunched flight of these birds conjures up depictions of prehistoric pterodactyls. Watch for mergansers and loons in the lake and eagles and hawks soaring overhead. While exploring a Nitinat Lake pocket beach I encountered an eagle gorging on a freshly caught salmon. The eagle's scream of rage at having to delay a feeding echoed over the lake as the bird flew off. (It returned later.) You'll often see jellyfish floating about and starfish or sea anemones precariously perched on sunken rocks. Keep an eye out for seals, especially toward the narrows. These animals sometimes startle paddlers.

A slender waterfall, Sitting Lady Falls, tumbles down a rocky slope west of Mount Rosander. A good camping spot lies south of the falls near Marchand Creek. At Daykins Bay, site of a former logging camp, a rock island makes a good rest stop. Near Nitinat Cone, Nitinat Lake constricts to begin its serpentine curve to the narrows. Here tidal currents will be evident. These waters can be treacherous, even for experienced paddlers.

Whyac, the old First Nations village on a rocky headland overlooking the Nitinat Narrows, is one of the west coast's earliest settlements. Near Whyac, powerful ocean tides surge in and out of Nitinat Lake. It takes upwards of twelve hours to complete one cycle. West Coast Trail hikers are ferried across the narrows by a private ferry service. A daily limit of eight pre-registered hikers can access the trail via a Nitinat Lake water taxi. (See Section Three: Trip 5.) First Nations reserves (indicated by small structures or forest clearings) are scattered along Nitinat Lake. Always respect these areas. As a courtesy, we always contact the Ditidaht Reserve prior to our trip for permission to paddle in the Nitinat Lake area.

Tackle the narrows just prior to slack water on an ebb tide. That's when the current is minimal, yet sea swell still affects water conditions in the narrows. Seas are rarely favourable for canoeists to continue beyond Whyac to Tsuquanah Point. You won't be able to stay long. Slack tide lasts for only five or six minutes. As the tide turns to flood and the currents increase, prudent paddlers abandon the often breaker-lashed open coastline and drift back toward the main part of Nitinat Lake.

The brief duration of slack water does not coincide with high or low tide. Consult the Tofino listings in the *Canadian Tide and Current Tables: Vol. 6* and make the current table calculation for estimated time of slack water at Nitinat Narrows. The shallow Nitinat Bar at the lake's mouth causes standing waves and pounding surf. Perilous whirlpools and upwellings below Whyac develop during peak tidal flows. Currents can reach eight knots.

The remains of the Lummi Bay cannery (built in 1921) sit in a bay near Whyac. A fish camp operated at Brown (Brown's Bay) Cove. Nitinat Lake was once the scene of a thriving salmon industry. Too many nets strung across Nitinat Narrows seriously diluted the salmon runs. Without a steady fish supply these facilities closed down. In the 1930s, a logging company blasted out rocks just inside the narrows, so boomed logs could be towed through the passage. While this helped the loggers, it became harder for smaller boats to enter and leave Nitinat Lake, since they could not utilize the points of rock in a zigzag course against the tidal flow.

Listen for the drone of the whistle buoy offshore, near Clo-oose. You might mistake its bellow for a foghorn, unless you hear it on a sunny day. The buoy is activated by waves and breakers. The weather on Vancouver Island's west coast can be unpredictable. Chilling fog banks can creep in from the Pacific to obscure any sense of direction. Knowledgeable use of a compass is crucial in these conditions. When travelling on Nitinat Lake, watch the weather, maintain a healthy respect for the sea, use common sense and know your own and your boat, kayak or canoe's limitations. Pick up *The West Coast Trail and Nitinat Lakes*, published by the Sierra Club of BC, for more information and maps covering Nitinat Lake and the Nitinat Triangle, to the northwest.

If the Nitinat Triangle is your paddling destination, the best jumping-off point is the BCFS Knob Point Recreation Site on Nitinat Lake's northwest shore. Cut off the Cowichan Lake/Port Alberni mainlines onto Hitchie Main, around 2.5 km from the Nitinat Junction. This is also the turn for the Nitinat hatchery. (See Section Two: Trip 5.) The road runs just over 9 km along Nitinat Lake's northwest shore to Knob Point.

Paddlers still get a taste of Nitinat Lake on the 5-km journey from Knob Point to a small bay just south of Hobiton Creek. The mouth of Hobiton Creek is a Ditidaht First Nations Reserve. Visitors must respect this area. No camping is permitted. You have to portage to Hobiton Lake via a rough trail. The creek is closed to paddlers to protect sensitive salmon habitat. Salmon run up the stream in the fall. Paddlers should continue beyond Hobiton Creek. In the small bay identified with an obvious triangular sign, watch for the red portage marker on a rocky point, just south of the creekmouth. BC Parks staff and volunteers periodically clear the path, but the portage has muddy sections and windfall. Make one trip with your canoe or kayak and a second backpacking your gear. Expect a two-hour portage.

There are some wilderness campsites on Hobiton Lake's north shore. In June, July and August firewood is scarce at these sites. Carry and use a portable campstove. Halfway down Hobiton's south shore, look for markers on the trees near a gravel beach area. A rough trail to Squalicum Lake starts here. It's a tough climb with a canoe. The Hobiton area has stands of old-growth timber. The lake is ideal for swimming and has good fishing. Everything from bait and bobber, spinning gear and flies will take trout. Hotspots are the mouths of the creeks that pour down from Hobiton Ridge, on the lake's north side. Lucky Hobiton Lake visitors will taste Hobiton's early-morning magic when gossamer mists hover just above the lake waters.

A second portage (from Hobiton Lake to Tsusiat Lake) starts at Hobiton Lake's southwest end. Expect deadfall, mudholes and steep, slick slopes. Wilderness campsites are located on Tsusiat Lake's north side. The best spot sits close to the southwest-end log jam, near the outlet stream. At Tsusiat Lake you can paddle to a lagoon on the lake's south side where the Ditidaht warriors hid their women and children from warring enemies. From a distance the lagoon's narrow entrance lies camouflaged by two small islands.

CONTACTS

- BC Forest Service (South Island Forest District): 250-724-9205
- MacMillan Bloedel (Franklin Operations): 250-720-4200
- Pacific Rim National Park Reserve (Ucluelet): 250-726-7721
- West Coast Trail Nitinat Lake Information Centre (seasonal): 250-745-3422

MAPS/GUIDES

- BC Forest Service Port Alberni District Recreation Map
- Guide to Forest Lands of Southern Vancouver Island (Lake Cowichan Combined Fire Organization)
- MacMillan Bloedel Recreation and Logging Road Guide to TFL 44
- West Coast Trail Map (ITM Publishing)
- National Topographical Series: 92C/10 Carmanah Creek (1:50,000); 92C/15 Little Nitinat River (1:50,000)
- Provincial Map: Regional Map #2 Parksville/Tofino (1:125,000)
- *Canadian Tide and Current Tables: Vol. 6* (Canadian Hydrographic Service)
- *Pacific Rim Explorer* (Obee/Whitecap)
- *The West Coast Trail and Nitinat Lakes* (Sierra Club of BC)

NEAREST SERVICES

Bamfield; Cowichan Lake area; Port Alberni. There is an emergency telephone at the Ditidaht Reserve.

Trip 5:
The West Coast Trail

IN BRIEF

The West Coast Trail was initially a lifesaving trail along part of Vancouver Island's rugged west coast known as the Graveyard of the Pacific. From its early-1900s origin the trail has evolved from a primitive path to a world-class wilderness hiking destination.

ACCESS

To the Pachena Bay trailhead: Follow logging mainlines from Port Alberni or Cowichan Lake to Franklin Camp. Take the Bamfield road from Franklin Camp about 41 km to Pachena Bay, near Bamfield. (See Section Two: Trips 5 & 6.) To the Gordon River trailhead: Take Highway 14 (West Coast Road) to Port Renfrew. (See Section One: Trip 1.) Follow the signposts to the Parks Canada Information Centre. To the Parks Canada Nitinat Lake Information Centre: Take the logging roads from either Port Alberni or Cowichan Lake to the head of Nitinat Lake and continue toward Carmanah Walbran Provincial Park and follow the signs. (See Section Two: Trip 5; Section Three: Trips 3 & 4.) Gravel mainlines are in good to fair shape. Industrial traffic may be encountered in some areas.

DESCRIPTION

The 75-km West Coast Trail stretches along Vancouver Island's rugged west coast from Pachena Bay (near Bamfield) southeast to Port Renfrew. Originally constructed as a life-saving trail for shipwrecked mariners, the hiking route is part of Pacific Rim National Park Reserve. The West Coast Trail is suited for experienced backpackers only.

Respect for the sea and a concise knowledge of tides is essential. Be up-to-date on tidal information, available in the *Canadian Tide and Current Tables: Vol.* 6, published by the Canadian Hydrographic Service. Consult the listings for Tofino. Note that tidal information is based on the assumption of calm seas. Winds and storms can cause a rise in tides. Be aware when travelling beach and sandstone-shelf routes.

The trail has been improved over the years with cable car and bridge river crossings, boardwalks, stairs, ladders and regular trail clearing. It is still a rugged wilderness hiking destination and should not be taken lightly. Allow a week to complete the trek without rushing. Be self-sufficient and geared for foul weather. Guard against hypothermia. Bring extra clothes, winter sleeping bags and a good tent that will withstand deluging rains and fierce winds. Not every traveller is adequately prepared for the often unyielding weather conditions on Vancouver Island's west coast. Severe storms, surging in from the Pacific Ocean, can pound the shoreline at any time of the year. Chilling fogs creep in even over the summer. Be prepared for the unexpected. Dampness and moisture in the early morning and evening can soak anything left out in the open. Keep your gear dry by stashing everything in plastic bags.

The northern section is considered the easiest; the southern half is more challenging. For that reason, many people who plan to hike the complete trail start at the Pachena Bay trailhead near Bamfield. By the time you hit the tougher stretches, packs will be lighter and you'll be conditioned by a few days hiking. Some visitors opt for a partial trip along the West Coast Trail. Overnighters head from Pachena Bay to Michigan Creek; others journey as far as Tsusiat Falls, a trail highlight.

From the Pachena Bay trailhead the trail meanders on an old road to the Pachena lighthouse. There are plenty of ups and downs. In the spring and fall, sea lions sun themselves on the rocks below the Flat Rocks lookout. Beyond the Pachena lighthouse is Michigan Creek, the first of the camping beaches. The boiler from the *Michigan*, a ship that went down in 1843, lies wedged on the rocks just offshore. Cable cars cross some creeks. In other places sheer headlands and treacherous surge channels preclude shore hiking. Take land routes to bypass these impassable sections and to avoid scrambling over slippery beach rocks. At one point the trail runs high above the jagged rocks that doomed the *Valencia* in 1906.

Steep ladders lead to the beach at Tsusiat Falls, the most popular camping destination on the West Coast Trail. Firewood may be scarce here due to the hundreds of tenters who throng to the area over the summer. Consider shoulder-season travel to help prevent summer overcrowding at popular destinations (such as the Tsusiat Falls or Michigan Creek campsites). Tsusiat Falls (18.3 m high) are often used as a navigational aid by boaters out on the open Pacific. At Tsusiat Point you'll pass Hole-in-the-Wall, a sea-carved archway in the rocks. At Nitinat Narrows, just east of Tsuquadra Point, hikers must be ferried across the tidal outlet to Nitinat Lake by a private ferry service. The fee ($15.00) is payable in cash.

Highlights on the West Coast Trail's south end include the Cheewhat River suspension bridge. Cheewhat translates as "river of urine." From its source at Cheewhat Lake the river meanders through bogland that gives a yellow tinge to the water. Other stops of interest are the Carmanah lighthouse, Carmanah and Walbran creeks and the highest point on the trail, east of Thrasher Cove. The trail ends/starts at the Gordon River ferry crossing, near Port Renfrew.

The West Coast Trail is open from May 1st to September 30th. Registration and park-use permits are mandatory. A trail user fee of $70 is payable at the trailheads. Visa, MasterCard, cash and debit cards are accepted. Registered hikers receive personal trip counselling, a detailed water-resistant trail map and the *West Coast Trail Preparation Guide*. A portion of the user fee goes toward trail maintenance. Seasonal Parks Canada registration and information centres are located at the Pachena Bay (Bamfield) and Gordon River (Port Renfrew) trailheads and at the head of Nitinat Lake. The first two are open daily from 9 a.m. to 5 p.m. The Nitinat Lake centre is open from noon to 5 p.m., seven days a week.

A daily quota governs overnight starts from the three trail access points. Hiking permits issued at the Pachena Bay or the Gordon River trailhead are limited to twenty-six each per day. Of these, twenty are available through advance reservation; the remaining six are issued to hikers on waitlists. Demand is high for waitlist permits; you could face a two- or three-day wait (or longer). You must register at the trailhead by noon on the day you are scheduled to hike. Arrive early, if possible. An additional eight pre-registered hikers per day may access the West Coast Trail at Nitinat Narrows via a private Nitinat Lake water-taxi service.

Reservations are highly recommended. Reservations may be made through Super Natural BC Reservation Service at 1-800-663-6000 (outside Canada and the USA at 250-387-1642) between 6 a.m. and 6 p.m., local time. This service begins each year on March 1st. The non-refundable reservation fee of $25.00 can be paid by Visa or MasterCard.

Air and bus service to the trailheads is available. Contact Parks Canada for listings. You can journey from Port Alberni to Bamfield (or vice versa) on the M.V. *Lady Rose*. Reservations are required from mid-June through mid-September. For current rates and schedule information, call Alberni Marine Transportation at 250-723-8313 (toll-free at 1-800-663-7192 April through September).

At the time of this writing (1998), some changes to the West Coast Trail regulations were pending. Nothing had been formalized as this book went to press. For updated information on the West Coast Trail, contact Pacific Rim National Park Reserve (Ucluelet): 250-726-7721.

CONTACTS

- MacMillan Bloedel (Franklin Operations): 250-720-4200

- Pacific Rim National Park Reserve (Ucluelet): 250-726-7721
- West Coast Trail Information Centre (seasonal): Nitinat Lake: 250-745-3422
- West Coast Trail Information Centre (Pachena Bay): 250-728-3234
- West Coast Trail Information Centre (Port Renfrew): 250-647-5434

MAPS/GUIDES

- West Coast Trail water-resistant map (Canadian Cartographics)
- Guide to Forest Lands of Southern Vancouver Island (Lake Cowichan Combined Fire Organization)
- MacMillan Bloedel Recreation and Logging Road Guide to TFL 44
- West Coast Trail Map (ITMB Publishing)
- National Topographical Series: 92C/14 Barkley Sound (1:50,000); 92C/10 Carmanah Creek (1:50,000); 92C/11 Pachena Point (1:50,000); 92C/9 Port Renfrew (1:50,000)
- Provincial Map: Regional Map #2 Parksville/Tofino (1:125,000)
- *Adventuring Around Vancouver Island* (Lebrecht/Noppe/Greystone)
- *Adventuring in British Columbia* (Nanton/Simpson/Douglas & McIntyre)
- *Blisters and Bliss, A Trekker's Guide to the West Coast Trail* (Foster/Aitken/B & B Publishing/Cloudcap)
- *Canadian Tide and Current Tables: Vol. 6* (Canadian Hydrographic Service)
- *Pacific Rim Explorer* (Obee/Whitecap)
- *The West Coast Trail and Nitinat Lakes* (Sierra Club of BC)

NEAREST SERVICES

Bamfield; Port Renfrew.

Trip 6:
Great Central Lake/Della Falls

IN BRIEF

Many Vancouver Island adventurers combine the challenge of big-lake paddling with wilderness hiking on the amphibious journey to the head of Great Central Lake and the hike up the Drinkwater Creek Valley to Della Falls, Canada's tallest cascade.

ACCESS

To Launch Point One: Take Highway 4 west from Port Alberni for about 10 km to the paved Great Central Road. (See Section One: Trip 5.) Turn right and carry on for 7.5 km to the Ark Resort, at the foot of Great Central Lake. To Launch Point Two: Follow Great Central Road to the Ark Resort and cut right onto MacMillan Bloedel's Ash River Road to cross the Stamp River bridge. Stay on the mainline for 6.5 km and turn left onto Branch 83. Continue for 9.3 km to an intersection with a secondary road, just south of Lowry Lake. Turn left for 1.5 km to a boat launch and wilderness campsite at the BC Forest Service Scout Beach Recreation Site, on Great Central Lake. (See Section Two: Trip 10.) Area logging roads are in good to fair shape.

DESCRIPTION

For paddling backpackers (or backpacking paddlers) nothing beats an amphibious wilderness adventure to the head of Great Central Lake and up the rugged Drinkwater Creek Valley to Della Falls, in southern Strathcona Park. Della Falls is the highest waterfall in Canada. It was named by Joe Drinkwater, after his wife. Joe and his brother constructed the first road into Great Central Lake and worked mining claims in the region in 1911.

To reach either of two launching points, take Highway 4 west from Port Alberni for just under 10 km to Great Central Road. Turn right and follow this paved road 7.5 km to the foot of Great Central Lake. (See Section One: Trip 5.) At the Ark Resort you can park your vehicle (for a small fee) and either paddle the complete length of Great Central Lake (33 km) to the Della Falls trailhead or hire the resort's water taxi. Currently (1998) the return trip via the water taxi costs $85.00 per person. Canoe rentals are also available. Contact the Ark Resort at 250-723-2657 for up-to-date rates and information. The lake has private floating cabins and some active logging areas to which equipment is barged. Be aware of other boat traffic.

For the second launching point, swing north at the Ark Resort, cross the Stamp River bridge onto MacMillan Bloedel's Ash River Road and continue for 6.5 km to Branch 83 and cut left. The route runs high above the north side of Great Central Lake with good viewpoints along the way. Stay on Branch 83 for about 9.5 km to an intersection, south of Lowry Lake. Turn left onto (unmarked) Branch 83D and continue for about 1.5 km to a natural boat launch and user-maintained campsite at the BC Forest Service Scout Beach Recreation Site on Great Central Lake. A 2.5-km trail extends from the campsite to Lowry Lake. (See Section Two: Trip 10.)

Great Central Lake (one of Vancouver Island's deepest, with depths of over 330 m) is widest near Thunder Mountain. The lake's aboriginal name, *moo-hulth* means "burned-off face." A dam at the foot of Great Central Lake creates sunken deadheads, stumps and trees along the shoreline that can be potential hazards for paddlers. Despite these dangers, stay close to shore in windy or wavy situations. Over the summer, strong winds generally come up by the early afternoon. Prudent paddlers start out just after dawn, though sometimes the Great Central Lake's fickle winds blow all night. Great Central Lake is extremely narrow at its foot and is bordered by steep mountains. Funnelled valley winds can create challenging paddling waters. Watch the weather carefully and be aware of quick-changing conditions.

When the whitecap wave trains are rolling you may have to hole up for a day or two. Always carry extra food and supplies, just in case. To make better time, many paddlers rig up a sail and take advantage of the winds. A group of scouts passed our lakepoint campsite one blustery afternoon with three canoes lashed at the gunwales and two billowing sails. In seconds they were swept past, but still managed to exalt the merits of viewing the Della Falls from the Love Lake Trail. They also told us where they had left some canned vanilla pudding at the lakehead trailhead.

Some visitors prefer to take their time en route to lakehead. You'll find good overnight campsites on points of land on Great Central Lake's north side. These tenting spots are limited. Clark Point is one of the best. Farther west, another stopping point is near a bay of dead trees. Along the lake's south shore look for a level spot in one of many small bays where streams enter the lake.

In some places Great Central Lake's shoreline drops off abruptly in a series of huge stone steps. When the sun beats down on the area, nothing beats a swim and a game of water Frisbee.

The lakehead is marked by old railway trestles in shoreline shallows. A stand of spindly dead trees marks the lake's west end. At the new dock, pull

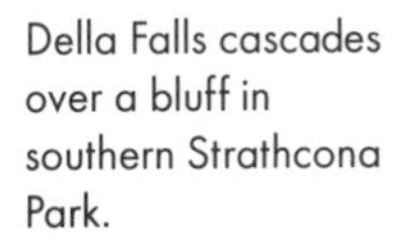
Della Falls cascades over a bluff in southern Strathcona Park.

in for the Della Falls trailhead campsite. A second landing is situated in the next bay. No overnight boat mooring is allowed. There are sixteen wilderness campsites here, a bear cache for food and a pit toilet. Some visitors base at the lakehead campsite and overnight up near the falls. Others make long day hikes.

The Della Falls Trail, about 16 km long, climbs 825 m up the Drinkwater Creek Valley. Hikers must be in good physical shape and geared for a wilderness setting. Better bridges make the creek crossings easier and safer and the trail is periodically brushed-out. Seasonal washouts and fast-growing trail vegetation can render the route indistinct in places. In the upper valley, June visitors may encounter impeding snows. August brings the best hiking weather, but the flow of Della Falls will not be at a peak.

The Della Falls Trail starts up the Drinkwater Creek Valley on an old railway grade. Apply your repellent before you near Swamper's Marsh and its ferocious mosquitoes. July is a bad month. Pesky no-see-ums can also be a problem. The trail's steady rise in elevation is occasionally broken by steeper sections. At the top of one sharp hill, hikers are treated to a high-level view of the Drinkwater Valley.

One possible campsite (within an easy day's hike to Della Falls) is at a gravel bar on Drinkwater Creek, close to an area of large boulders and rocks. Beware of sudden rises of the creek. Watch out for a prolific plant in this region, the Devil's Club. The needle-like spines of this plant can cause a severe allergic reaction for some people. At the second major bridge, if the weather co-operates, you'll see Della Falls in the distance. This is about three-quarters of the way in. Just ahead is what many consider the trail's toughest stretch, a rockslide zone.

The best upper valley camping spot is at the old sawmill site, near the start of the Love Lake Trail, a switchbacking route that climbs the steep slope on Love Creek's west side. At several points you can gaze across the valley at Della Falls. Farther along, experienced climbers can follow the routes to Mount Septimus and Mount Rousseau. *Hiking Trails III* (VITIS) has detailed maps and trail information on many backpacking and climbing routes in this region.

Continue upstream through more patches of Devil's Club to the base of Della Falls. The waters tumble 440 m over three ledges before fanning out into satiny ribbons at the rocky bottom. You only see the lower cascade from the base. The cold spray is welcome relief on a hot day, but protect your camera.

CONTACTS

- Ark Resort: 250-723-2657
- BC Forest Service (South Island Forest District): 250-724-9205
- BC Parks (Strathcona District): 250-954-4600
- MacMillan Bloedel (Sproat Operations): 250-720-4100

MAPS/GUIDES

- BC Forest Service Port Alberni District Recreation Map
- BC Parks Strathcona Provincial Park brochure
- MacMillan Bloedel Recreation and Logging Road Guide to TFL 44
- National Topographical Series: 92F/5 Bedwell River (1:50,000); 92F/6 Great Central Lake (1:50,000); 92F/7 Horne Lake (1:50,000)
- Provincial Map: 92F/SW Kennedy Lake (1:125,000)
- *Adventuring in British Columbia* (Nanton/Simpson/Douglas & McIntyre)
- *Adventuring Around Vancouver Island* (Lebrecht/Noppe/Greystone)
- *Hiking Trails III* (VITIS)

NEAREST SERVICES

Port Alberni area.

Trip 7:
The Willemar Lake Region

IN BRIEF

The Willemar Lake area is an excellent destination for anglers, wilderness campers and paddlers. Willemar Lake is the gateway to the Forbush lake chain at the headwaters of the Puntledge River. A portage trail connects the Forbush lakes with Willemar Lake, although some people line up the river rather than portaging. At the head of Forbush Lake, the Puntledge Valley Trail leads to stands of giant Douglas fir, within Strathcona Provincial Park.

ACCESS

From Port Alberni: Take logging mainlines from the foot of Great Central Lake to the Willemar Lake access road, near Comox Lake's south end. From Courtenay: An industrial mainline follows the west side of Comox Lake to the Willemar cut-off, about 5 km south of the Cruickshank River bridge. (See Section Two: Trip 10 for details on the logging roads from Port Alberni to Courtenay.) Gravel mainlines are in good to fair shape. There are steep hills and rough sections. Public access on some arteries is restricted to between 6 p.m. and 6 a.m. weekdays. Best times to travel are on weekends and holidays. Call ahead for current road and hauling information. The area is subject to seasonal fire closures.

DESCRIPTION

The Willemar Lake region, located just south of Comox Lake, nestles in the rugged terrain near Rough and Tumble Mountain and the Comox Gap. The Willemar Lake access road is about 5 km south of the Cruickshank River bridge, along the Alberni/Courtenay backroads. Roads at Comox Lake's south end have been improved of late with new culverts and bridges to facilitate area logging. (See Section Two: Trip 10.) The Willemar Lake access road winds 3 km along the Puntledge River's west side to Willemar Lake. After prolonged heavy rains watch out for muddy sections and deep waterholes.

There are a few user-maintained campsites and a natural boat launch at Willemar Lake. To reach them, bear right at a fork as you approach the lake. The short left fork dead-ends at the Puntledge River. An unsafe bridge has been removed, but a single timber support remains, as do a number of

Rugged mountains border Willemar Lake.

walk-in campsites on the far side of the river. In the heat of the summer even the chilling glacial waters of the Puntledge River feel good. The natural beauty of wilderness camping areas like Willemar Lake is easily tarnished by careless campers. Don't leave behind any litter. Remember to leave your campsite tidy for the next visitor.

Hikers can follow the old road beyond the bridge site and climb a steep western slope on Mount Hennessy. Highlights are several viewpoints west over Willemar Lake and its mountain-glacier backdrop and a waterfall (more easily heard than seen) on Nimnim Creek. This stream drains Nimnim Lake and cascades down to Willemar Lake's east side.

Willemar Lake curves around the base of Rough and Tumble Mountain and is affected by funnelled winds that surge through the sheer topography to create rough boating conditions. Keep an eye on the weather at all times, as Willemar Lake's moods vary. A calm lake may turn windswept in minutes. During severe storms, waves of 2 m in height have been reported on neighbouring Comox Lake (1,620 ha).

Scenic Willemar Lake (82 ha) contains cutthroat trout and also Dolly Varden (char) and kokanee salmon. Spring and fall anglers have good success utilizing small spinners, spoons, bait and bobber or trolling a wet fly. Anglers may find action near the creekmouths, using a shrimp imitation on a sinking line. Best fishing occurs in the spring and fall. Sunset is a preferred time to cast out for the trout. Be precise with your aim; a slight misjudgement may result in a snagged lure or hook. Both the shoreline bushes and the lake's floating deadheads have voracious appetites for terminal tackle.

There is a small wilderness campsite (best suited for small dome tents) where the Puntledge River enters the lake's west end. Rogue Willemar Lake deadheads sometimes pile up in this area. Near the Puntledge River mouth look out for logs that are swept around by incoming currents. Standing waves can develop at the rivermouth when contrary wind-induced wave trains meet the Puntledge River's incoming current.

For the Forbush lake chain, paddle up the Puntledge River shallows. At times the current may negate any paddling efforts. In drier summer months, paddlers must line up parts of the channel. If the Puntledge River is too high for travel or you simply don't want to line up-river, use the 200-m portage trail, on the left bank a short distance upstream from Willemar Lake. At the west end of Forbush Lake, near a wilderness campsite bordered by alder, you'll find the start of the Puntledge River Trail. The trail (marked by the Comox District Mountaineering Club) leads along the upper Puntledge River to forests of bigleaf maple, magnificent stands of Douglas fir and a waterfall, all within a remote corner of Strathcona Park.

CONTACTS

- BC Forest Service (South Island Forest District): 250-724-9205
- MacMillan Bloedel (Sproat Operations): 250-720-4100
- TimberWest (Oyster River Operations): 250-287-7979

MAPS/GUIDES

- BC Forest Service Port Alberni District Recreation Map
- Comox Valley Map (Comox Valley Chamber of Commerce/Comox Valley Ground Search and Rescue Association)
- MacMillan Bloedel Recreation and Logging Road Guide to TFL 44
- TimberWest Courtenay Logging Road Guide
- National Topographical Series: 92F/11 Forbidden Plateau (1:50,000); 92F/6 Great Central Lake (1:50,000)
- Provincial Maps: 92F/NW Buttle Lake (1:125,000); 92F/SW Kennedy Lake (1:125,000)
- *Hiking the Ancient Forests of British Columbia and Washington* (Stoltmann/Lone Pine)
- *Hiking Trails III* (VITIS)

NEAREST SERVICES

Courtenay; Port Alberni.

Trip 8:
Hiking Forbidden Plateau

IN BRIEF

Many first-time backpackers start out with hikes in the Forbidden Plateau region of Strathcona Provincial Park. Visitors can day-hike in the sub-alpine area or overnight at designated park campsites. Well-defined trails lead to fishing lakes, spectacular mountain scenery and seasonal displays of wildflowers.

ACCESS

To the Paradise Meadows trailhead: Turn off Highway 19 and follow the Mount Washington signposts onto the much-improved Mount Washington Road, that intersects TimberWest's Duncan Bay Main just outside of Courtenay. (See Section Two: Trip 11.) To the Forbidden Plateau (Wood Mountain) trailhead: From Highway 19 follow the signs to the Forbidden Plateau (Wood Mountain) ski lodge. The roads are paved up to the ski areas and trailheads. There are some steep hills and narrow sections.

DESCRIPTION

The trails on Forbidden Plateau, part of Strathcona Provincial Park, are Vancouver Island's most popular hiking destination. For backpackers and naturalists, Forbidden Plateau offers a variety of destinations accessed via well-defined hiking trails. The area is close to Courtenay and provides novice hikers with a place to test his or her skills on day hikes or overnighters into sub-alpine terrain. Seasoned hikers make longer journeys into alpine meadows or up various mountain and ridge routes. The trail up Mount Albert Edward (2,093 m), the highest peak on the plateau, offers stunning views.

There are two trailheads for the Forbidden Plateau area and both are accessed from Highway 19 near Courtenay. It's around 19 km to the Forbidden Plateau (Wood Mountain) ski lodge and the Becher Trail that winds in to Slingshot and McKenzie meadows, near Douglas and McKenzie lakes, each with wilderness campsites. At this point hikers are about halfway in to Kwai Lake, centrally located on the plateau. Allow at least seven hours' hiking time to Kwai Lake via the Becher Trail.

Mount Washington's Paradise Meadows trailhead begins near the nordic skiing lodge (about 18 km from the base of Mount Washington Road). From here it's less than an hour up to the plateau. Area trails (used by cross-country skiers over the winter months) are well marked by BC Parks and the Comox District Mountaineering Club. Many sections consist of wood chips. A short loop trail runs through the meadows. From Paradise Meadows two routes climb up to Lake Helen Mackenzie. One goes by Battleship Lake to the junction with a trail that winds along Lake Helen McKenzie's north shore. South of Battleship Lake, the trail passes Kooso and Lady lakes to several meadows and tarns (small mountain lakes) en route to Croteau Lake. A trail climbs nearby Mount Elma.

Beyond Croteau Lake is beautiful Murray Meadows. Remember to stay on the trails at all times to minimize damage to fragile vegetation. Near the end of Murray Meadows, you can cut south onto the Becher Trail and then take the cut-off for Mariwood Lake. This picturesque lake is dotted with tiny islands. Less than half an hour beyond Mariwood Lake is the Lake Beautiful region, consisting of various-sized lakes and ponds. A waterfall tumbles over a rocky ledge into Lake Beautiful. The trail continues southwest to a Cruickshank Canyon viewpoint. Legends tell of hairy giants emerging from Mount Albert Edward ice caves to toss victims off the sheer cliffs into the maw of Cruickshank Canyon.

At the Becher Trail junction, near Murray Meadows, swing west for Kwai Lake and one of three wilderness campsites within Forbidden Plateau's designated core area. BC Parks levies overnight camping fees at these sites. Check with BC Parks (Strathcona District) for current updates. No fires are permitted within the core area. Kwai Lake and the two other camping locations (Lake Helen MacKenzie and Circlet Lake) have pit toilets.

Visitors who base at Circlet Lake's designated campsite wait for favourable weather before they tackle the challenging hike up Mount Albert Edward. The Mount Albert Edward route (marked by rocks and ribbons) goes straight up. A higher plateau offers much gentler elevation changes than those on the first section of the trail. Fog and clouds can engulf plateau trails. It is easy to become disoriented and lose one's bearings. Knowledgeable use of compass and altimeter may be required in these conditions.

From Circlet Lake you can day-hike to Moat Lake. Many hikers pack collapsible rods to sample Forbidden Plateau's rainbow trout fishing. The larger lakes are the ones to try. Beyond Moat Lake, experienced hikers can follow a route that crosses Mount Frink and hooks into the Circlet Lake/ Mount Albert Edward route. Other nearby hiking spots are Hairtrigger Lake (one of my favourite day-hiking destinations, on a ridge west of Kwai Lake) and Amphitheatre Lake, up in behind McPhee and Circlet lakes.

You can return to Paradise Meadows via Lake Helen Mackenzie's west

Small dome tents are ideal for forbidden plateau hikes.

side and complete a Forbidden Plateau loop. From the Hairtrigger/Kwai Lake junction the trail passes the Park Ranger station and several meadows before dropping suddenly near Mount Brooks. At Lake Helen Mackenzie cut northeast for the trailhead, or take the route that curves along Lake Helen Mackenzie to its northeast end and a beautiful wilderness campsite, close to Battleship Lake. This location is a popular weekend camping spot.

For first-time hikers, Forbidden Plateau trails provide relatively safe access to alpine or sub-alpine regions. If possible, travel with someone who knows the area. Consult the comprehensive BC Parks *Strathcona Provincial Park* pamphlet prior to your hike. The information includes trail distances and approximate hiking times. You may encounter striking contrasts in plateau weather conditions. Warm weather is ideal for a swim in many high-altitude lakes. When rain and fog swirl into the region, a pesky bug problem lessens, but the mists also obliterate the outstanding mountain vistas. Be sure to carry insect repellent and an antidote for bites. Mosquitoes, no-see-ums, black flies and deer flies are problem pests.

Camp only in designated park campsites and secure your food carefully at night; marauding mice are common. When cooking in camp be ready for sudden whiskey jack invasions. Carry and use a portable stove. Please remember to practise low-impact camping. Leave no litter behind when you leave. Everyone's efforts are needed to ensure Forbidden Plateau's fragile alpine and sub-alpine beauty.

CONTACTS

- BC Parks (Strathcona District): 250-954-4600

MAPS/GUIDES

- BC Parks Strathcona Provincial Park brochure
- Comox Valley Map (Comox Valley Chamber of Commerce/Comox Valley Ground Search and Rescue Association)
- National Topographical Series: 92F/11 Forbidden Plateau (1:50,000)
- *Adventuring Around Vancouver Island* (Lebrecht/Noppe/Greystone)
- *Hiking Trails III* (VITIS)

NEAREST SERVICES

Courtenay area.

Trip 9:
The Sayward Forest Canoe Route

IN BRIEF

A series of twelve Sayward Forest lakes connected by BC Forest Service portage trails comprise the Sayward Forest Canoe Route, northwest of Campbell River. Should you choose to paddle only part of the complete circuit, you can access the 47.2-km route at several put-in and take-out points.

ACCESS

From the junction of Highway 19, Highway 19A and Highway 28, near the Campbell River bridge, stay north on Highway 19; continue 14.5 km to MacMillan Bloedel's Menzies (Salmon River) Main, the gateway to the Sayward Forest. (See Section One: Trip 8). Head west on Menzies Main for 9.5 km to the Morton Lake Provincial Park access road. Swing right and continue 6.5 km to the park and the nearby Mohun Lake boat launch. (See Section Two: Trip 12.) Area BC Forest Service and logging roads are in seasonally good to fair shape. Active hauling may be frequent on some mainlines.

DESCRIPTION

The Sayward Forest Canoe Route, a 47.2-km loop of lakes, rivers and portage trails in the Sayward Forest, is an excellent choice for paddling adventures. And you don't have to complete the whole circuit. Water access points are many along area backroads, and there are countless BC Forest Service user-maintained wilderness campsites to choose from.

The Sayward Forest Canoe Route was established by the BCFS in 1977-78. They constructed a series of portage trails to link various lakes: Mohun, Twin, Amor, Surprise, Brewster, Gray; Whymper, Fry, (Lower) Campbell, Gosling, Higgins and Lawier. Some portages follow old logging roads and railbeds. (Decades ago the Sayward Forest was ribboned with logging rail lines.) A few new trails were punched through to create the paddling link. Portages (indicated by signposts and orange markers or ribbons) total about 7 km in length and are seasonally maintained and cleared. All but two are wheelable (they are suitable for canoe wheel attachments that make portaging easier).

The BCFS recommends you begin the canoe loop at the boat launch on Mohun Lake's upper east shore. This popular put-in point, close to Morton Lake Provincial Park, has a large parking area. From Campbell River head north on Highway 19 for 14.5 km to MacMillan Bloedel's Menzies (Salmon River) Main, the primary route to the Sayward Forest. (See Section One: Trip 8.) Continue west on the mainline for 9.5 km to the Morton Lake Provincial Park access road. It's 6.5 km from here to the campsite. (See Section Two: Trip 12.)

From the Mohun Lake boat launch, head in a counter-clockwise direction to take advantage of current flow in the river stretches. The second-longest portage trail, and one with some elevation gain, links Mohun Lake with the Twin Lake swamps, a series of marsh and ponds connected to Twin Lake. If area beavers are active, there will be less portaging in this section. You can reach the BCFS two-site Twin Lake campsite from Highway 19 via Mohun Lake West Road. (See Section One: Trip 8.)

From Twin Lake, portage over the hump to Amor Lake. There are two water-access-only campsites here (Sterling Island and Sterling Beach). The Mister Canoehead campsite, in a bay on Amor Lake's south end, can be reached by water or the portage trail from Surprise Lake. Travellers can turn off Highway 19, near Roberts Lake, to wind in to Amor Lake from the north. Bumpy secondary roads lead to a BCFS recreation site, on the lake's southwest arm. Parking is limited here. (See Section One: Trip 8.)

Surprise Lake sits just behind a rise south of Amor Lake. Paddle to Surprise Lake's south end and the start of the longest portage (over 2 km) on the paddling route. Some sections are subject to seasonal flooding. The trail follows an old spur to Brewster Lake's northeast tip. The BCFS recommends paddlers keep to the portage trail and avoid the temptation to follow the Long Lake Main logging road. It's over 5 km from the Brewster Lake put-in to the log jam and the logging road bridge at the lake's south end. Here there are a number of BCFS recreation sites. (See Section Two: Trip 12.) A short portage may be required around the log jam. Watch out for "wrap-around trestle."

You can paddle, portage or line from Brewster Lake, through Gray Lake to Whymper Lake. You don't have to be a whitewater expert to navigate the four sets of rapids (two above Gray Lake, one between Gray Lake and Whymper Lake and the last just north of Fry Lake). Adequate water levels are required. Over the summer, low water in some stream sections may require lining. Scout ahead carefully for boulders, sweepers and old railway pilings that might pose dangers. If there's any doubt as to your capabilities or water conditions, play it safe and portage around the dubious chutes. Log jams at Gray Lake's south end may force paddlers onto the portages.

There are many access points along the Sayward Forest Canoe Route.

Just before the stream widens into Fry Lake, the canoe route goes under the road bridge near the junction of Gray Lake Road and Campbell Lake Road. You can access this intersection (and the BCFS Orchard Meadow Recreation Site on Fry Lake's north side) from Highway 28, via Strathcona Dam. Some travellers venture in along Campbell Lake's north shore. (See Section Two: Trip 12.) Take care when paddling near the Fry Lake snags. A narrow waterway (somewhat prone to bathtub chop) links Fry Lake with Campbell Lake. Watch for submerged stumps in both lakes.

Campbell Lake is the largest lake in the circuit. Be aware of regular water release from Strathcona Dam that induces lake current. Campbell Lake, like Brewster, Gosling and Mohun lakes, can become windswept very quickly. Keep an eye on the weather and stay close to shore in rougher conditions. Parallel Campbell Lake's northwest shore to pass a number of BCFS recreation sites, plenty of fishing spots and shoreline coves. It's a little under 8.5 km to the Gosling Bay wilderness campsite.

The BCFS Gosling Bay Recreation Site, west of Loveland Bay Provincial Park, has five campsites and a natural boat launch on a rocky lakefront. From Gosling Bay take the one-kilometre portage (a steady climb on an old road) to Gosling Lake. The four-site wilderness campsite on the lake's southern fringe has a small float. Remember to watch the winds when you head north on Gosling Lake.

At Gosling Lake's north end, portage across Camp 5 (Brewster Lake) Road for the swamp channel to tiny Higgins Lake. Watch for deadheads in Higgins Lake. Another portage at the north end of the lake leads to Lawier Lake. From Lawier Lake's tip, the portage route follows an old road to MacBlo's Menzies Main, close to the tiny Mohun Lake Recreation Site, about 13 km west of Highway 19. Cross the mainline for Mohun Lake. The paddle up Mohun Lake to the starting point at the east-shore boat launch is one of the circuit's longest. Some paddlers camp on the island at Mohun Lake's south end.

The BCFS regularly updates the *Sayward Forest Canoe Route Recreation Map*. This informative brochure has details on area campsites, safety hints and paddling/portaging distances and approximate times. You can pick up a copy at its Campbell River District office or local tourist information centres.

CONTACTS

- BC Forest Service (Campbell River): 250-286-9300
- MacMillan Bloedel (Menzies Operations): 250-287-5000

MAPS/GUIDES

- BC Forest Service Campbell River Forest District Recreation Map
- BC Forest Service Sayward Forest Canoe Route Recreation Map
- Campbell River Search and Rescue Society Logging and Highway Road Map
- MacMillan Bloedel Campbell River/Sayward Recreation and Logging Road Guide
- National Topographical Series: 92K/4 Brewster Lake (1:50,000); 92K/3 Quadra Island (1:50,000)
- *Adventuring Around Vancouver Island* (Lebrecht/Noppe/Greystone)
- *Adventuring in British Columbia* (Nanton/Simpson/Douglas & McIntyre)

NEAREST SERVICES

Campbell River area.

Trip 10:
Schoen Lake Provincial Park

IN BRIEF

Schoen Lake Provincial Park is known for its spectacular mountains, meadows, waterfalls and rushing streams. The rugged peaks of Mount Schoen (1,862 m) tower over beautiful Schoen Lake. You can camp at the lake's west-end campsite and test the fishing, or boat or paddle to the eastern shore for wilderness hiking on the Nisnak Lake Trail. This challenging route winds down to Schoen Lake from a starting point along MacMillan Bloedel's Upper Adam Road.

ACCESS

To the Nisnak Lake trailhead: Just under 10 km from the Sayward Junction, turn right off Highway 19 (near Keta Lake) and backtrack across the highway on the logging road bridge. (No left turns are permitted from the highway.) (See Section One: Trip 9.) Head south on Upper Adam Road for 21.4 km to the parking area on the left of the mainline. Upper Adam Road is in seasonally good to fair shape. There are steep hills. Cable gates may be encountered in some areas. Active logging may restrict public entry. Check with MacMillan Bloedel for current access restrictions.

To the Schoen Lake Provincial Park campsite: Take Highway 19 about 54.5 km beyond the Sayward junction to the signposted Schoen Lake/Mount Cain turn, just less than 11 km east of Woss. (See Section One: Trip 9.) Follow the signs about 14 km to the park campsite. The park access road is in good to fair shape. Turnarounds are limited, particularly closer to the campsite. The route is subject to seasonal fire closures, washouts and snow blockages.

DESCRIPTION

Schoen Lake Provincial Park is one of my favourite places on Vancouver Island. The area has good fishing, paddling and boating, wilderness hiking and stunning mountain scenery. You can hike in to Schoen Lake via the Nisnak Lake Trail. Backpacking anglers head to Nisnak Lake (less than a hour away) and isolated casting spots beneath Mount Schoen's imposing five peaks. The rough trail runs through pristine sub-alpine meadows and stands of old-growth forest to a wilderness campsite on Schoen Lake's eastern fringe.

To reach the Nisnak Lake trailhead, head north from the Sayward Junction on Highway 19. A little under 10 km from the Sayward turn (just beyond the Keta Lake rest area), Upper Adam Road crosses the highway. (See Section One: Trip 9.) No left turns are allowed off Highway 19 here, so cut right and double back over the highway on the logging road bridge. Call MacMillan Bloedel's Kelsey Bay Operations beforehand about access restrictions on Upper Adam Road.

The road enters old growth near the eastern fringe of Schoen Lake Provincial Park. When park boundaries were finalized in 1977, provision was made to allow two logging roads within the park. MacBlo's Upper Adam Road was punched through in the early 1980s to connect with Moakwa Main. A Canadian Forest Products road skirts Schoen Lake's southwest corner. Constructed to access timber in Schoen Creek Valley, the narrow right-of-way is high above the lake and can't be seen from the water. The placement of the road leaves intact an old fire trail through old growth closer to lakeside.

A small clearing on the left at km 21.4 serves as a parking area for the Nisnak Lake Trail. This trail, best suited for experienced hikers, is hard to locate at its start and on the Nisnak Lake approaches. The 7-km route leads from Upper Adam Road, through the park's sub-alpine meadows, alongside Nisnak Lake and down the Schoen Creek Valley to three wilderness campsites in a cedar grove at Schoen Lake's east end. The trail is infrequently maintained. Hikers should be prepared for torrential rains, wet conditions near the meadows, deadfall, slippery logs at tricky creek crossings and some strenuous hiking. Negotiating an extensive alder slide on Nisnak Creek's south side can be tiring for some.

The first part is flagged through to the meadows. At times, you may have to spread out to locate tree ribbons that sporadically mark the route. It's best to tackle the Nisnak Lake Trail with someone who is familiar with the area and conditions. That way you'll have more time to enjoy your hike instead of trying to figure out where you are.

At Nisnak Meadows, behind two wetland tarns, a captivating waterfall tumbles down Mount Schoen's South Peak. To get nearer to the waterfall requires a 2-km climb via elk trails in the drainage route. Beyond the meadows, closer to Nisnak Lake, it's easy to lose the trail. Patience and good balance are needed when carrying a full pack around (and sometimes on) slick deadfall. Some hikers wear caulked boots. In the mature forest surrounding Nisnak Lake, the prime camping spot (only large enough for a small dome tent) lies near a small stream on the north shore.

The trail continues around the end of the lake to cross Nisnak Creek. As it begins a descent to Schoen Lake, the route becomes more obvious. Beyond the big alder slide, almost 200 m wide, the trail veers away from the stream to eventually emerge on Schoen Lake's northeastern shore and a wilderness campsite in a cedar grove. (Paddlers and boaters access this site from the park's camping area at Schoen Lake's west end, 5 km away.) Some hikers continue north from the cedar-grove campsite on an unimproved route (once a trapline) to the Compton Creek Valley. *Hiking Trails III* (VITIS) contains details on the Nisnak Lake Trail and other park hiking routes.

To reach Schoen Lake Provincial Park's established campground, on Schoen Lake's west end, watch for the signposted cut-off on Highway 19, about 54.5 km beyond the Sayward Junction. RVs and larger trailered boats are not advised on the 13.7-km route, which narrows and roughens closer to Schoen Lake. Two creek crossings (where new bridges now stand) are subject to seasonal washouts. Fire closures or snow may also block the road.

Reset your vehicle's trip meter to zero at the highway cut-off and follow the signs. Just under the 2-km mark, keep right for the park. A little over the 5-km mark the road splits. A left climbs up to Mount Cain Regional Park, a winter skiing area and popular summer hiking destination. For more information on Mount Cain Regional Park, contact the Regional District of Mount Waddington (Port McNeill) at 250-956-3301. Keep right at the fork and continue another 8.5 km along the Davie River's north side for the Schoen Lake Provincial Park campsite.

The camping area has ten user-maintained campsites, pit toilets and a rough boat launch. Schoen Lake (242 ha) contains cutthroat and rainbow trout. Even when the fish don't bite, the mountain views make it a delight just to be on the water. Campsite quiet hours are between 10 p.m. and 7 a.m. A signpost and map detail the park and area hiking routes. Remember that park trails are not maintained. Use them at your own risk. One trail starts near the campsite and crosses a Davie River log jam to follow an old fire trail along the south shore of Schoen Lake to Schoen Creek. Expect deadfalls and muddy sections. The route is hard to pick up from the campsite. Markers and ribbons indicate the trail, yet it's still easy to lose your way farther up the Schoen Creek Valley. Some visitors canoe, kayak or boat 5 km to the cedar-grove wilderness campsite at Schoen Lake's northeast end and hike up to Nisnak Meadows. Anyone planning a foray by water should note that the waters of Schoen Lake are often quite rough.

CONTACTS

- BC Forest Service (Port McNeill): 250-956-5000
- BC Parks (Strathcona District): 250-954-4600
- Canadian Forest Products (Woss): 250-281-2300
- MacMillan Bloedel (Kelsey Bay Operations): 250-282-3100

MAPS/GUIDES

- BC Forest Service Port McNeill Forest District Recreation Map
- Canadian Forest Products Englewood Logging Division (TFL 37) Recreation Map
- MacMillan Bloedel Campbell River/Sayward Recreation and Logging Road Guide
- National Topographical Series: 92L/8 Adam River (1:50,000); 92L/1 Schoen Lake (1:50,000)
- Provincial Map: 92L Alert Bay (1:250,000)
- *Adventuring Around Vancouver Island* (Lebrecht/Noppe/Greystone)
- *Hiking Trails III* (VITIS)
- *Parks of British Columbia and The Yukon* (Paquet/Maia Publishing)

NEAREST SERVICES

Sayward; Woss.

Trip 11: Paddling the Tahsish/Kwois

IN BRIEF

A trip to Tahsish/Kwois, now a provincial park, entails west-coast inlet and river travel. Experienced wilderness paddlers can journey up the Tahsish River (some sections must be lined or portaged) to the confluence with Kwois Creek. Canada's tallest known western hemlock (75.6 m) is located nearby. Some area spruce trees rival those of the Carmanah Valley. Logging roads, near Nimpkish Lake's south end, lead about 47 km from Highway 19 to the Tahsish Inlet launch point.

ACCESS

Take the Zeballos turn on Highway 19, 21 km north of Woss. (See Section One: Trip 10.) Gravel mainlines are in good to fair shape. Be prepared for narrow sections, steep hills and sharp rocks. Heavy industrial traffic may be encountered. Call the logging companies prior to your trip for the safest public travel times. Roads may be subject to seasonal fire closures.

DESCRIPTION

A paddling destination that still retains its sense of isolation lies at the head of Tahsish Inlet, a Kyuquot Sound coastal indentation. It's easy to confuse Tahsish with Tahsis. Both names come from the aboriginal *tashee*, which translates as "trail" or "path." Tahsis sits at the head of Tahsis Inlet, on Nootka Island's east side. The Tahsish/Kwois region is to the northwest, near Fair Harbour.

In 1862, the first recorded crossing of Vancouver Island by a European began at the Tahsish estuary. As part of a coastal survey headed by Captain George H. Richards of HMS *Hecate*, Lieutenant Phillip Hankin and Surgeon-Lieutenant Charles Wood set off to explore the Tahsish Valley. Led by Native guides, they followed a Kyuquot elk-trail trading route to the Nimpkish Valley. The first expedition was halted by surging high waters and impossible river crossings. The second attempt via Atluck, Huson, Anutz and Nimpkish lakes to Fort Rupert was a success.

Woss-based Canadian Forest Products has logged in the upper Tahsish Valley; TimberWest has worked along the Artlish River. From Highway

19, 47 km of Canfor and TimberWest logging roads access a TimberWest industrial site on Tahsish Inlet, near the Artlish River mouth. Travel these narrow routes after weekday working hours (6 a.m. to 6 p.m.) to avoid industrial traffic. Call the logging companies beforehand for current hauling information and best public access times.

Take the Zeballos turn (on Highway 19, between Port McNeill and Woss) and reset your vehicle's trip meter to zero. Just over the 9-km mark, turn right onto Atluck Road, and follow the signs for Atluck Lake and the user-maintained campsite co-managed by the BC Forest Service and Canfor. (For more information on area backroads and fishing and camping destinations, see Section One: Trip 10.)

Continue on Atluck Road to follow Atluck Lake's north side to lakehead (km 19). Just past Welch Road the mainline splits (km 20.5). Atluck Road swings to the right. Keep left on Artlish Road to climb a steep switchback. Continue along the north fork of the Artlish River to pass Apollo Road. In the lower Artlish River Valley the route goes through stands of old-growth forest broken by cutblocks, and parallels the Artlish River to Tahsish Inlet. Deep river pools near the estuary are a highlight. A little under the 47-km mark you'll reach the gravel boat launch and dock at a TimberWest industrial site, opposite a range of mountains called False Ears.

The distance from the launch point to the head of Tahsish Inlet is approximately 5 km. Strong winds can surge up the channel and whip up the whitecaps. When contrary winds battle currents from the Tahsish and Artlish rivers, inlet waters are at their worst. There is a broad shallows at the Artlish rivermouth and many large stumps. Be weather-wise and time your saltwater journey carefully. Carry a fresh water supply and treat any drinking and cooking water obtained from creeks and streams.

There are few wilderness camping spots on these shores. You'll find one or two possible wilderness tent sites at the head of Tahsish Inlet, east of the First Nations Reserve. Time your visit to coincide with the lowest high-tide cycle of the month. Refer to the *Canadian Tide and Current Tables: Vol. 6* to calculate inlet tides. Remember to choose your tidal-zone campsite wisely. Practise low-impact camping and leave no evidence of your stay. Build any fires below the high-tide mark. The head of the inlet is a great place to watch eagles, seals and loons.

From the Tahsish River estuary you can hike up the Tahsish River flood plain on riparian-zone game trails, or paddle and portage upriver through a series of navigable stretches and deep pools to the confluence with Kwois Creek, the Tahsish's primary tributary. The lower Tahsish Valley is a favourite wintering range for Roosevelt elk and deer. Each fall black bears and eagles throng to the estuary. The Tahsish River, top salmonid producer on

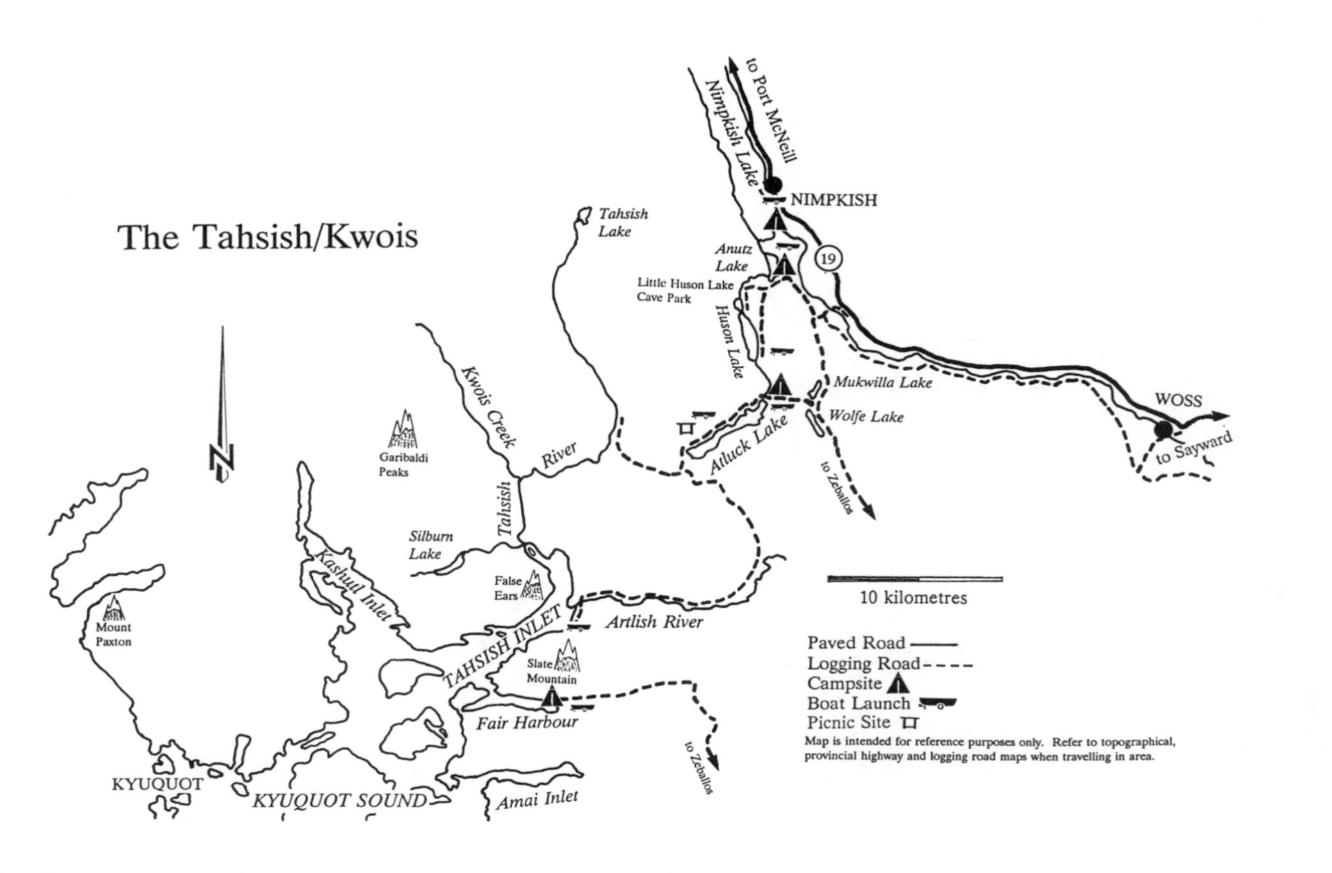
The Tahsish/Kwois
to Port McNeill
Nimpkish Lake
NIMPKISH
19
Tahsish Lake
Anutz Lake
Little Huson Lake Cave Park
Huson Lake
Mukwilla Lake
Wolfe Lake
Atluck Lake
to Zeballos
WOSS
to Sayward
Kwois Creek
River
Garibaldi Peaks
Tahsish
Silburn Lake
False Ears
Kashutl Inlet
Mount Paxton
TAHSISH INLET
Artlish River
Slate Mountain
Fair Harbour
to Zeballos
KYUQUOT
KYUQUOT SOUND
Amai Inlet
10 kilometres
Paved Road
Logging Road
Campsite
Boat Launch
Picnic Site
Map is intended for reference purposes only. Refer to topographical, provincial highway and logging road maps when travelling in area.

A journey to the Tahsish/Kwois requires river and inlet travel.

northwest Vancouver Island, contains cutthroat and rainbow trout and a small run of summer steelhead. The river gravel beds are the spawning grounds for five species of salmon.

From the estuary the Tahsish River splits in two and rounds the river island that marks the boundary of a 64-ha ecological reserve. About half a kilometre up the right fork, shallow water and a tangle of fallen trees block the way. The left channel passes old trees with immense roots that plunge into the estuary's tidal waters. Giant cedar, fir, spruce and hemlock, many centuries old, fringe the riverbank. Tackle this section on a flood tide to take advantage of higher water levels. The tide backs up the Tahsish River for quite a distance. Eventually a gravel bar halts paddling progress. Portage over to the main river channel, just below the mouth of Silburn Creek. Out of sight of inlet logging, visitors are surrounded by virgin forests and the murmur of the river, giving the illusion of stepping back in time.

River travellers should note that the Tahsish River and Kwois Creek flood plains are extremely unstable and subject to flash flooding. Most of the river-valley floor is under water during wet weather. Be ready for sopping feet from lining through rocky channels and pushing the canoe around gravel bars. Some paddlers don neoprene booties. On hot, windless summer days, biting flies haunt the river valley. Pay particular attention to the persistent presence of "old green eyes," the horsefly, and its close cousin, the deerfly.

Below the confluence with Kwois Creek the Tahsish River swerves to create a large jade pool. It's a pristine setting for fly casting. The surface of a slow back eddy can be alive with swarms of bugs. Allow a three-hour paddle and portage from tidewater to the Tahsish/Kwois river junction, but conditions will vary. Farther upstream, sheer canyons and impeding waterfalls geographically cut off the unlogged lower Tahsish River Valley (and the adjoining Silburn and Kwois watersheds) with the already-logged upper valley. Close to where the creek and river join, the forest harbours large spruce and one of Canada's largest known western hemlock (75.6 m).

CONTACTS

- BC Forest Service (Campbell River): 250-286-9300
- BC Forest Service (Port McNeill): 250-956-5000
- Canadian Forest Products (Woss): 250-281-2300
- North Island Forestry Centre 250-956-3844
- TimberWest (Beaver Cove Division): 250-928-3023

MAPS/GUIDES

- BC Forest Service Campbell River Forest District Recreation Map
- Canadian Forest Products Englewood Logging Division (TFL 37) Recreation Map
- Pacific Forest Products Recreation and Logging Road Guide to the Forest Lands of West Vancouver Island (depicts logging roads west of Atluck Lake to Tahsish Inlet)
- National Topographical Series: 92L/3 Kyuquot (1:50,000); 92L/7 Nimpkish (1:50,000); 92L/2 Woss Lake (1:50,000)
- Provincial Map: 92L Alert Bay (1:250,000)
- *Canadian Tide and Current Tables: Vol. 6* (Canadian Hydrographic Service)

NEAREST SERVICES

Nimpkish; Port McNeill; Woss.

Trip 12:
Raft Cove Provincial Park

IN BRIEF

Raft Cove Provincial Park's sandy west-coast beach and spectacular seascapes near the mouth of the Macjack River attract many hikers. The majority of visitors day-hike to the beach; some carry in overnight gear and camp on the beach. The short but rugged 1.2-km route to the beach is usually slippery and muddy.

ACCESS

From Port Hardy, follow the logging roads for 46 km to Holberg. Continue on San Josef Main to Ronning Main, a little over 12 km west of Holberg. (See Section Two: Trip 16.) Cut left onto Ronning Main for about 10 km to Branch 700. This spur dead-ends at the parking area near the Raft Cove trailhead. Ronning and San Josef mainlines are active hauling roads. On weekdays be prepared to back up to roadside pull-outs to avoid off-road logging trucks. Check ahead with Western Forest Products for safest travel times. The mainlines are in seasonally good to fair shape. Watch for sharp rocks. Secondary roads may require a 4 x 4 or high-slung vehicle. Deactivated roads may be impassable.

DESCRIPTION

Raft Cove Provincial Park, located south of San Josef Bay, was established in 1990 and includes 405 ha of forest donated by Western Forest Products. Raft Cove features a wild, exposed sandy beach at the Macjack River estuary. Cape Palmerston's rocky headlands dominate the beach's north end. Commerell Point's jagged isthmus lies to the south, close to the Macjack rivermouth.

Early Cape Scott pioneers (among them Willie Hecht and the Boytle family) settled in the Raft Cove area in 1913. A trail ran up the coast to Cape Palmerston and northeast to San Josef Bay. A second route headed east to the San Josef wagon road. The majority of homesteaders eventually left. Willie Hecht moved to Holberg, but his old trapping cabin still guards the Macjack River's south side.

Holberg residents and area loggers were familiar with Raft Cove prior to the creation of Raft Cove Provincial Park. A beach access was flagged through from a 1984 cutblock spur near Ronning Creek. The route went through boglands and quagmires and could prove very muddy. Slippery deadfall made caulked boots essential for hiking safety. At the Macjack River you could look for an old canoe and paddle downstream to the beach or wait for low tide and hike down the river. Hikers also faced two tricky river crossings. A second challenging hiking route off Ronning Main parallelled Graham Creek to the rocks at the beach's north end. Today, the designated park trail begins at the end of Branch 700, a Ronning Main spur.

To reach Raft Cove Provincial Park, drive 46 km on the logging roads from Port Hardy to Holberg. Continue west on San Josef Main for just over 12 km to the intersection with Ronning Main. (See Section Two: Trip 16.) Reset your vehicle's trip meter to zero and swing left onto Ronning Main. The road runs through cutblocks and patchy old growth to Branch 700 (km 10.2). Cut left here to a dead end near the Raft Cove trailhead.

The 1.2-km trail starts with a creek crossing and then cuts through an unlogged coastal old-growth forest of hemlock, western red cedar and Sitka spruce. There are muddy sections, slippery log crossings and blowdowns. In favourable weather it's about forty-five minutes to Raft Cove. Many visitors day-hike to the beach, but others carry in overnight gear. Raft Cove's forested beach spit is bordered on one side by the Pacific Ocean, on the other by the Macjack River. When beach tides are high, tenters may be forced to set up camp in the trees at the end of the spit.

Whenever I visit Raft Cove Provincial Park it usually rains. At any time of the year, systems can surge in from the Pacific Ocean to pelt this part of northern Vancouver Island with deluging showers. Even day hikers should carry full raingear and a tarp to provide shelter should the weather turn inclement. The exposed nature of Raft Cove makes it susceptible to cold, blustery Pacific Ocean winds. Dress warmly.

The best freshwater source is over on the Macjack River's south side, near Willie Hecht's old trapper's cabin. Wait for low tide and wade across the river on its firm sandy bottom. You may get your feet and legs wet in the effort. Know the tides; you don't want to be cut off by a flood tide should you spend time exploring the coastline to Commerell Point. Tide information is available in the *Canadian Tide and Current Tables: Vol. 6*, published by the Canadian Hydrographic Service.

With favourable low tides, hikers can access the beach's north end sea-carved arch or head up the Macjack River on its exposed sand flats. Watch for black bears scavenging in the tide zone. You're most likely to see only their tracks (along with cougar and wolf prints) in muddy riverbanks. Some visitors simply beachcomb to the mouth of the Macjack River and watch incoming swells battle river currents. The Macjack River can be accessed from a WFP logging road north of Topknot Lake, and then canoed or kayaked to its mouth. Fallen trees and logs may block sections of the river. Experienced ocean kayakers paddle to Raft Cove via the San Josef River and San Josef Bay.

CONTACTS

- BC Forest Service (Port McNeill): 250-956-5000
- BC Parks (Strathcona District): 250-954-4600
- Western Forest Products (Holberg): 250-228-3362

MAPS/GUIDES

- BC Forest Service Port McNeill Forest District Recreation Map
- Western Forest Products Visitors' Guide to Northern Vancouver Island
- National Topographical Series: 102I/9 San Josef (1:50,000)
- Provincial Map: 92L Alert Bay (1:125,000)
- *Canadian Tide and Current Tables: Vol. 6* (Canadian Hydrographic Service)
- *Hiking Trails III* (VITIS)

NEAREST SERVICES

Holberg.

Trip 13:
Cape Scott Provincial Park

IN BRIEF

Cape Scott, on the extreme northern tip of Vancouver Island, is known for violent storms, torrential rains and surf-lashed beaches. The region's rich history includes two failed attempts at settlement near the turn of the last century. Today, Cape Scott Provincial Park's trails are a hiker's gateway to west-coast wilderness. Anglers who strap a collapsible rod onto their backpacks will discover an extra treat – the park's challenging and often secluded trout fishing.

ACCESS

From Port Hardy take the logging roads for 46 km to Holberg and continue about 18.5 km, on San Josef Main, to the park. (See Section Two: Trip 16.) Gravel mainlines are usually in good to fair shape. Secondary roads may require a high-slung vehicle or 4 x 4. Deactivated roads may be impassable. During weekday working hours (usually 6 a.m. to 6 p.m.) access on some routes, particularly those closer to Holberg, may be restricted due to active logging or fire closures, or for public safety. Check with Western Forest Products in Holberg or Port McNeill for current hauling and area road conditions.

DESCRIPTION

Cape Scott's first white homesteaders were Danes, who settled at Hansen Lagoon and Fisherman Bay between 1897 and 1907. After these failed efforts, a second influx of a thousand newcomers arrived in 1913. They came from the United States, eastern Canada and diverse parts of Europe to seek land available for pre-emption. A corduroy wagon road, linking Cape Scott with San Josef Bay and the Holberg area, would ensure access to markets. Over the years, work on the crucial artery progressed slowly. The wagon-road dream was finally abandoned due to continual government delays, the outbreak of WWI (which depleted the area's young men) and the region's austere geography and weather. By 1918, only a few scattered settlers remained.

To reach Cape Scott Provincial Park, take Highway 19 to Port Hardy (500 km from Victoria; 390 km from Nanaimo). (See Section One: Trips 3,

6, 8, 9 & 10.) On the way, stop in at the North Island Forestry Centre on Highway 19, near the Beaver Cove turn, for area logging road maps and information on a variety of forest tours. (This office is open seasonally from June through August.) About 2 km south of Port Hardy, take the Holberg/ Cape Scott/Winter Harbour cut-off on Highway 19 and reset your vehicle's trip meter to zero. Expect industrial vehicles and logging trucks on the gravel roads from Port Hardy to the park. Exercise caution and always drive with your headlights on. (See Section Two: Trip 16 for a detailed look at the run from Port Hardy to Cape Scott Park.)

Parts of Cape Scott Park are within the Quatsino rainforest and have an average annual rainfall of 375-500 cm. Periods of extended dry weather are rare. Visitors must be prepared for torrential rains and gale-force winds. July and August are usually the driest months; even then, strong Pacific weather systems can make hiking miserable. Carry reliable raingear and be equipped for severe conditions. The use of sturdy hiking boots is recommended on the often muddy trails. Use a staff for balance and to probe questionable quagmires. Hikers must have current tide information, available in the *Canadian Tide and Current Tables: Vol. 6* (Canadian Hydrographic Service). The BC Parks *Cape Scott* brochure features safety tips, a good map, general hiking times and historical information. (Note that BC Parks regulations prohibit any motorized transportation within park boundaries without a permit. These restrictions include float planes and helicopters.)

San Josef Bay:

The Cape Scott parking lot is the starting point for both San Josef Bay and Cape Scott hikers. A journey to San Josef Bay, the most popular and easiest of Cape Scott's beaches to reach, once took upwards of two hours. The route through marshy land on San Josef River's north side is now much improved with a chip-bark trail and boardwalks. Side trails on the way in go to riverside casting spots. A steep, unimproved trail extends from San Josef Bay, up Mount St. Patrick (the highest point in the park) and over to Sea Otter Cove and Lowrie Bay. Allow approximately five hours to complete the 10-km trip to Sea Otter Cove. It's a farther 2 km to Lowrie Bay. Note that the head of Sea Otter Cove can be inundated at high tide, so be up-to-date on tidal information.

The Cape Scott Trail:

Cape Scott hikers veer north at the marked junction halfway to San Josef Bay. Eric Lake, the largest body of freshwater within the park, is a popular day-trip destination for hikers and anglers alike. The old wharf at the lake's south end or the gravel bar near the campsite, halfway along Eric

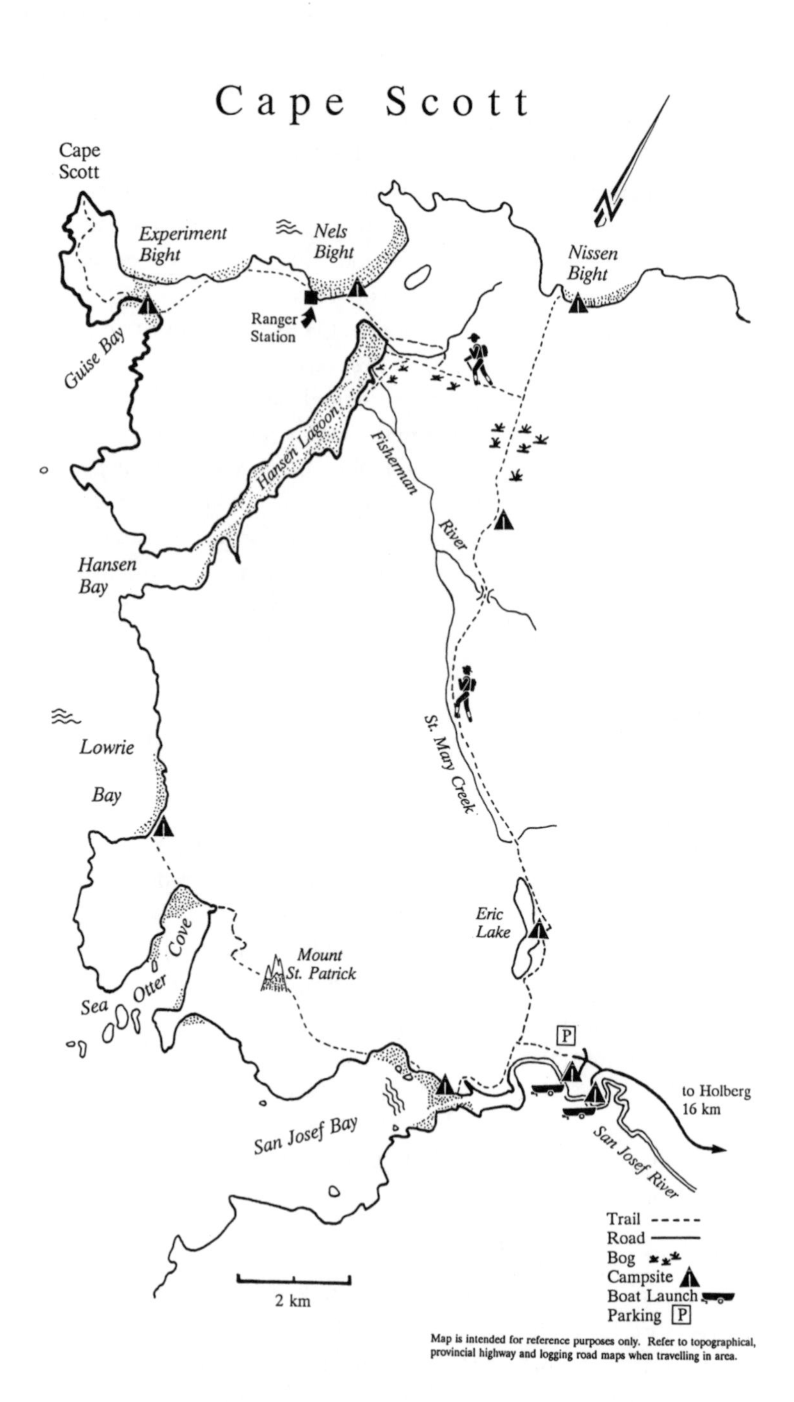
Cape Scott
Cape Scott
Experiment Bight
Nels Bight
Nissen Bight
Ranger Station
Guise Bay
Hansen Lagoon
Fisherman River
Hansen Bay
Lowrie Bay
St. Mary Creek
Eric Lake
Cove
Sea Otter
Mount St. Patrick
P
to Holberg 16 km
San Josef Bay
San Josef River
Trail
Road
Bog
Campsite
Boat Launch
Parking
P
2 km
Map is intended for reference purposes only. Refer to topographical, provincial highway and logging road maps when travelling in area.

Lake's eastern shore, are good places to cast the often windblown waters for feisty cutthroat trout. At the campsite (about an hour's hike in) you'll find food hangers (bear caches) installed as safeguards against nighttime scavengers. Similar devices are located at Nels Bight, Nissen Bight and Guise Bay.

The Fisherman River bridge is about halfway to the big-surf beach at Nels Bight. Beyond the river crossing the rainforest opens up into lowlands and bogs. Hikers sometimes use an old BC Parks cabin at the Donaldson farm site for an emergency shelter. Years ago, people encountering the next series of bogs had to proceed on a tedious zigzag course to escape boot-swallowing mudholes and deep waterholes. The route has since been upgraded with boardwalk. Many park bridges and boardwalks are strategically located in the wetlands and bogs to protect sensitive vegetation and prevent trail deterioration; that the trails are made safer for travel is a secondary benefit.

There is a park information signpost at the Nissen Bight cut-off. Just before this trail junction, a short path (marked by two crumbling fence posts) leads to the gravestone of William Christensen. William, the adopted son of an early Cape Scott settler, died at the age of thirteen from a normally minor wound – a cut foot. Lack of proper medical attention at the isolated Danish settlement and heavy seas prevented sending the boy by small boat to the nearest hospital in Alert Bay, 112 km away. The epitaph on the granite grave marker reads: "The sun went down while it was yet day."

The Cape Scott Trail swings left at the Nissen Bight turnoff to run west through what was the heart of the Cape Scott community. Watch for the flattened ruins of the community hall and overgrown vestiges of the Spencer Farm, abandoned in 1956. The trail emerges at the head of Hansen Lagoon into a wide expanse of diked grassland. In the fall, this area teems with migratory Canada geese. To successfully reclaim land from the sea to accommodate cattle grazing, two dikes were built. The first, completed in 1899, was soon breached by a high tide. A mound of rocks, extending 720 m out into Hansen Lagoon, marks its location (near the middle arm of Fisherman River). The second dike, finished in 1905, lies due west of the Hansen Lagoon signpost.

If you've brought a fishing rod this far, you're probably heading to the Fisherman River, where it enters Hansen Lagoon and splits into three arms. For me, nothing compares with a few hours of casting at the rivermouth, in a wilderness setting virtually unchanged from the days of the Danish settlements. Remember to approach the overhanging riverbanks with stealth so as not to spook the skittish cutthroat; make your first cast long. Keep straight ahead at the Hansen Lagoon signpost and head for the dike. A path then veers into the forest to access Fisherman River. Watch for bear sign. Be careful at the tidal river crossings. Time your visit for the ebb tide to avoid flooding waters in the river and lagoon grasslands that can render the trail impassable for a time. On a really low tide (and with the help of high-topped rubber boots) you can work your way up the lagoon from the north arm of Fisherman River to the dike.

For Nels Bight, bear right at the lagoon signpost and enter the timber to skirt the head of Hansen Lagoon. Nels Bight, with a 2-km stretch of sand, is the largest of Cape Scott's beaches – and the park's most popular campsite. First-time visitors usually set up camp here and day-hike to the cape lighthouse. Seasonal staff base at Nels Bight in a private BC Parks cabin to engage in bridge and boardwalk construction, extensive drainage work (to keep trails dry) and ongoing brush clearing and blowdown removal. Staff also educate hikers through warning markers, information signposts and direct contact on the trails.

Nels Bight to the Cape Scott Lighthouse:

The 16-km return hike to the Cape Scott lighthouse begins near the ranger cabin at the west end of Nels Bight. The route to Experiment Bight, Guise Bay and the cape sometimes follows an old jeep road dating back to WWII, when a radar station operated in the area. Older planks of the roadway can be slippery in damp conditions. The first beach en route to the Cape is Experiment Bight. From its sands you can see the Cape Scott lighthouse and foghorn. The trail to Guise Bay starts where the sand ends and the rocks begin. Watch for marker floats secured to shoreline branches.

At the crescent shores of Guise Bay, the trail follows the beach to an isthmus of dunes at the Sand Neck. From the narrow height of land here you can see both the east and west coast of Vancouver Island. From the Sand Neck the trail climbs a plank road to the Cape Scott lighthouse. Built in 1960, the facility is one of many threatened with automation. Lighthouse staff were directly involved in a life-saving rescue in early 1996, reinforcing the need for manned lighthouses. Respect the privacy of lighthouse staff. They cannot provide fresh water to hikers.

Beyond the lighthouse, follow the boardwalk and numerous sets of stairs to two suspension bridges spanning sea-carved gorges. Near the foghorn, at the very tip of Vancouver Island, a cliffside viewpoint opens up on a jagged seascape, the reef-strewn Scott Channel and the Scott Islands. The Scott chain, a regional breeding ground for sea lions, is home to cormorants, murres and puffins.

The Sand Neck Coastal Route:

Take the supply road to the start of a rough coast trail that leads to the Sand Neck and, farther along, to Experiment Bight. This route accesses tiny pocket beaches and coves via game trails and headland by-passes. At high tide some sections of the route are cut off for a time. Thick coastal salal, muddy slopes and windfall may slow hiking progress. Bears often wander along this less-travelled coastal route. If you spot any recent bear sign, talk loudly, bang a pot or tap nearby trees with a staff to alert any trailside bear of your presence.

Nissen Bight:

From the main Cape Scott Trail cut right at the park information signpost onto the Nissen Bight Trail. At the bottom of Lard Hill (very slippery at times due to its clay base) the trail forks. A tiny path to the left runs into Fisherman Bay, a semi-protected gravel beach often visited by black bears. Occasionally, commercial fishing boats overnight in the bay and then head back out at first light. Keep right at the fork for Nissen Bight. Take care climbing over the logs to the beach. Nissen Bight's water supply is located about a kilometre away, at the beach's east end. To reach the stream you can wait for lower tides and cut along the hard sand. If the tide is flooding, you may have to hike up near the beach cusps (alternating gravel ridges and troughs of smaller pebbles and sand). Where the sand ends, continue around the rocky point (slippery logs must be negotiated) and along the pebbled shoreline to the waterhole. Remember to boil or treat your water. BC Parks discourages travel in non-designated coastal areas. Only experienced, well-prepared hikers should contemplate going beyond the waterhole. Sections of the shoreline are periodically severed by incoming tides.

The provincial government has purchased a coastal strip running from Nissen Bight, near the park's northeast boundary, to Shushartie Bay. Surveys here and on Ministry of Forest lands extending southeast to Duvall Creek, close to Port Hardy, are the first step in the creation of the proposed North Coast Trail. This rugged extension to Cape Scott Park, estimated at 65 km long and requiring three to four days to hike, would offer spectacular seascapes and extensive camping beaches.

Some hikers journey to Cape Scott Park just once; others return again and again to tackle the muddy trails and explore new areas. For these travellers, a single taste of Cape Scott's wilderness atmosphere and striking beauty just isn't enough.

CONTACTS

- BC Forest Service (Port McNeill): 250-956-5000
- BC Parks (Strathcona District): 250-954-4600
- North Island Forestry Centre (Beaver Cove): 250-956-3844
- Western Forest Products (Holberg): 250-288-3362
- Western Forest Products (Port McNeill): 250-956-3391

MAPS/GUIDES

- BC Forest Service Port McNeill Forest District Recreation Map
- BC Parks Cape Scott brochure
- Western Forest Products Visitors' Guide to Northern Vancouver Island
- National Topographical Series: 102I/16 Cape Scott (1:50,000); 102I/9 San Josef (1:50,000)
- *Adventuring in British Columbia* (Nanton/Simpson/Douglas & McIntyre)
- *Adventuring Around Vancouver Island* (Lebrecht/Noppe/Greystone)
- *Canadian Tide and Current Tables: Vol. 6* (Canadian Hydrographic Service)
- *Hiking Trails III* (VITIS)
- *Parks of British Columbia and The Yukon* (Paquet/Maia)

NEAREST SERVICES

Holberg.

Map Sources

BC Forest Service
Vancouver Forest Region
2100 Labieux Road
Nanaimo, BC V9T 6E9
ph: 250-751-7001; fax: 250-751-7190
(BC Forest Service recreation maps are available for the Duncan, Port Alberni, Campbell River and Port McNeill forest districts. The Duncan/Port Alberni districts have merged and are managed under the South Island Forest District in Port Alberni.)

Canadian Hydrographic Service
Chart Sales and Distribution Office
9860 West Saanich Road, PO Box 6000
Sidney, BC V8L 4B2
ph: 250-363-6358; fax: 250-363-6841
(marine charts and tidebooks)

Crown Publications Inc.
521 Fort Street
Victoria, BC V8W 1E7
ph: 250-386-4636; fax: 250-386-0221
(federal and provincial maps; marine charts)

Island Blueprint
905 Fort Street
Victoria, BC V8V 3K3
ph: 250-385-9786; toll-free: 1-800-661-3332; fax: 250-385-1377
(federal maps; marine charts and tidebooks)

Maps BC
Surveys and Mapping Branch
4th Floor, 1802 Douglas Street
Victoria, BC V8V 1X4
ph: 250-387-1441; fax: 250-387-3022
(Maps BC distributes aerial photos. It no longer produces provincial maps – smaller scale charts: 1:100,000; 1:125,000; 1:250,000. Limited stock of these charts is still available at some map dealers.)

Nanaimo Maps and Charts
8 Church Street
Nanaimo, BC V9R 5H4
ph: 250-754-2513; toll-free: 1-800-665-2513
fax: 250-754-2313; toll-free fax: 1-800-553-2313
(federal maps; marine charts and tidebooks)

Mountain Meadows Sporting Goods
368 Fifth Street
Courtenay, BC V9N 1K1
ph: 250-338-8732; fax: 250-338-1823
(federal maps)

Robinson's Sporting Goods
1307 Broad Street
Victoria, BC V8W 2A8
ph: 250-385-3429; fax 250-385-5835
(federal maps; marine charts and tidebooks)

Spinners Sports
Discovery Harbour Shopping Centre
1436 Island Highway
Campbell River, BC V9W 8C9
ph: 250-286-6166; toll-free: 1-888-306-4444; fax: 250-286-3404
(federal maps; marine charts and tidebooks)

LOGGING COMPANIES

Most logging companies offer Vancouver Island logging road recreation guides. These can usually be picked up at regional offices (during normal working hours) or by mail from their head offices.

Canadian Forest Products Ltd.
Englewood Logging Division
Woss, BC V0N 3P0
ph: 250-281-2300; fax: 250-281-2485

MacMillan Bloedel Ltd.
925 West Georgia Street
Vancouver, BC V6C 3L2
ph: 604-661-8671 (Public Affairs); fax: 604-687-5345

North Island Forestry Centre
PO Box 130
Port McNeill, BC V0N 2R0
ph: 250-956-3844; fax: 250-956-4448
(Open seasonally from June through August, this office stocks a variety of recreation and logging road maps for northern Vancouver Island.)

Pacific Forest Products Ltd.
#1000 – 1040 West Georgia Street
Vancouver, BC V6E 4K4
ph: 604-640-3400; fax: 604-640-3480

TimberWest Canada Ltd.
2300 – 1055 West Georgia Street
Vancouver, BC V6E 3P3
ph: 604-654-4600
Some logging road guides to its Vancouver Island divisions are available from local company offices. A number of its maps may be in limited supply or out-of-print.

Western Forest Products Ltd.
Suite 2300, 1111 West Georgia Street
Vancouver, BC V6E 4M3
ph: 604-665-6200; fax: 604-665-6268

Other Information Sources

Capital Regional District Parks
490 Atkins Avenue
Victoria, BC V9B 2Z8
ph: 250-478-3344; fax: 250-478-5416
(Many brochures on CRD regional parks are available.)

Outdoor Recreation Council of British Columbia
#334 – 1367 West Broadway
Vancouver, BC V6H 4A9
ph: 604-737-3058; fax: 604-737-3666
(It distributes many pamphlets related to the outdoors.)

Regional District of Mount Waddington
PO Box 729
Port McNeill, BC V0N 2R0
ph: 250-956-3301; fax: 250-956-3232
(It has information on north Island regional parks.)

- BC Parks provides a variety of brochures and maps of Vancouver Island provincial parks. Copies are available at Travel Info Centres and park offices.
- For general information call BC Parks (Victoria): 250-387-4550.
- For specific details on south Island parks call BC Parks (South Vancouver Island District): 250-391-2300.
- For information on north Island parks call BC Parks (Strathcona District): 250-954-4600.
- BC Provincial Parks Campsite Reservations:
  1-800-689-9025 (in Vancouver, dial the last seven digits only). Reservations are accepted for the following Vancouver Island parks: Bamberton; Cowichan River; Englishman River Falls; French Beach; Goldstream; Gordon Bay; Miracle Beach; Rathtrevor.
- For toll-free calling to many provincial government offices contact Enquiry BC: 250-387-6121 (outside Greater Victoria 1-800-663-7867.)
- For information on BC Ferries routes and schedules call: 250-386-3431 (reservations and information); 250-381-5335 (24-hour schedule information).
- The Campbell River Search and Rescue Society publishes a logging and highway map that covers the Campbell River, Sayward, Oyster River and Buttle Lake areas.
- The Comox Valley Chamber of Commerce and the Comox Valley Ground Search and Rescue Association publish a Comox Valley map that includes area logging roads and hiking trails.
- Mussio Ventures' *Backroad Mapbook Volume II: Vancouver Island* is a one-volume mapbook depicting Vancouver Island backroads. This publication lists Vancouver Island freshwater and saltwater fishing destinations, provincial parks and hiking, mountain biking, camping and paddling spots.
- The Vancouver Island Trails Information Society publishes *Hiking Trails I, II & III*, three books that cover the Victoria area, southeastern Vancouver Island and central and northern Vancouver Island trails, respectively.

- Many adventurers book guided interpretative hikes, available from a variety of tour companies. Victoria's Coastal Connections is known for its Southern Vancouver Island outings.

Anglers will be interested in the following publications, which give information on Island lakes, access roads and fishing opportunities.

- *BC Freshwater Fishing Directory & Atlas,* published and updated annually by *BC Outdoors* magazine.
- *Guide to Freshwater Fishing on Vancouver Island,* published by Ministry of Environment, 1995.
- *Guide to Island Rivers,* published by *Island Angler*, 1994.
- *Island Angler,* published monthly by Andrew Kolasinski.
- *Island Fish Finder Magazine,* published monthly by Rosebrugh Holdings Ltd.
- *Steelhead & Freshwater Fishing Guide (Vancouver Island,)* published by Pacific Rim Publications.
- *25 Favourite Lakes of Southern Vancouver Island,* published by the Haig-Brown Fly Fishing Association (Victoria) 1992.

Suggested Reading

Akrigg, G.P.V. and Helen B. *British Columbia Place Names*. Victoria: Sono Nis, 1986.

Baikie, Wallace. *Strathcona: A History of British Columbia's First Provincial Park*. Campbell River: Ptarmigan Press, 1986.

Blier, Richard K. *Island Adventures, An Outdoors Guide to Vancouver Island*. Victoria: Orca Book Publishers, 1989.

Blier, Richard K. *More Island Adventures, An Outdoors Guide to Vancouver Island*. Victoria: Orca Book Publishers, 1993.

Bruhn, Karl. *Best of BC Lake Fishing*. Vancouver/Toronto: Whitecap Books, 1992.

Dowd, John. *Sea Kayaking: A Manual for Long-Distance Touring*. Vancouver: Greystone, 1997.

Environment Canada. *Marine Weather Hazards Manual, West Coast Edition*. West Vancouver: Gordon Soules Book Publishing, 1992.

Goldberg, Kim. *Where To See Wildlife on Vancouver Island*. Madiera Park: Harbour Publishing, 1997.

Graham, Donald. *Keepers of the Light*. Madiera Park: Harbour Publishing, 1992.

Graham, Donald. *Lights of the Inside Passage*. Madiera Park: Harbour Publishing, 1992.

Guppy, Walter. *West Coast Ventures, Mine-Finding on Vancouver Island*. Victoria: Cappis Press, 1988.

Hall, Del. *At The End of the Trail From Victoria*. Victoria: Cougar Press, 1989.

Hall, Del. *Island Gold*. Victoria: Cougar Press, 1990.

Hayman, John. *Robert Brown and the Vancouver Island Exploring Expedition*. Vancouver: University of British Columbia Press, 1991.

Hudson, Rick. *A Field Guide to Gold, Gemstones & Mineral Sites of BC, Volume I: Vancouver Island*. Victoria: Orca Book Publishers, 1997.

Ince, John and Kottner, Hedi. *Sea Kayaking Canada's West Coast*. Vancouver: Raxas Books, 1982.

Jones, Robert H. *Tangled Lines and Patched Waders*. Victoria: Horsdal & Schubart, 1995.

Jones, Robert H. *Warped Rods and Dull Hooks*. Victoria: Horsdal & Schubart, 1997.

Lebrecht, Sue and Noppe, Susan. *Adventuring Around Vancouver Island*. Vancouver/Toronto: Greystone Books, 1997.

Lee, David and Thirkell, Keith. *Four-Wheeling On Southern Vancouver Island, Victoria To Tofino*. Madiera Park: Harbour Publishing, 1997.

McKnight, George. *Sawlogs on Steel Rails*. Port Alberni: Port Alberni Seniors' History Committee, 1995.

Merriman, Alec and Taffy. *Logging Road Travel: Vols. I & II*. Sidney: Saltaire Publishing, 1977-79.

Meyer, Kathleen. *How to Shit In The Woods*. Berkeley: Ten Speed Press, 1994.

Obee, Bruce. *The Pacific Rim Explorer*. North Vancouver: Whitecap Books, 1995.

Nanton, Isabel and Simpson, Mary. *Adventuring In British Columbia*. Vancouver: Douglas & McIntyre, 1996.

Neering, Rosemary. *Backroading Vancouver Island*. Vancouver/ Toronto: Whitecap Books, 1996.

Nicholson, George. *Vancouver Island's West Coast 1762-1962*. Vancouver: George Nicholson's Books, 1981.

Pacquet, Maggie. *Parks of British Columbia and the Yukon*. North Vancouver: Maia Publishing, 1990.

Payne, David. *Island Cycling, A Cycle Camper's Guide to Vancouver Island*. Victoria: Orca Book Publishers, 1996.

Petersen, Lester R. *The Cape Scott Story*. Langley: Sunfire, 1985.

Pojar, Jim and Mackinnon, Andy. *Plants of Coastal British Columbia*. Vancouver: Lone Pine Publishing, 1994.

Poole, Michael. *Ragged Islands*. Vancouver/Toronto: Douglas & McIntyre, 1995.

Pratt-Johnson, Betty. *Whitewater Trips for Kayakers, Canoeists and Rafters on Vancouver Island*. Vancouver: Soules Book Publishers, 1984.

Priest, Simon. *Bicycling Vancouver Island & The Gulf Islands*. Vancouver: Douglas & McIntyre, 1984.

Rogers, Fred. *Southern Vancouver Island Hiking Trails*. Surrey: Heritage House Publishing Company, 1995.

Scott, R. Bruce. *Breakers Ahead*. Sidney: Review Publishing House, 1970.

Scott, R. Bruce. *Barkley Sound: A History of the Pacific Rim National Park Area*. Victoria: Fleming Review Printing, 1972.

Scott, R. Bruce. *People of the Southwest Coast of Vancouver Island*. Victoria: R. Bruce Scott, 1974.

Scott, R. Bruce. *Bamfield Years: Recollections*. Victoria: Sono Nis Press, 1986.

Seagrave, Jayne. *Provincial and National Park Campgrounds in BC*. Langley: Heritage House, 1997.

Sierra Club of BC. *The West Coast Trail and Nitinat Lakes*. Vancouver: Douglas & McIntyre, 1992.

Smith, Ian. *The Unknown Island*. Vancouver: Douglas & McIntyre, 1973.

Snowden, Mary Ann. *Island Paddling*. Victoria: Orca Book Publishers, 1997.

Stedham, Glen. *Bush Basics: A Common Sense Guide to Backwoods Adventure*. Victoria: Orca Book Publishers, 1997.

Stoltmann, Randy. *Hiking the Ancient Forests of British Columbia and Washington*. Vancouver/Edmonton: Lone Pine Publishing, 1996.

Thomson, Richard E. *Oceanography of the British Columbia Coast*. Ottawa: Canadian Special Publication of Fisheries and Aquatic Sciences 56, 1984.

Turner, Robert D. *Logging By Rail*. Victoria: Sono Nis Press, 1990.

Vancouver Island Trails Information Society. *Hiking Trails I: Victoria & Vicinity*. Victoria: Vancouver Island Trails Information Society (11th ed. edited by Susan Lawrence), 1993.

Vancouver Island Trails Information Society. *Hiking Trails II: Southeastern Vancouver Island*. Victoria: Vancouver Island Trails Information Society (12th ed. edited by Richard K. Blier), 1997.

Vancouver Island Trails Information Society. *Hiking Trails III: Central and Northern Vancouver Island and Quadra Island*. Victoria: Vancouver Island Trails Information Society (8th ed. edited by Jim Rutter), 1996.

Walbran, John T. *British Columbia Coast Names*. Vancouver: Douglas & McIntyre, 1977.

Watmough, Don. *Cruising Guide to British Columbia, Vol. IV: West Coast of Vancouver Island Cape Scott to Sooke*. Vancouver: Maclean Hunter, 1984.

Wells, R.E. *There's A Landing Today*. Victoria: Sono Nis Press, 1988.

Weston, Jim and Stirling, David. *The Naturalist's Guide to the Victoria Region*. Victoria: Victoria Natural History Society, 1986.

Yorath, C.J. and Nasmith, H.W. *The Geology of Southern Vancouver Island*. Victoria: Orca Book Publishers, 1995.

Zuehlke, Mark. *The Vancouver Island South Explorer*. Vancouver/Toronto: Whitecap, 1994.

Note: Some of the above may be out-of-print.